BR 1806

BRITISH MARITIME DOCTRINE

Second Edition

By Command of the Defence Council

NAVAL STAFF DIRECTORATE
D/NSD 2/10/1

LONDON : THE STATIONERY OFFICE

© Crown Copyright 1999

Published with the permission of the Ministry of Defence on behalf of the Controller of Her Majesty's Stationery Office

Applications for reproduction should be made in writing to The Copyright Unit, Her Majesty's Stationery Office, St Clements House, 2-16 Colegate, Norwich, NR 1BQ

First Edition 1995

ISBN 0 11 772910 8

BR 1806

BRITISH MARITIME DOCTRINE

Second Edition

FOREWORD BY
Admiral Sir Michael Boyce KCB OBE ADC
First Sea Lord and Chief of Naval Staff

The First Edition of this book, launched in 1995, was a great success and drew plaudits from its wide international readership. I believe that this new edition is a worthy successor, retaining the excellent substance that was at the core of the First Edition while moving on and placing that still essential core in an up to date context.

Since 1995 we have tested our overall defence posture in a succession of operations as well as through the mechanisms of the Strategic Defence Review (SDR); both have served to confirm the utility of maritime power as expressed in our maritime doctrine. The outcome of the SDR reflected the need to continue the shift in emphasis away from the long-standing confrontation of the Cold War years towards the use of our armed forces in the wider and, in many ways, more complex range of tasks that accompany the expeditionary nature of our role that the times in which we now live demand. Not only have we moved away from a military strategy of pre-disposition in Northern Germany and the North Atlantic, but we have also embraced the emerging doctrine of Peace Support Operations (PSOs). This process is both an intellectual and an operational challenge because the term 'peace support' requires the contingent threat of the application of force, as operations in the Balkans graphically illustrate. So, while we may find ourselves engaged in a wide range of operations under the heading 'PSO', it is important that we retain the ability to apply force as we did in the Gulf in 1990/91 and in December 1998. Nor must we forget that it is often our ability to conduct higher intensity operations that gives us the scope to deal with the lower intensity challenges that most PSOs represent.

I reiterate a theme that was stressed in the First Edition: doctrine must not be rigid, either in terms of its periodicity of review or the message that it must convey about flexibility of approach. Doctrine is not, nor must be allowed to become, dogma. This book demonstrates well the ways in which enduring principles have proved sufficiently adaptable to accommodate the needs of the new security circumstances we face. The final chapter reflects the thinking behind the Maritime Contribution to Joint Operations, the Royal Navy ís new operational concept that signals the full extent of the shift away from anti-submarine operations in the Eastern Atlantic towards littoral operations almost anywhere in the world. I expect all naval professionals, at whatever level, to apply their minds to the complexities inherent in our new focus but to do so in a challenging way. I firmly subscribe to the view that the only way to confirm the appropriateness of our way of thinking is to seek out its flaws; we must certainly not fall into the trap of using only that evidence that supports our instinctive conclusions. For that reason, this new edition of BR1806, like its predecessor, is not simply the official line to take. It is also the agreed starting point for healthy discussion about the nature and limits of our profession and the operations we may have to conduct in support of our national interests worldwide. I commend it to all on that basis and look forward with anticipation to any debate it generates.

CONTENTS

Page		
	Editor's Introduction	
1	Chapter 1 -	Maritime Doctrine in Context
13	Chapter 2 -	The Maritime Environment and the Nature of Maritime Power
33	Chapter 3 -	Concepts Governing the Use of Maritime Power
51	Chapter 4 -	The Application of Maritime Power
77	Chapter 5 -	Maritime Logistics and Supply
89	Chapter 6 -	Maritime Command and Control
109	Chapter 7 -	Planning and Conducting a Maritime Campaign or Operation
141	Chapter 8 -	Maritime Operational Capability
159	Chapter 9 -	Summarising the Maritime Contribution to Joint Operations
172	From Trafalgar to Today: A Bibliographical Essay on Doctrine and the Development of British Naval Strategic Thought	
187	Editorial Consultative Board	
188	Abbreviations	
191	Glossary	
239	Index	

EDITOR'S INTRODUCTION

This new edition of *BR1806* follows the 1998 Strategic Defence Review (SDR). However, the SDR has not resulted in significant changes to maritime doctrine at the *military-strategic* level. The doctrinal principles contained in *BR1806* are enduring and, although there is clearly a relationship between policy and doctrine at the strategic levels, changes in policy will not necessarily have an immediate effect on doctrine. Indeed, fundamental principles of military doctrine are influential in the sense that they contribute to defining the limits of policy by helping to inform political decision makers about the strengths, weaknesses, advantages and disadvantages of military options. It is only policy shifts over extended periods that ultimately shape grand-strategic doctrine which, in turn, has an influence on military-strategic doctrine. Nevertheless, the SDR was an important process that has set the current policy context for doctrinal development. Importantly, the SDR confirmed the direction in which Britain's security policy has been going since the end of the Cold War, rather than heralded any significant change to it. That direction is away from a substantial physical commitment on the continent of Europe, consisting of largely static, defensive forces, towards an expeditionary posture in which strategic mobility and flexibility are the principal features. The 'continental strategy' of the Cold War has given way to a new maritime strategy in which the doctrinal principles discussed in this book assume an enhanced significance.

When the previous edition of *BR1806* was published in 1995, the joint military-strategic level **British Defence Doctrine (BDD)** had not yet appeared. The work that has since been done on *BDD*, as well as on **The United Kingdom Doctrine for Joint and Multinational Operations (UKOPSDOC)**, has not only had a developmental effect on the style and substance of *BR1806*, it has also allowed a reduction in the amount of contextual information needed in this new edition. Much of the strategic policy and conceptual content of the Introduction and first two chapters of the 1995 edition has, therefore, been removed.

GENERAL CONCEPTS AND PRINCIPLES APPLICABLE TO MARITIME FORCES

The general concepts that determine the ways in which all of the UK's maritime forces are applied in support of national interests are discussed in detail in **BDD**. Concepts related to the use of military force, such as *deterrence, coercion, destruction, constraint and disruption*, are endorsed and also defined in the Glossary at the back of this book. Also accepted are the notion of a spectrum of conflict, the concept of limitation and the methods by which it is achieved, and the concept of intensity. Types of conflict, ranging from general war to terrorism, are acknowledged with the caveat that, while general war may be considered unlikely, it must still be included for doctrinal as distinct from policy reasons.

From the comments so far, it will be clear that, while **BR1806** continues to stand, and can be read, on its own as a comprehensive statement of British maritime doctrine, the more enthusiastic student of the subject should also study the latest **Statement on the Defence Estimates** and **BDD** to place maritime operations in the broader politico-strategic and doctrinal context.

THE JOINT APPROACH TO BR1806

Despite the inherently *joint* nature of maritime operations at the *operational* and *military-strategic levels*, there are important differences between the ways in which land, air and sea forces operate. The need for a clear articulation of maritime doctrine has to be met by those who have a deep professional understanding of the maritime environment. For that reason it has until now been appropriate for the *Naval Staff* to prepare this book. However, the assistance of Army and RAF representation on the Editorial Consultative Board has been regarded as essential and readers will certainly detect a greater tendency to deploy joint language and terminology in this new edition. This reflects both doctrinal and institutional developments since the 1995 edition was drafted. The publication of both **BDD** and **UKOPSDOC** has also moved joint thinking forward. The establishment of the Permanent Joint Headquarters (PJHQ) for the conduct of joint operations and the Joint Services Command and Staff College (JSCSC) for the command and staff training of officers have also both had an influence on joint thinking.

The SDR has further moved this process forward and has included one important new institutional development with the establishment of the Joint Doctrine and Concepts Centre (JDCC). An early decision in relation to the JDCC was that it would have responsibility for the production and promulgation of all joint doctrine, in particular at the operational and military-strategic levels. The maritime doctrine contained in this book is joint: in essence it is military-strategic level doctrine viewed from a maritime perspective. It is, therefore, entirely appropriate that in future it should be the JDCC that will have responsibility for its production. This edition of **BR1806** will therefore be the last written under the auspices of the Naval Staff. All future editions will be both written and published under the JDCC's auspices. The Assistant Chief of Naval Staff (ACNS), the Commander-in-Chief Fleet and the various staffs and organizations with an input to maritime doctrine will continue to be represented on the Editorial Consultative Board and future editions will continue to require Navy Board endorsement before publication.

APPLICATIONS OF MARITIME POWER

When **BDD** was being drafted, in the latter part of 1996, it became obvious that it would not be possible to use **BR1806's** categorisation of operations (*Military, Constabulary* and *Benign*) for non-maritime purposes. There was, for example, reluctance to apply the word 'constabulary' to military operations conducted ashore. Nevertheless, it is certainly the case that navies have traditionally been employed in policing functions to a very much greater extent than have armies or air forces. Fishery protection, anti-piracy and drug interdiction operations are classic examples of 'constabulary' operations that are routine functions for navies around the world. It has also been suggested that the use of the word 'benign' for essentially philanthropic activities has the unfortunate effect of implying that all operations not categorised as Benign might be regarded as malign. However, the use of a word like 'benign' to describe an activity does not necessarily imply that all other activities are, by definition and by default, 'malign'. Criticisms of the three categories have not, therefore, been persuasive and each continues to be discussed in detail in the chapter on the Application of Maritime Power (Chapter 4).

THE STRUCTURE OF BR1806

BR1806 is designed to be read as a logical progression from chapter to chapter. However, a reader who is broadly familiar with the subject matter but is investigating a specific topic will find that individual chapters stand largely on their own, with some of the more important principles illustrated and stressed in more than one chapter - this is deliberate repetition and not poor editing!

Chapter 1 discusses the nature of *doctrine* and places maritime doctrine within a general context. It reflects, in particular, the tone and content of the *Navy Board's* most recent statement on the development of maritime doctrine, which was promulgated within the Naval Service in **Defence Council Instruction RN 158/97**.

Chapters 2 to 9 are arranged logically and, in effect, in three separate sections . Chapters 2 to 4 deal with the fundamental principles and represent the core doctrinal chapters of the book. Chapter 2 describes the maritime environment, the distinctive features of the sea and the attributes of maritime power. Having set the scene, Chapter 3 examines specifically maritime doctrinal concepts, in particular *sea control* and *maritime power projection*, and considers styles of warfare in the maritime environment. Chapter 4 covers the application of maritime power and the range of maritime *military* tasks that can be conducted at sea and from the sea, as well as the *constabulary* and *benign* tasks that are also important functions, especially in peacetime.

Having dealt with the core of maritime doctrinal principles and concepts at the *military-strategic level*, the second part of the book describes the principles of maritime logistics and support (Chapter 5), how *command and control* is executed (Chapter 6) and, finally, the ways in which maritime *operations* and *campaigns* are planned and conducted (Chapter 7). These three chapters move the discussion from the *military-strategic level* towards the *operational level* and represent the essential link between what is contained in the main part of this book and what is contained in **Fighting Instructions**, the RN's principal operational and tactical level doctrine publication.

The penultimate chapter of the book defines operational capability and, in so doing, describes the UK's current maritime capabilities (Chapter 8). Finally, Chapter 9 summarises the contribution of maritime forces to joint operations in a free standing, though summary essay which also serves to place the UK's maritime forces in a politico-strategic and doctrinal context.

GLOSSARY

One of the most successful aspects of the previous edition of *BR1806* was the extensive glossary that was included at the end of the book. A great many readers from around the world have commented very positively about the extremely wide range of definitions contained therein and this has therefore been retained, improved and updated to reflect developments since 1995. As in the 1995 edition, terms included in the Glossary are printed in italics in the main body of the book.

FURTHER READING

The main purpose of *BR1806* is educational. It provides a starting point for the study of the principles underlying maritime doctrine and a general introduction to the academic study of maritime strategy and its influence on international relations. The book itself has been compiled drawing on previous experience and past analysis conducted by academics and professionals; their contribution should not be forgotten. For those with a wish to develop further their understanding of the subject, a bibliographical essay is provided immediately after Chapter 9. It contains reference to the principal available works, both classic and contemporary, together with brief comments on them. A well rounded naval officer who aspires to a sound understanding of his profession, its development and its context, will need to be familiar with the range of works quoted.

FEEDBACK

Finally, before proceeding with the substance of this book, it is important to acknowledge the role of feedback in the process of doctrinal development. This new edition of *BR1806* has benefited from comments received about the content, style and presentation of its immediate predecessor. Such comment is greatly valued and encouraged. While the principal readership of this book will undoubtedly be serving officers within the UK's *Naval Service*, whose opinions are especially important, others with a view can be assured that their feedback will be most gratefully received. The address for feedback is:

Head of Defence Studies (Royal Navy)
Naval Staff Directorate
Ministry of Defence
Main Building
Whitehall
London SW1A 2HB

The Nelson Touch

Nelson is well known for simple instructions, such as his use of the signal "close action" - usually interpreted as "engage the enemy more closely" - and his sentence in his memorandum before Trafalgar that "No captain can do very wrong if he places his ship alongside that of the enemy". It is easy to be misled by the apparent simplicity of these instructions. In reality they reflected a confidence that his subordinates were completely familiar with contemporary naval doctrine, amended sometimes by Nelson himself. Nelson, who was a great believer in delegation, expected his subordinates to use their intelligence, seamanship and understanding of his intentions to do much better in outmanoeuvring their opponents. Importantly he devoted much time and effort discussing with his captains how he pictured forthcoming battles. As a result, they were able to take independent action in support of Nelson's objectives, without further reference to him. Of course, if all else failed, they knew that there was a minimum that he expected of them and, if they had to resort to it, knew that they would not be judged "very wrong" in so doing.

Battle of the Nile 1st August 1798. Captain Thomas Foley's initiative (GOLIATH) in leading a column of ships inshore of the French line, thus exposing them to fire from two directions, transformed Nelson's almost certain victory into a strategic rout.
Picture courtesy of the National Maritime Museum Greenich.

Battle of the Nile. The French flagship L'ORIENT blows up.

MARITIME DOCTRINE IN CONTEXT

Chapter 1

In the Royal Navy, the existence of formal doctrine can be traced back to the original edition of *Fighting Instructions*, issued to the Fleet in 1672, and to a code of tactical signals promulgated during the Commonwealth in 1653. The development of maritime tactical doctrine is thus a well established process going back over 300 years. The Royal Navy's current *tactical* and *operational* doctrine is still promulgated in *Fighting Instructions*. It is also subjected to regular review as technology and equipment is developed and enters into service and as a consequence of both operational experience and the analysis of operational and exercise performance. By its nature, much of this doctrine is specialised, is essentially the domain of those involved in tactical and operational decision-making and is not very widely disseminated. Indeed, some aspects of tactical and operational doctrine are sensitive and are covered by appropriate security classifications.

However, once we move up the hierarchy, from the *tactical* and *operational* levels to the *military-* and *grand-strategic levels*, doctrine becomes less the exclusive business of the deep military specialists and more the legitimate interest of any with a professional, academic, political or social stake in the use of military power. There is also an especial need to recognise that, for reasons of motivation, morale, commitment and professional operational understanding, junior military ranks need to have access to an understanding and interpretation of the strategic context in which their profession is expected to operate.

The emergence of *military-strategic level* maritime doctrine can be traced back to the late nineteenth century and the early years of the twentieth century. Arguably, until Alfred Thayer Mahan applied his mind to the subject, there was little, if any, structured, academic thought given to the attributes of maritime power and how it might best be applied in support of national interest. If one accepts the dictionary definition of 'doctrine' as "that which is taught", then the conclusions of Mahan and those of a number of distinguished British maritime strategic thinkers could be credited with the doctrinal label. In the UK, perhaps none was so influential as Sir Julian Corbett, in particular the views he expressed in his profoundly important book **Some Principles of Maritime Strategy**. If, however, we restrict 'doctrine' to that which is officially promulgated, the only higher level maritime doctrine that has been acknowledged officially in the UK has been that contained in the various editions of **BR1806**. This was originally called **The Naval War Manual**, its last appearance under that title being in 1969 (previous editions dating from 1948 and 1958).

In 1995, the new **BR1806** was published under a different title: **The Fundamentals of British Maritime Doctrine**. The use of the word 'doctrine' in the title reflected a trend within the UK armed forces as a whole. The new **BR1806** complemented similar publications published by the Army and the RAF to form a stable of documents dealing with *military-strategic level* doctrine. Eventually, in 1996, the individual Services' doctrinal books were joined by the military-strategic level joint doctrine publication, **British Defence Doctrine**. This latter has itself provided the higher level framework from which *operational level* joint doctrine cascades.

A JOINT APPROACH

This leads neatly to a point of profound importance. Maritime doctrine as discussed in this book is not simply 'naval doctrine'. While this edition of **BR1806** has been edited within the *Naval Staff* in the Ministry of Defence and is, in that sense, a single-Service statement of doctrine, it is not, nor could it be, concerned solely with matters of a naval nature. The maritime environment is inherently *joint*. Air power is as vital to operations at sea as it is to the conduct of military operations ashore. Naval forces themselves exist to influence events ashore; they have never operated strategically in an exclusively naval environment. This book is not, therefore, about 'sea power'. It is, rather, about the maritime dimension of *joint* operations. An air force fighter aircraft and an army infantry battalion may well be components of a maritime force because the word 'maritime' refers to the environment in which they are operating not to that institutional part of the UK's armed forces that might be providing them. Indeed, although 'joint' has traditionally meant forces from two or more of the Services operating together, increasingly the phrase 'joint operations' is coming to mean operations conducted across environmental boundaries regardless of how many of the Services are engaged.

Since the Cold War the focus of maritime attention has undoubtedly shifted towards *littoral* operations in support of operations ashore. For this reason there is an increasing emphasis placed on joint operations and the concomitant need for each Service to understand the modus operandi of the other two. Joint operations in the littoral present a complex mix of opportunities and challenges that will at times be difficult to meet. However, the Royal Navy's traditional, 'Nelsonian' flexibility of approach and its instinctive reliance on initiative to achieve maximum effect sit very easily with the *manoeuvrist* culture that guides military operations today.

Despite the shift of focus towards the *littoral*, it is essential that the deep water environment and the continuing need to be able to conduct open ocean sea control operations is not neglected. In particular, the submarine threat may have changed but it has not disappeared. The UK's maritime forces must retain their ability to carry out effective anti-submarine warfare (ASW) operations,

MARITIME DOCTRINE IN CONTEXT

especially in support of ballistic missile carrying submarine (SSBN) deployments but also in the often (though not necessarily) shallower waters of the *littoral*. Maritime doctrine at all levels reflects operational imperatives in deep water as well as in the littorals.

HMS SUTHERLAND

THE PURPOSE OF MARITIME DOCTRINE

Doctrine is a framework of principles, practices and procedures, the understanding of which provides a basis for action. Maritime doctrine fulfils this function for the use of military power at and from the sea. The doctrine contained in this book covers principally the strategic and, to a certain extent, the *operational levels* of military planning, both in conflict and in the peacetime applications of military power. In general terms, the main purpose of maritime doctrine, at all levels, is to derive the greatest benefit from current maritime forces in support of national policy. However, in achieving this aim it also serves a number of subsidiary purposes.

It has internal educational and training functions which contribute to the professionalism of the UK's maritime forces and the men and women who serve in them. There is a particular emphasis on the education of the officer corps and the *Navy Board* has instructed that all officers in the RN and RM should undergo formal study of the fundamental principles of maritime doctrine contained in *BR1806*. This commences during New Entry courses at Britannia Royal Naval College (BRNC), Dartmouth and the Commando Training Centre, Royal Marines (CTCRM), Lympstone and continues during the Initial Staff Course (ISC) and Advanced Command and Staff Course (ACSC) at the Joint Services Command and Staff College (JSCSC). By the time officers reach subsequent mid-career staff appointments, on *Flag*, Ministry of Defence or *joint* staffs, they should be familiar with the principles underlying the use of maritime power. All officers receive a personal copy of the book and all warrant officers on promotion are also made aware of its contents.

In so far as it produces a way of thinking about the utility of maritime power and the conduct of *operations*, doctrine also has a professional motivational function through providing maritime forces with clear statements about their roles and objectives. At the *military-strategic level*, doctrine also informs the wider defence community (including politicians, industrialists, academics, etc), as well as interested members of the general public, about the roles and political utility of maritime forces.

Increasingly in recent years, the *Operational Requirements* (OR) staff in the MOD have used doctrinal terminology in articulating the need for equipments to provide operational capabilities and there is an important role for doctrine, particularly that at the *military-strategic level*, in informing the OR process. In examining the overall utility of a joint asset (an aircraft carrier, for example) it is necessary to assess its characteristics and likely employment in relation to doctrinal principles applicable in all relevant operational environments.

THE NATURE OF DOCTRINE

Within the UK's armed forces the general definition of military doctrine is very similar to that used in NATO. To quote *BDD*, it is: "fundamental principles by which military forces guide their actions in support of objectives. It is authoritative, but requires judgement in application". The second part of that definition is intended to convey the message that doctrine should not develop the rigid authority of dogma but should remain flexible. This theme was reinforced by the then First Sea Lord, Admiral Sir Jock Slater, in his Foreword to the 1995 edition of *BR1806*. He remarked that maritime forces "must be

Ch 1
MARITIME DOCTRINE IN CONTEXT

careful to avoid a dogmatic approach in thinking about the principles that govern maritime actions" and that "we must retain our reputation for innovation and for responding to political changes and technical opportunities".

Doctrine must be flexible in two senses, therefore. First, it must convey the importance of initiative and not discourage commanders from challenging received wisdom when appropriate. Second, it must be subject to regular formal review to ensure that the accumulated wisdom being promulgated in the form of doctrine is as robust and relevant as possible. However, in conducting regular review, care must be taken not to make change for change's sake. At the *military-strategic level*, the fundamental principles will probably change only very rarely. In contrast, at the *tactical level*, doctrine will clearly be directly affected by current challenges and capabilities; tactical doctrine is equipment, threat and environment driven.

THE HIERARCHY OF DOCTRINE

Maritime doctrine does not exist in a vacuum. As has already been mentioned above, **BR1806** is but one of a stable of doctrine publications at the *military-strategic level*. For a thorough understanding of the ways in which military forces are utilised in support of national policy there is no substitute for studying the range of doctrinal publications now available. Apart from **British Defence Doctrine** there is **British Military Doctrine** and **Air Power Doctrine**. At the operational level there is **UKOPSDOC**. As far as maritime doctrine is concerned, for those with access to it, there is also **Fighting Instructions** at the operational and tactical levels. **BR1806** is related to all of these publications. In the hierarchy it sits immediately above **Fighting Instructions** and alongside the other single-Service publications. There is a form of symbiosis existing between all such documents and the development of maritime doctrine through the publication of this book will have an influence on the development of the others.

Finally, the importance of NATO doctrine, while it exists in a separate hierarchy outside that for UK national doctrine, must be acknowledged. A great deal of the doctrine applied at the operational and tactical levels by the UK's maritime forces is agreed with Allies and promulgated in NATO publications. It is UK policy that it's

Ch 1
MARITIME DOCTRINE IN CONTEXT

national doctrine should be consistent with NATO doctrine other than in those exceptional circumstances when the UK has elected not to ratify the relevant NATO doctrine. With the UK as the principal European maritime power, UK influence on the development of NATO maritime doctrine is profound; so much so, indeed, that a similar symbiosis exists between UK and NATO maritime doctrine to that which exists between UK maritime doctrine and other publications in the UK national doctrinal hierarchy. A similar linkage also exists between NATO and UK *joint doctrine*.

HMS INVINCIBLE

Ch 1
MARITIME DOCTRINE IN CONTEXT

LEVELS OF MILITARY OPERATIONS

BDD recognises the different levels at which decisions are made and at which operations are conducted. They include the *grand-strategic, military-strategic, operational and tactical levels*. ***BR1806*** promulgates maritime doctrine at the military-strategic level but in so doing also discusses relevant aspects of the operational level. As already stated, the RN's operational and tactical levels of maritime doctrine are promulgated in ***Fighting Instructions***, With much additional tactical doctrine contained in NATO publications.

At each level, consideration has to be given to the types of operations that are to be conducted and the extent to which force needs to be applied to achieve political and military objectives. Ultimately, the UK's maritime forces must be capable of operating within the extremes of violence typical of those associated with general war. While general war is currently considered to be an unlikely eventuality, the intensity of violence associated with it cannot be dismissed to the same extent. High intensity operations may be required to achieve success in conditions falling well short of general war. Maritime forces must be able to function in high intensity situations and survive them in order to ensure success. The tendency for lower intensity operations to escalate, and for original limited objectives to expand, means that reserves of combat capability will be necessary to provide higher level decision-makers with an adequate range of options. Maritime forces must, therefore, be equipped and trained to allow for escalation to a higher intensity of operations than those for which they may originally have been deployed.

THE INFLUENCE OF LAW ON MARITIME OPERATIONS

Regardless of the level, intensity and type of maritime operations being conducted, including routine peacetime activities, they must be carried out within the limits imposed by international law and, where appropriate, within the limits imposed by either UK domestic law or that applying in other jurisdictions. Notwithstanding the inherent right of self defence, legal restraints on all maritime operations will be reflected in the *Rules of Engagement* (ROE). Royal Navy warships invariably operate with promulgated ROE, including during the conduct of routine peacetime activities.

1/1. The Principles of War

Essential to the art of military leadership and command is the ability to learn from one's own experience and that of others. The *Principles of War* are a distillation of experience and a simplification of complex and sometimes contradictory ideas. They are broad precepts for the conduct of armed conflict. They should be used to inform all military strategic and operational decisions rather than as a planning checklist. The ten Principles recognised by the armed forces of the UK are described in detail in ***BDD***. They are illustrated below:

Selection and Maintenance of the Aim

In the two world wars, shipping was a key element of Allied strategy. In both wars, the Germans attempted to disrupt this by submarine attack. There was a belated recognition in 1917 that protection of shipping rather than futile hunting operations was vital to this struggle and a convoy system was adopted in 1939.

Maintenance of Morale

During the sustained 'island-hopping' operations against Japanese held islands in the Pacific during the Second World War, an important American element was carrier air power. Many operations had submarines stationed off the islands to serve as search and rescue ships. This not only preserved a valuable asset but helped keep morale high.

Security

In mid-1943 a substantial defeat had been inflicted on German U-boats in the mid-Atlantic. Intelligence permitted a continuing assessment to be made that no large-scale assault on convoys was likely to occur for some time. This assurance allowed the switching of assets to other operations.

Surprise

During operations against Iraq in 1991, allied forces posed the possibility of an amphibious assault more or less directly against

Kuwait City. However, the Iraqi perception that it would take place was bolstered by certain deliberate Allied manoeuvres to reinforce the impression, tying down significant Iraqi land forces in the Kuwait area. The surprise, when the allied offensive came was that it did not include an amphibious element.

Offensive Action

Convoy operations to North Russia 1941-5 were often subject to a high level of surface threat from German surface warships. Although often materially and numerically superior to their British opponents they were nearly always driven off by determined offensive actions, allowing passage of the convoys and minimising damage to them.

Concentration of Force

In 1939, German warship raids caused considerable concern. One of these, the pocket battleship Graf Spee was very dangerous and a concentration of cruisers, each individually much inferior to the German, engaged her off the River Plate estuary in December 1939. A combination of determination and guile ensured the neutralisation of the German ship but the key to the success of the engagement was the concentration of a force which could easily have been defeated piecemeal.

Economy of Effort

British mining of the central Baltic in the area of the Bay of Gdansk in the Second World War brought results out of all proportion to the effort. Mines averaging fewer than 600 per year were laid by aircraft. Not only did these inflict a significant number of casualties but they also created enormous amounts of disruption, particularly affecting the German submarine trials and training programmes - a strategic outcome for a tactical effort.

Flexibility

In November 1965, Rhodesia made a unilateral declaration of independence and the United Kingdom responded by establishing a trade embargo. Within a few days an aircraft carrier despatched from

Singapore was able to supply airborne monitoring of the ports used by Rhodesia, well in advance of any significant land-based effort and not tied to Host Nation Support (HNS). Longer-term monitoring was established by means of a frigate patrol.

Co-operation

In 1982 during the Falklands War and again in 1998 in operations in the Gulf, both Royal Navy Sea Harriers and Royal Air Force Harriers were embarked on board a CVS enhancing the range of capabilities deployed for operations.

Sustainability

Long-range operations during the Falklands War posed considerable logistic problems, being conducted many thousands of miles from a significant base. The rapid establishment of the extensive Support Unit on Ascension Island, together with the forward deployment of support ships permitted high-intensity military operations for as long as was necessary.

Sustainability

Ch 2

HMS IRON DUKE

THE MARITIME ENVIRONMENT AND THE NATURE OF MARITIME POWER

Chapter 2

The maritime environment is the principal factor influencing the nature and attributes of maritime power. How those attributes are applied in any given set of circumstances will, of course, depend on the understanding and skill of those commanding maritime forces. It is a truism to say that maritime commanders need a thorough understanding of both the environment in which they are operating and the attributes of those forces under their command. What this chapter sets out to do is expose the nature of the maritime environment, in all its principal facets, and then identify the attributes of those forces that operate within it.

Ch 2

THE MARITIME ENVIRONMENT AND THE NATURE OF MARITIME POWER

THE MARITIME STRATEGIC ENVIRONMENT

Seventy percent of the earth's surface is covered by sea and over two-thirds of the world's population lives within 100 miles of it. Over 150 of the 185 member states of the UN are coastal states. Since the 1970s they have extended their jurisdiction out to sea, in many cases as far as 200 nautical miles and in some cases well beyond that. Most human maritime activity - shipping, fishing, oil exploration etc - is conducted within that 200 mile coastal zone. What this means is that a substantial proportion of the world's economic and political activity is being conducted in a narrow strip of land and sea on average no wider than 300 miles. This is often referred to as the 'littoral'; it is certainly that area within which *littoral* operations will be conducted.

Strictly speaking, therefore, the maritime environment consists of a combination of land and sea and, of course, the airspace and outer space above both. However, the word 'maritime' is to do with the seas and it is on that element of the maritime environment that the discussion in this chapter will concentrate.

The maritime environment has five dimensions of *military-strategic* relevance: economic, political, legal, military and physical. These are not listed in any order of importance, nor should they be regarded as distinct from each other. One can examine each dimension in turn but, in so doing, will inevitably see aspects of the other four, as is certainly the case with the discussion which follows.

The Economic Dimension

Economically, the traditional use of the sea is as a medium for transport. Ships still account for 99.5% of trans-oceanic trade, the volume of which has increased by a factor of eight since 1945; and it continues to increase. Maritime trade will certainly remain the principal means by which raw materials and manufactured goods are transported between supplier and customer nations. One third of that trade is in oil and petroleum products, about half of that originating in the Middle East, most going to either Western Europe or Japan. Other cargoes of note are iron ore (9% of seaborne trade), coal (8%) and grain (5%). The remainder, can be classified as 'other dry cargoes' (fruit, meat and manufactured goods). It is almost a cliche to refer to the UK's heavy reliance on seaborne trade, but it is heavily reliant, as is the European Union as a whole.

Maritime trade reflects the increasingly interdependent and complex nature of the modern world and the operation of an intense free-market environment. Ships belonging to a company registered in one nation may be registered under the flag of another; they may also have multinational crews with conflicting loyalties. Shipping companies themselves may be components of international conglomerates, as may the owners of the cargo being carried. As a consequence, the identification of beneficial ownership and appropriate state responsibility for protection of shipping, together with interest in its employment and safety, are often complex matters. These complexities are of concern to the UK in connection with its own trading activities. However, they are also relevant when it comes to applying economic sanctions, through *embargo* operations.

Fishery Protection

Fish provides about 25% of the world supply of animal protein. The bulk of the world catch is taken in the relatively shallow waters of the continental shelf, within 200 mile *exclusive economic zones* (EEZs). About 75% of the total catch comes from the North Atlantic and Arctic, North Pacific and the west coasts of Africa and the Americas. Approximately 70% of the total annual European catch is taken from within the UK's Extended Fishery Zone (EFZ). The control of fishing and the management of fish stocks is problematic, with most fishing nations deploying fleets to grounds within other states' EEZs. For some states, fishing can represent a substantial proportion of their economic activity. Over-fishing is today a major feature of almost all world fisheries, with stocks declining as technology makes fleets more efficient. Scarcity of fish and over-fishing produce potential for dispute. To prevent over-fishing, more rigid and better policed regimes are required.

Nothing has motivated coastal states to extend jurisdiction more than the prospect of hydrocarbon riches on the continental shelf. This has also created potential for dispute. While maritime boundary disputes are generally resolved peacefully, there are some whose political, legal and economic complexity defy negotiated resolution. The reason for crisis in the South China Sea, for example, is related (though not exclusively) to the prospect of substantial oil or gas fields in the region. Oil is a diminishing resource and will continue to be a highly attractive commodity of which states will wish to take full advantage.

Also within the economic dimension are illicit activities that can undermine the security of coastal regions and also threaten UK interests, both at home and abroad. The trafficking in illegal narcotics is perhaps the greatest criminal threat to our security in the long term and piracy remains a threat in a number of regions around the world.

The Political Dimension

The modern political dimension of the maritime environment took shape largely during the 1970s. For a great many coastal states, especially those in the developing world, the waters adjacent to their coasts represented the only prospect for expansion. The extension of sovereignty was often a political act which happened to have some economic consequences, rather than something which was done for objective, calculated economic benefit. Many states, especially small island territories, having asserted their rights to claim sovereignty over offshore resources, now find themselves without the wherewithal to police their *maritime domains* and manage their maritime resources effectively. Disputes over boundaries may be motivated more by political symbolism than by pragmatic calculation of costs and benefits.

Some states are increasingly regarding their maritime domains as part of their territory when, legally, territorial sovereignty is both restricted to a maximum of 12 nautical miles from the coast and limited by the rights of other states to exercise innocent passage. This is especially important in the context of international straits and archipelagic waters that define strategic choke points in which the coastal states have no right to suspend innocent passage. The extension of territorial jurisdiction has increased the likelihood of disputes over freedom of passage and use of *littoral* seas, with traditional maritime powers, including the UK and the US, resisting further restrictions on *high seas* freedoms. The US reactions during the 1980s to Libyan claims in the Gulf of Sirte are good examples.

The Legal Dimension

All of this leads to the legal dimension, the main framework of which is the **1982 UN Convention on the Law of the Sea (1982 UNCLOS)**, of which the UK became a party in 1997. The UNCLOS process has transformed the maritime environment, which has become far more complex in the legal sense. Those conducting maritime operations need to understand its complexities and should be familiar with the contents of the guidance contained in the **RN's Handbook on the**

HMS SOMERSET visits St Petersburg 1998

Law of Maritime Operations (BR3012). This provides guidance on both the rights and obligations of all states enshrined in *1982 UNCLOS*, including precisely what is and is not permitted in the various jurisdictional zones that coastal states may now claim as elements of their *maritime domains*. Commanders of maritime forces cannot function legally without an instinctive feel for the restrictions imposed on them in *internal waters, territorial seas, contiguous zones, exclusive economic zones* and on the *continental shelves* claimed by coastal states. They will not be able to take full advantage of maritime mobility without a similar understanding of the rights of *innocent passage, straits transit passage* and *archipelagic sea lanes passage*.

International law provides free and legal access for ships up to the territorial seas of nations and rights of innocent passage for the purpose of either traversing territorial waters without entering internal waters, or proceeding in either direction between the high seas and internal waters.

Law has a tendency to breed more law and there is little doubt that the legal dimension will continue to develop. Pressure for more law is currently focused on environmental concerns, which may further restrict ship movements and undermine flag state rights. There is a need for more effective policing of the existing regime, in particular in relation to fisheries and drug interdiction, but this has to be balanced against the need to retain freedom of navigation.

The Military Dimension

The Peloponnesian Wars, fought in the fifth and fourth centuries BC, pitted Athenian maritime power against continental Sparta; already the seas had a military dimension to them. This is not changing and shows no sign of doing so, despite marginal attempts to demilitarise the oceans. There are over 150 navies worldwide, ranging from the one remaining superpower navy at one end of the spectrum, to tiny, heavily resource constrained coastal policing forces from the developing world and former Soviet states, at the other. Between those two extremes there is a considerable variety of expertise and ability. Navies of medium capability continue to develop and increase in number, those of India and Japan being good examples of maritime forces being consolidated, while that of China, impressive though it is in numbers, has some way to go before it emerges as a powerful force. What is important to realise, of course, is that relatively minor maritime powers can pose threats of significance, especially in the context of lower intensity maritime operations. With the bulk of maritime military operations likely to be concentrated in the *littorals*, small, fast vessels armed with relatively unsophisticated surface to surface missiles can complicate *sea control* calculations. Once open hostilities break out, this type of threat can be dealt with reasonably effectively by a competent and well packaged maritime force; it is in those periods of rising tension, when states are flexing their muscles and the atmosphere is one of ambiguity and caution mixed with firm assertion of rights, in which the presence of such vessels generates most concern. Add to them a conventional submarine threat and the maintenance of adequate sea control becomes considerably more complex.

The military dimension of the oceans has a technological angle to it, but one that must be heavily caveated. Navies are equipment intensive armed forces and modern warships are sophisticated weapons platforms linked to one another in *task groups* by equally sophisticated *command and control* systems. But technology is no panacea. Relatively unsophisticated vessels (the small fast attack craft and conventional submarines mentioned above, for example) can tie up the most sophisticated task group and seriously threaten its mission.

At the other end of the scale is the problem associated with highly sophisticated navies trying to operate with the less well provided. This is a problem that is being highlighted by the increasing need for individual navies to operate together in multinational forces. Difficulties of interoperability have been encountered when attempting to put forces together under the auspices of well established alliance arrangements within NATO and the WEU. They are made even more complex when multinational forces are coalitions of willing nations' navies operating with different procedures and doctrine related to different equipments and capabilities. Concern is being expressed in particular about the future compatibility of US Navy systems and those available in other navies. Multinational maritime operations require compatibility in both equipment and doctrinal terms.

The Physical Dimension

Last but not least is the physical dimension. A comprehensive knowledge of the physical environment in which maritime forces are to operate is essential, as geographic, oceanographic and meteorological conditions will affect their ability to conduct operations.

Ch 2

THE MARITIME ENVIRONMENT AND THE NATURE OF MARITIME POWER

The most obvious point to make is that the oceans provide access to all parts of the globe, with the exception of those regions at the core of the large continents, in particular Asia. With 85% of states having a coastline, the almost ubiquitous quality of the seas is one of their most important features.

The operating areas of maritime forces range from the deep waters of the open oceans (known colloquially as blue water) to the more confined and often - although not invariably - shallower waters of *littoral* regions, estuaries and rivers (frequently, though misleadingly, referred to as 'brown water'). Perhaps the most significant physical characteristic, however, is the position of the land bordering the sea. This may seem a trite point but it is of great import and consequence. Maritime choke points are but one manifestation of this factor. The Straits of Gibraltar, of Bab-el-Mandeb, of Hormuz, of Malacca and Formosa, are but five of the seventeen or eighteen most strategically significant in the world. The greatest cluster is in and around Indonesia, the Philippines and the South China Sea. The closure of significant straits in that region could increase deployment distance and times by substantial amounts for a US Navy Carrier Battle Group, for example, needing to deploy from Japan into the Indian Ocean and on into the Gulf.

Weather can have a significant *tactical* or *operational* impact and, in so doing, influence *military-strategic* decision-making. The campaign in the South Atlantic in 1982 was weather dependent and a delay much beyond the dates during which the conflict was conducted might have turned the balance of advantage towards the Argentinians with decisive effect; seasonal fluctuations in weather can have strategic significance. The effect of high sea states on flying operations and sonar performance are examples of ways in which operations may be made more difficult. However, these conditions will also affect an enemy. Skilful seamanship and well rehearsed tactics and procedures can reduce these effects. Adverse conditions can also be used to advantage; a submarine, for example, can use poor sonar conditions to avoid detection. The mobility of maritime forces may allow them to move to an operating area where conditions are more favourable. An aircraft carrier can, for instance, seek out and exploit a local window in poor visibility to continue flying operations. Expertise in oceanography and meteorology and comprehensive hydrographic support is vital if a commander is to exploit the maritime environment fully and minimize its adverse effects. The ability to carry out *Rapid Environmental Assessment (REA)* in times of crisis and increasing tension is an essential part of a maritime force's range of combat capabilities. Increasingly, environmental analysis is becoming embedded in the range of warfare disciplines present in a well balanced and capable maritime force.

THE MULTI-DIMENSIONAL MARITIME BATTLESPACE

Maritime forces must be capable of influencing events and actions above, on and below the surface of the sea. The oceans provide three dimensional space in which maritime forces can manoeuvre. They are an international arena for the demonstration of capability and the will to use force or apply influence. Currently, a threat can be posed from any direction and a recognised maritime picture must be established through comprehensive surveillance. All systems, including space and air based area sensors, must be co-ordinated to maintain a continuous, reliable and timely flow of useful data. The sea is, however, largely opaque to many sensors. It can therefore be used as a hiding place, for example by ballistic and cruise missile firing submarines.

Surface ships can be detected by satellite or air surveillance, but it is often hard to locate and identify targets with sufficient certainty to engage them, especially if they are not radiating. In open waters, attacking forces will usually have wide options for manoeuvre and may pose a diverse, unpredictable threat which places large demands on defending forces, particularly if the attacking force has a balance of offensive and defensive capabilities. This can favour the offensive, though defending forces can concentrate strength around units at risk, thus increasing the options for offensive manoeuvre. The possibility of drawing the attacker to his destruction can, in certain circumstances, redress the balance in favour of the defensive. Indeed an engagement might be positively welcome in providing an opportunity to inflict *attrition* on the enemy.

Future trends and interests are increasingly likely to be found in the *littoral* regions of the world, nominally those areas of land and sea which are susceptible to influence at and from the sea. The proximity of land places certain limitations on freedom of movement, avenues of approach and on both offensive and defensive options. There may be no alternative to passing through geographic choke points or waters in which surveillance and defence options are difficult and the possibility of low-cost surprise attack enhanced. The *littoral* environment will generally favour forces that can exploit limited warning time to their advantage, particularly when *sea denial* units are linked by sophisticated computerised counter surveillance systems. Thus, surveillance and weapon systems must be capable of dealing with the more complex littoral region and confronting the particular problems encountered when crossing environmental boundaries.

ATTRIBUTES OF MARITIME POWER

Success in a major operation will usually require the *joint* integration of sea, land and air forces to ensure the application of the right tool at the right place at the right time. Individual military units need to co-operate and complement each other to achieve the common aim. Commanders of *joint* forces have to be able to recognise the distinctive attributes of each of the components, in order to play each to its strengths, especially important in the conduct of a *manoeuvrist* campaign. Maritime forces have distinctive operational attributes.

Access

Over two-thirds of the world is covered by the sea and this allows maritime forces to exploit the oceans as a strategic medium for their relatively unhindered deployment to the most significant areas of interest and threat. Not only does access of this sort allow for intervention at a time and place of political choosing, very often maritime forces will routinely be in close proximity to crises as they are developing. Three-quarters of all states have a coastline and even many of those that are landlocked will be accessible from the sea with the co-operation of neighbouring coastal states.

Mobility

Maritime forces can move hundreds of miles per day over more than two-thirds of the world's surface, allowing access to the most

CVS/MCMVs deployed in the northern Gulf 1998

significant area of human, military and economic activity. Mobility enables maritime forces to respond from over the horizon, becoming selectively visible and threatening to potential adversaries. It also adds a critical dimension to all *joint operations*.

Versatility

Warships can easily change their military posture, undertake several tasks concurrently and be rapidly available for re-tasking. They can present a range of flexible and well calibrated political signals. Furthermore, maritime command, control and information systems at the *strategic, operational* and *tactical* levels offer uniquely sensitive, flexible opportunities to complement diplomacy. The UK's maritime forces are also routinely operating with other nations' maritime forces, providing a flexibility of force packaging that transcends the limits of our own capabilities. There is, of course, a corollary to versatility in support of diplomacy. Those states being signalled may misunderstand the level of threat being posed, and concurrent diplomatic activity may be required to resolve unintended ambiguity. The elements of versatility can be summarised as:

Flexibility in Response Ships at high *readiness* are always manned and provisioned for hostilities and their systems and crews can respond rapidly to contingencies by progressing quickly from peacetime cruising, through enhanced readiness, to a more combatant posture if required. This is particularly important as high impact episodes can occur in scenarios traditionally considered as low intensity situations.

Adaptability in Roles An individual warship of frigate size and above will have defensive and offensive capabilities in all three dimensions (air, surface and sub-surface). It can, therefore, operate in a variety of operational environments. Warships can be formed into *task forces* and *task groups* in which their individual characteristics combine to provide a mutually supportive, powerful and versatile combination of offensive and defensive capabilities. This, in turn, allows the group to operate at higher threat levels where conditions might be beyond the capability of a single ship.

Joint and Multinational Attributes Maritime forces have traditionally taken part in operations involving other services and the crossing of environmental boundaries. By the very process of providing an amphibious capability for a multi-threat environment, the UK's maritime forces regularly practise *joint operations*. Maritime operations are joint by definition, as balanced naval forces, comprising air, land, in the form of amphibious elements, and integral naval power under a composite command structure, typify. They can provide afloat headquarters, logistics, area surveillance and denial platforms and facilities for joint forces offering advantages in flexibility, sustainability and access. Indeed, forces delivered into theatre by sea as part of an amphibious *task group* are configured tactically and deployed ready for use; they are not merely transported. They are available for a joint *task force* commander to be afloat or ashore - depending on the nature of an operation. Their integral combat power can be increasingly decisive in the shaping and sustaining of most modern operations. British maritime forces comprise discrete national units well practised in operating in multinational groups, either within NATO or in ad hoc coalitions. Inherent mobility allows maritime forces to assemble easily and the use of NATO and multinational doctrine and procedures allow multinational groups to co-operate and combine with the minimum of planning and preparation.

Multinational maritime forces benefit from frequent periods in company to exercise and develop their full operational effectiveness.

Sustained Reach

Maritime forces have integral *logistic* support, including repair and medical facilities. The range and *endurance* that these provide, give individual maritime units autonomy and sustained *reach*, which is the ability to operate for extended periods at considerable distance from shore support. *Reach* is enhanced by the provision of *organic* and *consolidation* tankers, supply and repair vessels. Only a maritime force so equipped can exploit the full potential of maritime power. If reach is to be sustained for an extended period, a *roulement* of replacement forces may be required. Seaborne logistic support provided by *sea basing* is an important element in sustaining *joint* operations, particularly those engaged in full *manoeuvre warfare*.

FORTs VICTORIA and GEORGE in Bahrein 1998

Resilience

Warships are designed to absorb substantial damage before they become non-operational. While a loss of capability through damage will degrade operational performance, a ship is designed with this in mind and her company trained to restore systems to use as quickly as possible. They are also designed to operate within areas contaminated through the use of weapons of mass destruction (WMD) with minimum degradation to their operational capability.

Lift Capacity

Sealift permits land and amphibious forces to transit and *poise* in theatre, and then enables joint power to be brought to bear ashore. Furthermore, it may often be the only practicable means of deploying mass (significant land and air forces, their battle winning equipment and logistic support) into a theatre of operations quickly and cheaply. For the UK, all major operations necessitate some maritime support to deploy, re-supply, withdraw, or re-deploy forces which have mass or have to deploy for extended periods. Although the *Royal Fleet Auxiliary* provides some sealift, a major operation relies for *lift* on ships taken up from trade, which may not necessarily be British registered or indeed readily available. An important duty for maritime forces is protecting the unhindered passage of this sealift.

Poise

Once in theatre, maritime forces can remain on station for prolonged periods, either covertly or overtly. They can retain or seize the initiative or signal political resolve, and act as a force for *deterrence* or active *coercion*. The ability of maritime forces to poise in international waters lessens the 'footprint', that is to say the political complications and military risks of deploying forces for extended periods on land. This unique capability to match the pace and reflect the tone of diplomatic activity is particularly useful in the dynamic and uncertain situations of the modern world. This is because poise exploits mobility, versatility, sustained reach, and lift capacity.

Leverage

Through suitable positioning and force packaging, maritime forces can provide maritime *leverage* to exploit access and to have an influence on events ashore disproportionately greater than the scale of force applied. Leverage is both a strategic and an operational concept, whose effects can be directly political or primarily military.

Political leverage involves the coercion of governments which, in advance of *hostilities,* is an aspect of naval diplomacy. By way of military example, at the strategic level, a maritime nation or coalition can use maritime and other expeditionary forces to shape and, if relevant, exploit the battlespace and expose an enemy's flank and rear. At the operational level, joint forces on a seaward front or flank can provide *manoeuvre from the sea* to attack, *distract* and tie down much larger forces ashore, *envelop* or otherwise achieve the *disruption* of an enemy.

2/1. The Impact of Maritime Power

In his book *The Leverage of Seapower* Colin Gray points to the ability of maritime power to "control the geo-strategic terms of engagement in war". While it is important to appreciate that this will not invariably be the case, as Gray goes on to say:

"Depending on who controls the sea, water is a highway or a barrier. The continuity of the world's seas and oceans translates into a global mobility and agility for maritime forces which can have no continental parallel. That mobility and agility has been used time and again, in all historical periods to achieve surprise and the full strategic advantage of surprise effect. Finally, and notwithstanding the several revolutions in transportation technologies for all environments over the centuries, superior seapower has enabled its owners to knit together coalitions with a total strategic weight greatly superior to those secured by dominant continental strength".

It is also worth recalling the words of the Duke of Wellington during the Peninsular War:

"If anyone wishes to know the history of this war, I will tell them it is our maritime superiority which gives me the power of maintaining my Army while the enemy are unable to do the same"

And to demonstrate that 'littoral warfare' is by no means an entirely new concept, the words of Thomas More Molyneux from his 1759 work on *Conjunct Operations* (conjunct meaning joint):

> "A military, naval and littoral war, when widely prepared and discretely conducted, is a terrible sort of war. Happy for that people who are Sovereigns enough of the sea to put it into execution. For it comes like thunder and lightning to some unprepared part of the world."

However, a balanced treatment will also accept the limitations of maritime power and who better to quote than Sir Julian Corbett, from his classic expression of British Maritime Doctrine, *Some Principles of Maritime Strategy* (1911). He argued that it was:

> "almost impossible that a war can be decided by naval action alone. Unaided, naval pressure can only work by a process of exhaustion. Its effects must always be slow, and so galling both to our own commercial community and to neutrals, that the tendency is always to accept terms of peace that are far from conclusive. For a firm decision a quicker and more drastic form of pressure is required. Since men live upon the land, and not upon the sea, great issues between nations at war have always been decided - except in the rarest of cases - either by what your army can do against your enemy's territory or else by the fear of what the fleet makes it possible for your army to do."

CONCLUDING COMMENTS

Maritime power, in the broadest of senses, is military, political and economic power or influence exerted through an ability to use the sea. Maritime power has traditionally been employed to control sea communications for the general economic welfare or survival of sea dependent states. Military maritime power has also an established ability to influence events on land through amphibious and ship launched land attack operations and as a component of joint operations. Maritime forces, in turn, can shape and exploit a battlespace to enable the introduction or integration of land forces and the staging of a major air campaign. This power projection capability has greatly expanded with the combined effect of modern sea-based and maritime aircraft, evolving amphibious techniques and the introduction of land attack missiles. Thus, while maritime power has demonstrated an integral air, sea and land impact the unifying factor is use of the sea.

There are two general maxims that can be discerned from a study of the use of maritime power throughout history (see Box 2/1). First, a continental power can win a war if it is able to secure military command at sea, achieve *sea denial*, or even just dispute command of the sea vigorously. Second, for a sea power or a maritime-dependent coalition, command of the sea provides the strategic conditions indispensable for success in war. These propositions explain the strategic dependence of both the UK and NATO on maritime power, particularly in the modern, interdependent world.

The maritime power that a maritime nation and alliance requires for security in the event of major attack can be used to protect national interests in situations of lesser intensity and impact. Thus, the forces and systems available for deployment around Europe can be seamlessly transferred to any area of national or alliance interest accessible from the sea. It can also provide opportunities to contribute to wider security and stability through conflict prevention and *conflict control*. Maritime forces can maintain presence without occupation; coercion without *embroilment*.

The utility of maritime forces in *joint operations* is most evident in the execution of a strategy designed to achieve objectives ashore by using access from the sea as a principal factor. Land forces may only be able to obtain access if they are landed by *naval forces*, creating the conditions for success through shaping and amphibious operations. Even when this is not the case, ground forces may be prevented from achieving their objectives unless maritime forces can safeguard their *lines of support*. Future operations will benefit from the ability of maritime platforms to support land operations by sea-basing. Movement of naval forces on the *high seas* can take place without prior diplomatic agreement. Furthermore, combat in open waters does not violate territorial integrity nor entail much risk of *collateral damage* to innocent parties. Maritime operations may therefore be conducted within a more flexible framework of political choice and risk than land operations. On the other hand a maritime force may include valuable units and there may be important political, psychological, and operational consequences if these are exposed to

Ch 2
THE MARITIME ENVIRONMENT AND THE NATURE OF MARITIME POWER

the possibility of *catastrophic* damage. The management of military risk is clearly an important element of any operation. The relatively unconstrained use of the seas allows the commander to manage risk to his force through choice of route and environment, and ease of extrication, conforming to the needs of political choice of time and space. In littoral waters, however, these options are likely to be more restricted, but are likely to be balanced by broader factors.

SIR TRISTRAM

2/2. Examples of Attributes:

These are all drawn from the landings in Normandy in June 1944 and the events of the succeeding months.

Access

A statement of the blindingly obvious, perhaps, but it was the sea that provided the medium through which the invasion force was able to gain access to the French coast. Very obviously, access, as an attribute, was linked in very closely with mobility.

Mobility

The inherent movement flexibility of a seaborne military force allowed the greatest possible choice of potential landing areas. In particular the force's great capability, meant that the choice of landing area was not merely restricted to the shortest possible sea crossing.

Versatility

During the landings some of the inshore fire support was obtained by innovative and improvisatory conversions of landing craft to produce a support squadron armed with guns, of up to medium calibre, and powerful bombardment rockets. These were later used to defend the beachead from German naval attack and were later to play an even more important role in the taking of Walcheren in the autumn.

Sustained Reach

Although by the later standards of the British Pacific Fleet and the Falklands in 1982 the distances were not as great. The sustenance of the ever-growing Allied land and air forces for several months until a deep-water high capacity port could be operated in late autumn 1944 was a considerable achievement.

Resilience

The planning for NEPTUNE had to take into account a number of adverse factors including weather and enemy measures from the air, on land and at sea; mines in shallow water and beach obstructions were particular hazards. The plans had not only to try and obviate these problems but allow for their effects. This was very successful.

Lift Capacity

On D-Day itself, 6 June, some 130,000 troops, their equipment and initial logistic support were landed. By the end of the month over 860,000 men, nearly 160,000 vehicles and over half a million tons of stores had been put ashore.

Poise

Poise is generally associated with forces at sea, but not always, In this case, it was exercised with much of the force still in harbour. In any event the potential to have gone to any one of several destinations at a time of Allied choosing demonstrated a very useful degree of poise.

Leverage

Following on from the point on poise, the ability to land in a number of alternative locations and at almost any time, as perceived by the enemy, was very useful. It tied up a much greater land force of limited land mobility than the five divisions actually delivered by Operation NEPTUNE, exerting a high degree of leverage.

Air Supremacy is a necessary precondition of command of the sea

CONCEPTS GOVERNING THE USE OF MARITIME POWER

Chapter 3

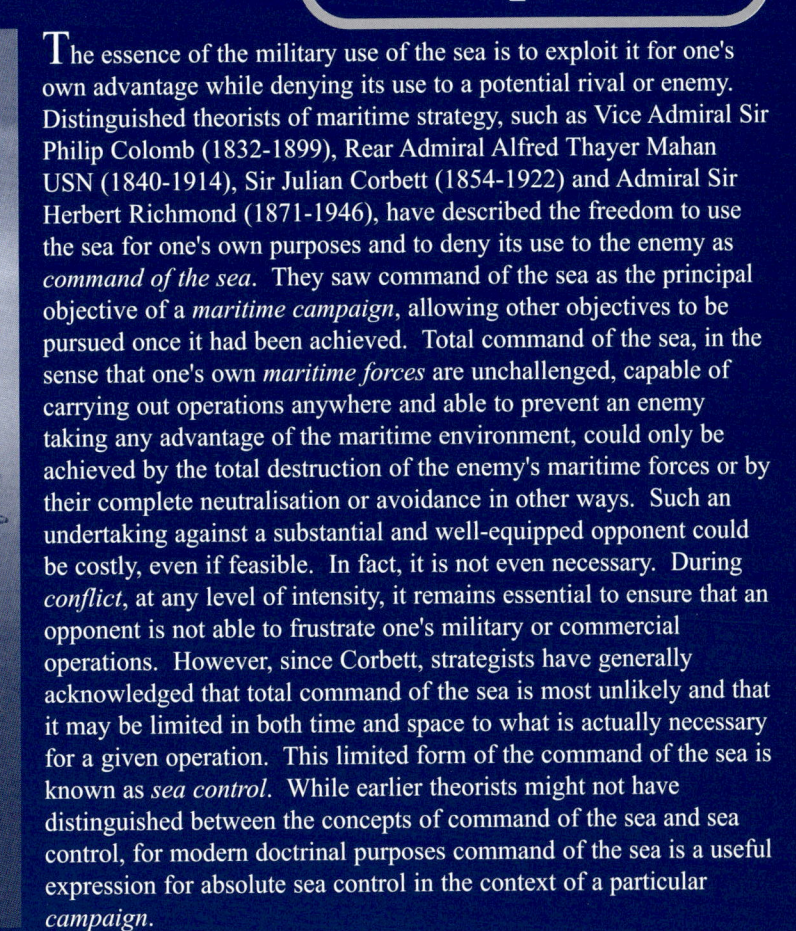

The essence of the military use of the sea is to exploit it for one's own advantage while denying its use to a potential rival or enemy. Distinguished theorists of maritime strategy, such as Vice Admiral Sir Philip Colomb (1832-1899), Rear Admiral Alfred Thayer Mahan USN (1840-1914), Sir Julian Corbett (1854-1922) and Admiral Sir Herbert Richmond (1871-1946), have described the freedom to use the sea for one's own purposes and to deny its use to the enemy as *command of the sea*. They saw command of the sea as the principal objective of a *maritime campaign*, allowing other objectives to be pursued once it had been achieved. Total command of the sea, in the sense that one's own *maritime forces* are unchallenged, capable of carrying out operations anywhere and able to prevent an enemy taking any advantage of the maritime environment, could only be achieved by the total destruction of the enemy's maritime forces or by their complete neutralisation or avoidance in other ways. Such an undertaking against a substantial and well-equipped opponent could be costly, even if feasible. In fact, it is not even necessary. During *conflict*, at any level of intensity, it remains essential to ensure that an opponent is not able to frustrate one's military or commercial operations. However, since Corbett, strategists have generally acknowledged that total command of the sea is most unlikely and that it may be limited in both time and space to what is actually necessary for a given operation. This limited form of the command of the sea is known as *sea control*. While earlier theorists might not have distinguished between the concepts of command of the sea and sea control, for modern doctrinal purposes command of the sea is a useful expression for absolute sea control in the context of a particular *campaign*.

SEA CONTROL

Sea Control is defined as the condition in which one has freedom of action to use the sea for one's own purposes in specified areas and for specified periods of time and, where necessary, to deny or limit its use to the enemy. There is likely to be a requirement for sea control across the spectrum of conflict. At the lower end of the spectrum, maritime forces may be used to ensure freedom of navigation by a *deterrent* presence in areas where illegal acts or constraints are being threatened or applied to merchant shipping. At the highest end it may be necessary to use a huge array of maritime power to eliminate an enemy's ability to challenge sea control over large areas of ocean. The need for *sea control* is not dependent upon the existence of a substantial threat. If there is any risk to freedom of action, sea control is necessary. If the risk is small, the capabilities that will be needed can be correspondingly modest.

Early achievement and retention of the necessary level of sea control will, almost invariably, be a component of any major maritime or *expeditionary campaign* or operation. However, there can be no absolute guarantee of protection from attack at sea unless command of the sea has been achieved. Sea control must be related to acceptable risk. For operations to take place, a working level of sea control must be achieved to provide sufficient freedom of action within an acceptable level of risk. If sea control remains in dispute in a certain area, each side will be forced to operate in the face of considerable risk. However, sea control is most unlikely to be an end in itself; it is essentially a necessary condition to allow use of the sea for further purposes.

Sea control comprises *control* of the surface and sub-surface environments and of the airspace above the area of control. The control of airspace is also one of degree. The minimum requirement for a successful operation is a *favourable air situation* although, to avoid an unacceptable threat to one's own forces, *air superiority* is highly desirable and often a necessity. *Air supremacy* is a necessary precondition of command of the sea.

The geographical extent of sea control may vary from local control around a single unit to domination of very large sea areas. In many cases, such as the protection of ports and anchorages, amphibious operations and providing support to the land battle, it must be achieved and maintained up to the shoreline. Air superiority may then be required across the shoreline and some distance inshore. Because of confinement and congestion, attaining sea control is a more complex task in *littoral* regions than it is in open ocean.

SEA DENIAL

Sea Denial is exercised when one party denies another the ability to control a maritime area without either wishing or being able to control that area himself. Classic means of achieving it are to lay a minefield or to deploy submarines to threaten enemy surface forces; a more recent method, particularly appropriate in *littoral* operations, is to mount surface to surface missile batteries along the coast to pose an unacceptable level of risk to enemy surface units.

Sea denial and *sea control* operations are not mutually exclusive. The denial of the enemy's freedom of action is a consequence of effective sea control operations. It is important to understand also that sea denial operations in one element or area of the maritime *battlespace* may be necessary to achieve sea control elsewhere. However, the concept is only applicable when full sea control is not exercised by choice or out of necessity. At the *operational* and *tactical levels*, a zone of sea denial may be used as part of the outer defence of a force or area, or as a way of *containing* enemy forces. At the strategic level, sea denial can be used in a *guerre de course* or sustained attack upon a nation's shipping to prevent reinforcement and to sap national morale and the ability to wage *war*.

BATTLESPACE DOMINANCE

Battlespace dominance embraces control over the environments of the entire *battlespace*; the surface, subsurface, air, land and information environments, and the electromagnetic spectrum. Achievement of battlespace dominance in an area will necessarily entail *sea control* of the sea portions of that area. The concept of battlespace dominance is useful in *joint*, especially in the *littoral* operations where there is a need to maintain freedom of action ashore as well as at sea.

FLEET IN BEING

A nation deprived of maritime superiority might choose, or be forced, to adopt a strategy of *fleet in being*. By avoiding confrontation with

Ch 3
CONCEPTS GOVERNING THE USE OF MARITIME POWER

Merlin - for ASW Sea Control operations

a superior enemy, a nation can preserve its own maritime forces while continuing to threaten those of the enemy. The risk of attack complicates the enemy's choice of options. The French adopted this approach during both the Seven Years War and under Napoleon. In the twentieth century the most obvious example of the conduct of a Fleet in Being strategy was that adopted by Germany through most of the First World War when, by keeping their major surface combatants away from decisive battle, they kept the British fleet tied down. The threat from a fleet in being can prevent superior opposing forces from establishing their desired levels of sea control by diverting forces to other tasks, such as blockade or *containment*, and as such is a method of *sea denial*. A fleet in being can *compel* the enemy to concentrate his forces in a valuable area, or around valuable units, cause him to route his passage to his disadvantage or to amend his operational plans. It may also prevent the enemy from doing other things with the forces needed to deal with the fleet in being.

COVER

An important function for the major elements of a maritime force to provide is 'cover'. This is the provision of support, if required, to less powerful units or detached elements of the force that are engaged in operations of their own, taking advantage of the wider *sea control* that the main force has achieved. An example of cover would be air support provided to mine countermeasures units operating independently in an area of high air threat, but needing to do so in order to prepare a route into a landing for an amphibious force. It is vital for the commander of a maritime force to recognise his responsibilities to provide cover for detached units and not fall into the 'out of sight, out of mind' trap.

3/1. Covering Force

A traditional function of the main striking forces available in the fleet has been the provision of cover to less powerful units. In both World Wars, the battlefleet based in Scotland provided cover for lighter forces engaged on convoy escort operations. During the Cold War, the NATO Striking Fleet of aircraft carriers and their supporting forces carried out a similar potential function. As a contemporary source put it:

> "The Covering Force, known to the Americans as the 'Strike Fleet', consists of heavy carriers, cruisers and A/S and A/A escorts, the whole forming a balanced force. The Covering Force is analogous to the Grand Fleet of the First World War and the Home Fleet of the Second. It is,

in fact, the umbrella under which we exercise command of sea communications."

(Vice Chief of the Naval Staff to the Permanent Under Secretary, Ministry of Defence, 19 August 1954)

Cover is still a relevant concept. During the Falklands Campaign of 1982, the nuclear powered fleet submarines provided cover for the carrier and amphibious task groups engaged in the re-occupation of the islands. After the Argentine cruiser GENERAL BELGRANO had been sunk by HMS CONQUEROR, the rest of the surface forces of the Argentine Navy, previously of major concern to the British carrier task group commander, remained in their home waters. This latter day 'battlefleet asset' was acting just as her battleship namesake had done in 1914-18, containing dangerous enemy striking forces so that other forces could maintain *sea control* against a reduced threat, and by so doing allowed for power to be projected successfully against Argentine forces on the islands.

MARITIME POWER PROJECTION

Sea control ensures freedom of action above, on and below the surface of the sea. The projection of maritime power is the application of maritime power from the sea to influence events on land directly. It exploits *sea control* to achieve access to the coast and deliver power ashore in the form of amphibious forces, *organic* aircraft, land attack weapons and special forces. Indeed, it can deliver a full range of combat capabilities at all stages of a land operation.

Maritime power projection is a concept that has broad application both during hostilities and for *crisis management*. In a crisis, power projection capability is an important contributor to *naval diplomacy*, providing the principal seaborne instruments for *coercion* and reassurance. The sailing of power projection forces demonstrates political resolve without a specific statement of commitment. They can poise at sea for long periods providing clear evidence of intent and purpose. A maritime power projection force can provide the main or the lead elements for an *intervention* operation and provide a mobile base for humanitarian, peace support or *non-combatant evacuation* operations. Maritime power projection forces are a part of the maritime component of a national *expeditionary* capability. During hostilities, maritime power projection forces can use the sea to provide access to territory that is less accessible by land and air and to apply *manoeuvre from the sea*.

'MANOEUVRE WARFARE' AND MARITIME DOCTRINE

This brings us neatly on to the relationship between concepts of maritime warfare and those applied to campaigns ashore, a relationship of some importance given the extent to which the dominance of the littoral battlespace involves operations across environmental boundaries.

In achieving and maintaining *sea control*, maritime forces operate at the *tactical* level in a multidimensional field. Sea control is normally a temporary condition and there is no direct parallel to the control of territory and the progressive advance across it. Concepts used in land warfare such as *lines of support* and *the forward line of own troops*, have no direct analogies in warfare at sea at the *tactical level*. A commander of a tactical formation is likely to have *organic logistics* in the form of tankers and stores ships and may feel detached from any 'lines of support'. In particular he is unlikely to be as constrained as a land commander by the movement of his logistic *consolidation*. This is not to imply that *lines of support* have no relevance at all at the tactical level. In maritime parlance, they are more generally known as *sea lines of communication* (SLOCs) and a tactical commander may have protection of shipping as his mission. But in such a context, the SLOCs concerned are likely to be strategic and his own organic logistics will obviate the need for him invariably and continuously to consider the protection of his own 'lines of support'.

However, in a *joint campaign* and, specifically, during power projection operations, concepts of land warfare become relevant. At the *operational* and *strategic levels*, maritime warfare acquires some of the geographic characteristics of land warfare. The geographic relationship of events at sea to those ashore will usually be important to the operational commander. The apportionment, sustainment and protection of maritime *logistics* at the operational level are of a similar concern to a maritime commander as those of ground forces to a land commander. The operational commander will have the problem of consolidating his logistic shipping and, perhaps, of setting up a separate tactical operation to protect consolidation shipping and reinforcements. It would be wrong to underestimate the distinctive nature of the maritime environment, in particular its vastness, featurelessness, absence of impediments to movement, and the difficulties of achieving and avoiding encounter. However, at the *operational* and *strategic level*, joint doctrinal concepts are likely to prevail. These demand careful study by maritime commanders and staffs. They could include campaign planning tools such as *main effort, centre of gravity, decisive points, tempo, simultaneity* and the *culminating point* (see Chapter 7). Maritime commanders also need to be fully conversant with the overarching concept of *manoeuvre warfare*.

HMS WESTMINSTER

Manoeuvre Warfare

Manoeuvre is a concept of particular importance having two distinct but related meanings, both derived originally from land warfare concepts. Firstly it describes one of the combat functions used in *joint operations*, in which context it is a phrase closely approximating in meaning to 'mobility'. However, it is in its second meaning that its relevance to this discussion is concentrated; that is to say, *manoeuvre warfare* as an overarching approach to the conduct of military operations. It is far more than merely the use of mobility or tactical manoeuvre, and the application of mobility does not necessarily imply a manoeuvrist approach (the left flanking sweep against Iraqi land forces in the Gulf War of 1991, for example, could be regarded as the use of mobility in the execution of an attritional campaign, not as convincing evidence of a manoeuvrist approach).

Manoeuvre warfare has been presented by some theorists as an alternative to *attrition warfare*. Instead of seeking to destroy an enemy's physical substance by the cumulative effect of superior firepower (attrition warfare), the goal of manoeuvre warfare is to incapacitate an enemy by disrupting his fighting system *(systemic disruption)* through the concentration of superior force against those elements of his fighting system most likely to cause the collapse of his will. Fundamentally the aim is to shatter both his moral and physical cohesion.

Theoretically, manoeuvre warfare offers the possibility of results disproportionately greater than the resources applied, and thus the chance of success for the weaker side. It may also be a very cost-effective style of warfare for a stronger opponent, allowing him to achieve success while minimizing losses. Importantly, however, it can also fail completely if disruption does not occur as predicted. In its purest form, therefore, manoeuvre warfare entails an element of inherent risk not present in an operational concept relying largely on overwhelming force as a means of destruction.

In reality, any *campaign* will contain elements of both manoeuvrist and attritional styles of warfare; they complement each other and are by no means mutually exclusive. The threat or actual delivery of selective but overwhelming *attrition* against a key vulnerability can bring about the systemic disruption sought by manoeuvre, while a series of successful manoeuvre actions at one *level of war* may bring about cumulative effects of destruction that wear down an enemy at a higher level.

Ch 3
CONCEPTS GOVERNING THE USE OF MARITIME POWER

3/2. Manoeuvre from the Sea

Two outstanding examples of manoeuvre from the sea in which the Royal Navy played significant parts were the landing at Inchon in 1950 during the Korean War and the employment of amphibious forces in the 1991 Gulf War. In September 1950, three months after the North Korean invasion of the South the Northern forces had driven the United Nations forces into an area about Pusan in the far south of the peninsula. US Marines covered by the gunfire of two British and two American cruisers, stormed ashore at the port of Inchon near the South Korean capital of Seoul which was soon recaptured. This surprise amphibious attack struck the Northern forces in the flank, cut their lines of communication and caused their rapid collapse and retreat. Only massive Chinese intervention saved the day for the communist cause. In the Gulf War two US Marine Corps brigades first carried out a *demonstration* landing in Oman, then *poised* at sea. The effect was to tie down five Iraqi divisions in defence of the Kuwaiti coastline. On both occasions Royal Navy warships assisted in providing escort and barrier defence. In the Gulf the Royal Navy also provided the key mine countermeasures capability.

Manoeuvre and Joint Operations

In its most effective form, *manoeuvre warfare* has both spatial and temporal effect. That is to say, it employs manoeuvre to both gain positional advantage and generate a faster tempo of operations than the opposition. The aim is to achieve a decisive initiative in the right place and at the moment of one's own choosing. In applying this approach the intention is to undermine the opposition's ability to co-ordinate an effective response, rather than to destroy all components of his military capability through incremental attrition. So, the true value of firepower is not measured by its aggregate potential but rather by its selective, targeted and surgical application against the opposition's critical vulnerabilities.

All forces have the potential to offer ways and means of enhancing the manoeuvrist approach. To do this most effectively, all must be allowed to play to their particular strengths. Maritime, land and air

Fleet submarine sails for patrol

forces have different but complementary attributes: the *access*, mobility, versatility, sustained *reach*, resilience, *lift* capacity, forward *presence*, *poise* and *leverage* of maritime forces; land forces' capacity for shock action, protection and the ability to take and hold ground; and air power's ubiquity, speed, responsiveness and reach. These are the inherent strengths and they must be used to overcome relative weaknesses, both those that are themselves inherent and those that arise for reasons of circumstance or situation. Land forces, for example, may experience difficulties on their own in achieving a manoeuvrist approach because the terrain and physical features may severely restrict mobility. In such circumstances, a combination of air lift and maritime mobility may enable ground forces to move significant distances and re-deploy to maximum manoeuvrist effect, catching the opposition unawares. The maritime environment is especially conducive to manoeuvre of this sort, presenting land commanders with opportunities to get around their own traditional and situational difficulties by lateral thinking and action across environmental boundaries.

Joint operations are not simply a matter of forces from different arms of the armed forces operating in the same theatre. The real essence of effective command of manoeuvrist operations is to recognise the relative strengths and weaknesses (both inherent and situational) of each component of the force and to play each to its strengths in support of the others. By doing that, the value of a joint force is more than merely the sum of its constituent parts.

Maritime Manoeuvre

Maritime manoeuvre is the ability to use the unique access provided by the sea to apply force or influence at a time or place of political choice, taking into account the conditions of the modern world and the advances offered by technology. Historically, as well as from the standpoint of modern *doctrine*, maritime forces do not have a choice between manoeuvrist and other styles of warfare. *Manoeuvre warfare* theory is the intelligent use of force and is a logical development of the Principles of War, especially the principles of surprise, flexibility, concentration of force and economy of effort. Maritime forces combine *mobility*, firepower, flexibility and responsive *Command and Control* systems in a manner ideal for the pursuit of a Manoeuvrist campaign. The historical debate is significant because it reveals some important doctrinal points:

Ch 3

CONCEPTS GOVERNING THE USE OF MARITIME POWER

- Success in modern warfare against a well-equipped enemy requires superior intelligence, a quicker decision-making cycle, flexible and agile forces and systems that can deliver selective firepower at great range.

- Intelligence must be involved in all operational decision making.

- Opportunities for systemic disruption at the strategic and operational levels should be sought.

- Strategic and operational surprise may be difficult to achieve against an enemy with similar or superior intelligence and surveillance capabilities.

- There will always be a trade-off between risk and return. At those points at which force is to be brought to bear against an enemy, risk should be minimized by achieving an adequate superiority of force and surprise.

- The development of Manoeuvre Warfare theory has been a stimulus for interest in operational art and the operational level of war. Indeed, many of the concepts of joint operational level doctrine are drawn from Manoeuvre Warfare theory, in particular that of the centre of gravity.

Manoeuvre from the Sea as a Combat Function

The ground combat function of manoeuvre seeks a position of advantage with respect to the enemy from which force can be threatened or applied. An important role of maritime power projection forces, particularly amphibious forces, is to provide manoeuvre from the sea in this sense. Firepower can create the conditions for successful manoeuvre by providing the protection to cover movement into a favourable position, by disrupting or deceiving an enemy so that he cannot effectively react, or by exposing vulnerabilities that can be exploited by manoeuvre. Speed of manoeuvre at sea will often surprise opponents ashore. A maritime force can move up to 400 miles a day, whereas land forces without the benefit of air or sea lift will often be lucky to move 30 miles (even in the German 'blitzkrieg' attack on France in 1940, the maximum advance achieved was 120 kilometers per day).

Seaking 4 launches from RFA ARGUS

PROACTIVE AND REACTIVE CHOICES IN MARITIME CAMPAIGNS

A maritime power projection operation is by definition a *proactive* operation in that it involves seizing the initiative by forward operations in which forces are moved to invite contact with the enemy. This is not to say that it is necessarily offensive. For instance, the mission may be to effect withdrawal or evacuation. In contrast the task of achieving sea control will present the commander with both proactive operational and reactive options in which the initiative is retained by drawing the enemy into contact.

The *offensive* is a course of action that forces the enemy to fight, if only to defend his own position; the *defensive*, in contrast, is a posture which forces the enemy to attack if he wishes to fight. Both the offensive and the defensive are relevant at every level of warfare. Convoy, to take the classic example, is tactically defensive but operationally offensive in that it obliges the enemy to fight in circumstances of one's own choosing; his only alternative is to abandon his strategic objective. It is extremely dangerous to confuse the offensive as a policy or course of action, with the offensive mentality. It has always been highly desirable, and usually essential for victory, that the commander and his subordinates should be endowed with an offensive (or aggressive) mentality: a determination to win whatever the difficulties, a trait in ample evidence in the characters of all the great commanders through history. But this attitude of mind has nothing whatever to do with the actual method of warfare being employed. Indeed, the offensive mentality is as necessary (if not more so) in defensive operations as it is when conducting an offensive.

3/3. The Balance of Offensive and Defensive: Convoy

One extremely good historical example of the ways in which military value can be derived from a subtle balancing of the offensive and defensive character of operations, is the use of convoying in both World Wars to defeat the submarine threat.

Before the First World War, it was thought that technological developments had made convoys obsolete. In the event, only the belated introduction of convoys in 1917 saved Britain from the U-boats. In the Second World War German submarine commanders only achieved their 'Happy Times' against independent shipping. When an ocean convoy system was fully introduced in 1941 and coupled with flexible routeing, linked to strategic intelligence, the overall level of individual U-boat kills declined, never to recover. When the Germans turned on the convoys in greater strength as their only alternative in 1942-3 they were only able to achieve successes at insupportable cost. Larger convoys proved less vulnerable than smaller, and released escorts to create groups to support convoys that intelligence revealed to be under threat. Concentrating forces around convoys at risk defeated the U-boats from 1943 onwards, and for the rest of the war the ocean convoy system remained a wall against which the Germans smashed themselves with diminishing effect.

The success of convoy was largely a result of its tactically defensive yet operationally offensive nature. Contrary to popular myth, convoys were not successful because they were more difficult to find than independently routed shipping. Indeed, their operationally offensive character depended on them being regarded by the enemy as a supremely attractive high value target that could be found. Their high value would attract the concentrated attention of their attackers. Defensive effort concentrated around the convoy would then be more effectively applied against attacking U-boats. This is precisely what occurred after 1941 in the North Atlantic. Essentially, the concentration of shipping in convoys was used to draw attackers into an anti-submarine warfare 'net'. The understandable popular assumption that convoys were successful in the past because they were difficult to find is, therefore, quite misleading.

Nevertheless, a slavish adherence to 'the offensive' can lead to important strategic and operational errors, such as the British failure to convoy in favour of 'hunting groups' during the First World War. A more useful analysis of modern maritime combat is the division into proactive and reactive elements. To be successful in maritime combat a commander must seize and maintain the initiative to force a response to his actions, thereby ensuring that engagements take place on his own terms. In doing so, the commander should exploit, where possible, the advantages both of reactive posture (for instance concentration of forces around the shipping at risk to draw the enemy to destruction) or proactive operations (such as the *distraction* of enemy forces).

A classic proactive method of achieving *sea control*, frequently advocated and used by the Royal Navy in the past and referred to earlier in this chapter, is to seek out the enemy to bring him to decisive battle thereby destroying his forces and eliminating his capability to challenge sea control. Other maritime operations can then proceed unthreatened. Historically this course was not simply a matter of *elan* but reflected Britain's qualitative and often quantitative superiority over its enemies. To be effective it will generally require a large *balance of advantage* in maritime forces. The enemy may also have the option of declining battle and operating a *fleet in being*. What is important to realise is that bringing the enemy to a decisive battle may well be the most effective option. Arguably, despite the espousal of manoeuvrist principles, most naval warfare, where there is no territory to take or hold, is essentially a matter of *attrition*. As the enemy's losses increase he becomes progressively less able to dispute the use of the sea. Battles are not the only route to victory but they matter because they offer the opportunity considerably to speed up the rate of attrition. As much may be achieved in an afternoon as in a year or more of generally successful warfare against an enemy who avoids decisive battle. By the same token, of course, battles are risky, for much may be lost instead of won. But, for the commander who is determined to win and has something like sufficient forces, battle is by far the quickest and often cheapest route to victory. Arguably, the Gulf War of 1991 was a classically offensive attritional campaign in every dimension of warfare waged: land, sea and air. That is not to ignore its manoeuvrist characteristics which complemented the largely attritional approach.

Proactive methods, other than the offensive, can be considered under the concept of military containment, which constitutes constraining an enemy's forces and reducing risk in areas outside those in which sea control is required. Containment can be achieved by *close* or *distant blockade*, the implicit threat of force (as with submarines and mines) or by *distracting* an enemy's maritime forces by posing an explicit overriding threat to his critical interests. Reactive methods of achieving *sea control* comprise the direct *screening* of formations and convoys, and the use of single or integrated defensive barriers of sub-surface, surface and air forces.

Because of the huge expanse and diversity of the maritime arena and its environmental complexity, the variety of air, surface and sub-surface threats, and vagaries in detection and prosecution of targets, no single system or layer of protection is likely to be adequate. For this reason, *sea control* is usually effected by a combination of proactive and reactive methods depending on time and space considerations. Probabilities of effectiveness of the various methods are thus aggregated to provide appropriate levels of protection and risk. This principle of defence in depth is demonstrated most clearly in the *layered defence* of a formation of high value.

NATO'S PRINCIPLES OF MARITIME OPERATIONS

While the *Principles of War* govern military operations in all environments, the Major NATO Commanders have defined four principles of maritime operations. They bring together the themes of this chapter, and capture the essence of both manoeuvre warfare and the proactive/reactive dilemma. The three that are particularly relevant to combat operations are: Seizing the Initiative; Containment; and Defence in Depth. The fourth is *Presence*, which is discussed in more detail in Chapter 4.

3/4. NATO's Principles of Maritime Operations: Examples

Seizing the Initiative

In November 1940, carrier-borne aircraft of the Mediterranean Fleet attacked major Italian units in harbour at Taranto causing severe damage to them. This decisive action redressed the balance of naval forces which had previous been weighted heavily in favour of the Italians.

Containment

During the Second World War, Germany possessed a small number of highly effective heavy warships. British policy was to keep these away from where they could do harm. Although it was generally impossible to prevent them from sailing, every subsequent effort was made to detect and destroy them. Latterly considerable efforts were made to neutralise them in harbour. By such means the threat was constrained and eventually eliminated.

Defence in Depth

The American Pacific operations during the Second World War were often conducted in an intense air threat environment. This was dealt with by a layered system of defence: attempting to deal with the aircraft at source where possible, airborne combat air patrol aircraft, medium calibre guns and, finally, a large number of close-range weapons.

Presence

The Armilla patrol which started in 1980 demonstrated to the nations of the Gulf area that the United Kingdom was concerned in the welfare of its national shipping in this volatile area. It was also an indication of wider British interests.

CONCLUSION

This chapter has been devoted to concepts related to the military or combat governed use of maritime force. Many of these concepts have application during sustained hostilities (war). However the concepts of *sea control* and *power projection* in their modern interpretation have relevance throughout the spectrum of conflict and in many operations that fall well short of war. The next chapter goes on to discuss the various applications of maritime power in which the concepts discussed in this chapter will be applied.

Ch 4

HMS OCEAN

THE APPLICATION OF MARITIME POWER

Chapter 4

The full range of operations in which the UK's maritime forces may become involved is extremely wide, including high intensity war-fighting at one extreme and essentially philanthropic humanitarian relief operations at the other. This broad range of operations can be broken down into distinct categories, each demanding a specific approach to the conduct of operations. There are also important legal distinctions which provide the basis for legitimate involvement in maritime operations and about which commanders need to be aware. The categorisation is not merely an academic exercise; it is important operationally and there is every reason for maritime doctrine to recognise its significance. There are three general categories into which UK maritime operations are grouped: *military, constabulary* and *benign*. These will each be described in turn. However, it is important also to realise two other contexts within which these three categories of operations may also fall: *Peace Support Operations* (PSOs), and *Military Assistance to Civil Authorities* (MACA). All maritime operations will fall into one of the three general categories; some may also be either PSOs or MACA.

THE MILITARY APPLICATION OF MARITIME POWER

A *military* use is one in which combat is used or threatened or which presupposes a combat capability. All war-fighting tasks require the military use of force. Less obvious perhaps are the uses of military force in support of diplomacy and in which forces are used to coerce, persuade or signal a message. Although under these circumstances combat may not be used or even envisaged, it is the combat capability of the forces that underpins their use.

The military applications of maritime power are governed by the concepts of *sea control* and *power projection* that were explained in Chapter 3. However, military applications of maritime power do not fall neatly and exclusively under either sea control or power projection headings, because a degree of sea control is an enabling requirement for most tasks in *conflict*, including those that are also forms of power projection. Nevertheless, a useful distinction can be made between applications of power at sea, of which sea control is the essence, and from the sea, which are broadly power projection tasks. What follows below is a brief summary of the applications of maritime power at sea (essentially sea control and protection of maritime trade) and its use to project power ashore. More detailed discussions are included in Chapter 7, in relation to the planning and conduct of maritime operations.

Maritime Power at Sea

Maritime power is applied at sea in both offensive operations conducted against enemy forces, and defensive operations conducted to protect friendly forces and maritime trade **(Force Protection)**. All involve **Sea Control** operations, which can be both *offensive* and *defensive* and may consist of elements of both. They may also contain aspects which, by their nature, are more akin to **Sea Denial**. Sea control operations will be conducted by any maritime task force, group, element or unit, all of which will aim to achieve an adequate level of sea control within their own areas of operations. However, **Area Sea Control Operations** are essentially geographic and are conducted using long-range surveillance and weapon systems over extended areas of sea.

4/1. Force Protection

The protection of high value units and logistics support at sea will normally depend on a wide range of factors in both multi- and single-threat environments. These factors will include the nature of the threat, its intensity, the characteristics of the environment, the protection resources available, and the importance and urgency of each mission. Each situation must be regarded as unique if the chances for success are to be maximised.

Emerging technology and concepts, particularly in the fields of surveillance, information, and platform design, have extended the range of available protection techniques. Integrated operational deception and tactical distraction, new generation sea-lift vessels capable of high speed transit, and a willingness to seek out manoeuvrist solutions, can all be used to route vulnerable assets away from potential threats. Threat avoidance will be as important as the ability to respond to attack. If tactical contact with the enemy is unavoidable, sufficient combat power must be provided to the force to allow it a reasonable chance of success. Given the high value and scarcity of modern warships and the complexities of the environment in which they have to operate, careful judgements will need to be made by commanders about the utility of various force protection techniques. Established methods such as convoying may prove as appropriate in certain circumstances as they have in the past, especially in a single-threat environment. However, in modern multi-threat environments traditional protection techniques may well not be the panaceas that history suggests they should be. Fundamentally, the modern multi-threat environment renders rigid dogmatic resort to historically proven doctrine especially dangerous. In this instance, the best lesson of history is not to assume that previous solutions will necessarily apply but to retain an open mind and a flexibility of approach.

At the *operational level*, **Interdiction of the Enemy's Maritime Forces** hampers the enemy's attempts at reinforcement or *manoeuvre from the sea* and frustrates his sea control and sea denial operations. Interdiction operations can be conducted against shipping and aircraft at sea, in harbour, in the air or on land, through the threat or use of attrition.

Blockade is a combat operation to prevent access to, or departure from, a defined area of an enemy's coast and waters. It can be used operationally as a method of achieving sea control or sea denial through containment. Strategically, it may also be used as an extreme form of sanctions enforcement and as an operation against the will of a nation or regime. During full hostilities, it can prevent reinforcement, re-supply, and maritime trade, and thus deprive an enemy of the national material and moral resources necessary to continue hostilities.

Containment is achieved by posing a threat to an enemy's critical interests so that he must retain maritime forces in their defence. The threat to these enemy interests may take the form of a direct challenge to his sea control forces or to his power projection forces that could threaten targets ashore. Containment of the Soviet Navy in this manner, in order to maintain freedom of action in the Atlantic and Pacific, was an important component of the US Navy's Forward Maritime Strategy of the 1980s.

The establishment of **Exclusion Zones**, the legitimacy of which is only guaranteed and unambiguous under international law when authorised by the United Nations through a Security Council Resolution, have served both military and diplomatic functions. In conflict, they offer a means of simplifying *sea control* through the promulgation of an intention to maintain *sea denial* over a specific area. In diplomatic terms they are a way of enhancing coercive action by declaring resolve to use combat if necessary. Clearly, to be credible, they must be enforceable and the rights and security of third parties need to be safe-guarded.

Sea control **Barrier Operations** can be conducted where geographic or oceanographic features or operational constraints will channel or concentrate enemy forces. With modern long range surveillance, maritime forces may now be tasked to provide area sea control and static **Layered Defence** of these areas, though the difficulty of achieving area sea control should not be underestimated. Maritime trade is important to the United Kingdom, NATO and the European Union. In peacetime, naval forces maintain freedom of the seas for maritime trade by general presence and, on occasion, by **Freedom of Navigation Operations**. This is in addition to the specific requirement of providing security to air and *sea lines of communication* in support of *a joint* or maritime *campaign*.

When there is a significant risk to maritime trade, the Government may offer specific protection to merchant ships through **Naval Control of Shipping** (NCS) measures. This protection and control is normally confined to voluntary participation by ships or ships' owners and operators within a clearly defined geographic region or regions under *Regional Naval Control of Shipping* (RNCS) and may be applicable within protected areas or exclusion zones. Governments may also choose to enforce compulsory NCS of their own flagged ships. Mobile NCS teams for RNCS provide a flexible response to any crisis affecting merchant shipping. So too do a range of other NCS measures including: the issue of navigational warnings, the provision of selected advisory briefings, **Accompanying, Escorting**, and, finally, the formation of merchant ship **Convoys**. NCS measures may also be used to monitor and control merchant shipping contributing to operations. In certain situations UK maritime forces may be called upon to protect ships of many nationalities carrying cargoes of interest to the UK and its allies.

Maritime Power from the Sea

Military force at sea contributes to what has traditionally been known as **Naval Diplomacy**; that is to say, the use of maritime forces as a diplomatic instrument in support of political objectives and foreign policy. It is the availability of force to back up and provide support to diplomatic efforts at various levels.

4/2. Naval Diplomacy

The backing up of diplomatic negotiations, conducted in a period of tension, by the deployment of a naval task group able to pose an often unstated but self evident threat, is a classical application of naval diplomacy. The deployment of the RN Task Force to the South Atlantic in 1982 was initially an example of naval diplomacy, with its steady passage south providing a clear threat of military force to back-up the diplomatic negotiations being conducted as an attempt to avert actual hostilities. Importantly, when the diplomatic efforts failed to achieve their aim (the removal of Argentinian forces from the Falklands without the UK having to resort to force), the military threat was subsequently converted into actual military action. Arguably, the UK's resolve in 1982 will have

> provided subsequent such uses of naval diplomacy with additional coercive influence. The deployment of an RN aircraft carrier with US carriers to the Gulf in the winter of 1997/98 was a further example of coercive naval diplomacy, the aim of which was to persuade Iraq to comply with the needs of UN weapons inspection teams. On that occasion naval diplomacy appeared to work, although further pressure, including air strikes at the end of 1998, had again to be applied on Iraq in response to its flagrant disregard of UN Security Council Resolutions.
>
> Doctrinally it is important not to confuse naval diplomacy with Defence Diplomacy (see Box 4/6). 'Naval diplomacy' is a term with a specific application. Defence Diplomacy is a Defence Policy Mission for the UK armed forces under which heading some naval diplomacy activities may well fall. However, some manifestations of naval diplomacy (as that in 1982) will be deliberately overtly coercive, even aggressive, in a way that Defence Diplomacy will never be.

The ultimate means of achieving this is through the maintenance of a secure **Strategic Nuclear Deterrent**, which is the responsibility of the Royal Navy; it is perhaps best regarded as permanent naval diplomacy having a grand-strategic effect. The UK's instruments of strategic nuclear deterrence are deployed at sea because the stealth of nuclear powered submarines makes them extremely hard to find and then destroy. They are not, therefore, liable to pre-emptive attack or counter-attack. Nuclear weapons have great *reach* and variable direction of attack when deployed in nuclear powered submarines. TRIDENT submarines also have the flexibility to provide the *sub-strategic* component of our deterrence forces. This allows for the delivery of nuclear attacks that are more limited than those that would form part of a strategic nuclear response. They are an intermediate level of response that allows for a flexible and essential element of our overall deterrent posture, providing the linkage between strategic and conventional *deterrence*.

Naval diplomacy is designed to influence the will and decision-making apparatus of a state or group of states in peacetime and all situations short of full *hostilities*. It can be used on the one hand to support or reassure and can be a significant contributor to *coalition*

Trident D5 launched from HMS VIGILANT

building. On the other hand, it can be used to deter and coerce trouble-makers.

Doctrinally, there are several ways in which naval diplomacy can be brought to bear on international politics. When it is exercised in a general way involving deployments, exercising and routine operations in areas of interest, it is known as **Presence**. A traditional way of demonstrating *presence* is by foreign port visits to impress upon local populations the state's interests and involvement in the region. There is no threat of force; instead the vessel and her ships company act as ambassadors, whose function is to make a favourable

Ch 4
THE APPLICATION OF MARITIME POWER

impression on the local population. Warships are unique in their international acceptability, access capabilities and ability to make this kind of impact. The presence of a naval vessel in an area may be the primary symbol of national commitment - for example, HMS ENDURANCE in Antarctica. *Presence* is both a national and an Alliance task; indeed, the contribution of presence to stability and deterrence is considered by the Major NATO Commanders to be so important that it has been adopted by NATO as a principle governing the use of maritime forces. The term *forward presence* is used to express a strategic decision to deploy forces for presence into or close to theatres of interest or concern.

Maritime forces can be used **Symbolically**, purely to signal a message to a specific government while not in themselves posing any threat to an opponent or providing significant military assistance to a friend. When a stronger message is required, naval diplomacy can take the form of the employment of carefully tailored forces with an offensive capability. This can act as a signal of will and greater force to follow, or encouragement of a friend or ally by providing some reinforcement. The threat or use of limited offensive action is **Coercion** which may be designed to deter a possible aggressor or to *compel* him to comply with a diplomatic demarche or resolution.

4/.3. Symbolic Use of Naval Force

"In order to clothe the arrival of our new Ambassador, Lord Halifax, in the United States with every circumstance of importance, I arranged that our newest and strongest battleship, the KING GEORGE V, with a proper escort of destroyers, should carry him and his wife across the ocean." Sir Winston Churchill on a decision made in 1941 before the United States had entered the Second Word War
(W S Churchill *The Grand Alliance*)

There may be occasions when the UK wishes to be in a position to influence events, particularly in the early stages of a crisis, but when specific policy objectives may be unclear beyond the need to declare interest and avoid *maldeployment*. In these situations **Preventive, Precautionary and Pre-emptive Naval Diplomacy** may be employed, with tailored maritime forces operating under carefully crafted *rules of engagement* poising in theatre for subsequent use when political objectives have been refined. In the language of PSOs, (see below) maritime forces may be significant contributors to *preventive deployments* for *crisis prevention*.

4/4. Non-Combatant Evacuation Operations

The use of maritime forces in evacuation operations was demonstrated during the civil war between government and rival factions in Aden in January 1986. The Royal Yacht, later supported by HM Ships NEWCASTLE, JUPITER and RFA BRAMBLELEAF, evacuated 1379 men, women and children of 55 different nationalities from the besieged town. The majority were evacuated by the Royal Yacht's own boats over an open beach.

When naval diplomacy fails, maritime forces may be required to use their military potential to resolve situations or protect national interests. The protection of UK citizens and others may necessitate the use of maritime forces in **Non-Combatant Evacuation Operations** (NEOs). Ultimately, if diplomacy breaks down completely, maritime forces may become engaged in **Combat Operations Against the Land** and **Support to Joint Operations** in a variety of ways. Maritime forces are capable of employing a range of amphibious operations that UK doctrine, promulgated in *UKOPSDOC*, has listed under four type headings: amphibious demonstration, amphibious raiding, amphibious assault and amphibious withdrawal (see the detailed discussion in Chapter 7). Maritime based aircraft can contribute to the *strategic air offensive, counter-air, anti-surface force* (land and sea), and *combat support air operations*, all of which may be supporting joint campaign objectives ashore. Submarines and, indeed, surface ships armed with *land attack missiles* can contribute to an attack on important shore targets. Naval systems can provide fire support to all operations, increasingly with greater range, accuracy and lethality. Maritime electronic capabilities can contribute significant intelligence, area surveillance and communications, and naval missiles provide air defence over littoral areas. Logistic support is also available to landed forces and structural and organizational improvements will enhance their capability for wider support of ground forces.

4/5. Maritime Operations in the Spanish Civil War

Modern maritime operations in support of diplomacy and humanitarian objectives are not new, but a return to the more traditional pattern of activities after the Cold War.

> Good examples of the 'traditional' patterns from earlier this century were the activities of the Royal Navy in the Spanish Civil War (1936-1939). British warships were used to prevent interference with shipping by Spanish warships not granted belligerent rights by the international community, to break illegal blockades, to deter Italian submarines from covertly sinking ships bound for Spain, to evacuate personnel threatened by one side or the other and to symbolise by their presence on patrol the principle of non-intervention.

Power projection forces (including special forces) may also be employed as part of a *sea control* campaign to destroy enemy forces in harbours, ports and air bases, and their *command* and *control* systems and logistics. Alternatively, they can be used to secure a land flank for sea control forces.

Maritime forces can also assist in the **Protection of Joint Forces** or territory by providing a sea based defensive barrier or by holding down a flank. Conversely, they can expand the maritime flank or defend it against an enemy manoeuvre from the sea. More specifically they can contribute to air defence, supplementing land-based forces or, within a *Joint Operations Area (JOA)*, supply total defence capability. Within this is the potential for sea-based forces to provide defence against theatre ballistic missiles, weapons of mass destruction and more static enemy indirect fire systems. Maritime forces can therefore provide support at all stages of a land operation.

Defence Diplomacy

'Defence Diplomacy' is an SDR initiative, very much in tune with the post-Cold War security environment. The SDR listed three specific Military Tasks that contribute most to the Defence Diplomacy Mission, each of which is described in terms that imply the use of military forces in a manner supportive of activities and initiatives underway in other states:

- Arms control, non-proliferation, and confidence and security building measures;

- Outreach activities designed to contribute to security and stability in Central and Eastern Europe, particularly Russia, through bilateral assistance and co-operation with the countries concerned;

- Other activities covering military assistance to overseas military forces and defence communities not otherwise covered by Outreach.

4/6. Defence Diplomacy - RUKUS

Defence Diplomacy is one of the eight core Missions of the UK's Defence Policy post-SDR. By its very nature and that of the Military Tasks included under its heading, it suggests a co-operative and helpful approach to other states as a means of improving relations. In that sense it is generally benign in its application.

In the year that this book is being published, the RN will be hosting the annual RUKUS Talks. These were initiated in the dying days of the Cold War at Adderbury in Oxfordshire and were originally unofficial and largely academic in tone. They involved representatives of the Russian Navy, the RN and the USN, as well as a number of academics and others with a naval interest. However, the success of the early Talks generated a momentum and they have emerged in more recent years as a regular, annual, official event involving all three navies, with each taking it in turn to host. In 1996 they were held in the UK, in 1997 the US Navy hosted them at the US Naval War College, Newport, Rhode Island and in 1998 they took place at the Kuznetsov Academy in St Petersburg. In 1999 it will again be the UK's turn to host them and they are due to take place at the Maritime Warfare Centre as this book is being published.

The aim of the original Adderbury Talks was to facilitate dialogue between East and West and they were, in that way, a form of unofficial confidence building measure. In contrast, the focus of the RUKUS Talks today is on achieving a practical and effective degree of tri-lateral maritime interoperability, by exchanging ideas and doctrine for use in multi-national Peace Support Operations. In that way they fit admirably within the Government's Defence Diplomacy initiative, with the accent on assistance and co-operation in an attempt to generate understanding and reduce tension.

Ch 4
THE APPLICATION OF MARITIME POWER

Maritime forces can become involved in such activities across a wide spectrum. These include the traditional activities associated with maintaining presence and supporting diplomatic initiatives in peacetime (port visits being the classic example). However, in recent years, following the break-up of the Soviet Union and the dissolution of the Warsaw Pact in particular, there has been a concentration of effort on relations with the states of eastern Europe. Some older Cold War initiatives remain in place with new focus, a good example being the RUKUS Talks (see Box 4/6). However, the main thrust of Outreach activities has taken shape since the early 1990s. Personnel from the UK's maritime forces have visited all the European states of the former Soviet Union. Advice and assistance has been given, for example, to the Baltic States (who now have a tri-lateral mine countermeasures squadron - BALTRON - following advice from NATO navies), to the Ukraine and to Georgia. The development of armed forces in new states presents a range of challenges. The UK's principal concern in providing advice and assistance is to help with the transition to balanced and responsible armed forces accountable to the political establishments in the new states. In providing such assistance we hope to achieve warm and positive relations with the states concerned and to develop military professionalism to the point where our maritime forces can operate effectively together and carry out humanitarian aid and other forms of Peace Support Operations. The accent is on generating a sense of 'maritime community' amongst the armed forces of the region.

RFS BESPOKOINY and HMS NORFOLK off Plymouth 1998

THE CONSTABULARY APPLICATION OF MARITIME POWER

Constabulary use is where forces are employed to enforce law or to implement some regime established by international mandate. Violence is only employed for self defence or as a last resort in the execution of the constabulary task. The ways in which force can be used will normally be prescribed in the law or mandate that is being enforced and there will be a general reluctance to employ violence. Combat is not, therefore, the principal means by which the mission is achieved, even though the situation may warrant combat preparations, in particular for self defence or as a last resort enforcement measure.

Embargo, Economic Sanctions and **Quarantine Enforcement** operations are normally carried out under international mandate, usually from the UN Security Council using Chapter VII of the *UN Charter*. As with other constabulary tasks, the level of force that may be used in enforcement must be mandated to ensure legality. Forces involved may be subject to counter-attack, so a level of overall local sea control may be required to ensure the protection of enforcement forces. These operations are normally used to restrict the egress of certain categories of cargo, with embargoes on arms entering states being of particular relevance in many cases. These tasks are distinct from blockade, which is a fully military application employed in war and which must fulfil the requirements of international law described earlier.

4/7. Freedom of Navigation Operations

If a state's claim to extended territorial seas is not accepted, or a state attempts to restrict the use of the high seas or international straits, it may be necessary to use maritime forces to demonstrate intent to use those waters. It may also be necessary to prevent a state from claiming customary rights in the future. Freedom of navigation operations are designed to influence a government and are therefore a form of naval diplomacy. They may be symbolic or coercive. In autumn 1963 the carrier HMS VICTORIOUS and supporting forces demonstrated the right and resolve to use the Sunda Strait between Java and Sumatra by conducting an overt transit during the campaign associated with Indonesian confrontation of Malaysia.

Ch 4
THE APPLICATION OF MARITIME POWER

Anti-Piracy Operations are *constabulary* operations involving the exercise of universal jurisdiction on the high seas. Within *territorial seas* they are a coastal state responsibility. Where piracy is rife and pirates are equipped with modern weapons and craft, the task has the same characteristics and requirements as other forms of protection of shipping including, perhaps, the need for robust *sea control* measures. The other principal form of criminal law enforcement task that is increasingly involving maritime forces, is **Drug Interdiction**. The Atlantic Patrol Task ship, when operating in the West Indies, spends a substantial proportion of its time on-station involved in these operations, protecting the interests of dependent territories and complementing allies' (US, French and Dutch) efforts in the region. While anti-piracy and drug interdiction operations are the most obvious examples of low intensity law enforcement operations, other possibilities should not be discounted. These include the **Interception of Illegal Immigrants** and **Counter-Contraband** operations mounted to combat the smuggling of a wide range of illicit goods, including weapons and explosives (a good example of the latter being the RN operations mounted off the coast of Northern Ireland since the early-1970s). Operations to counter gun-running may well be a part of a wider **Counter-Insurgency Operation**.

Royal Marine anti-piracy boarding exercise

The maintenance of law and order in coastal states' maritime domains has generated a range of tasks, especially since the substantial extensions of coastal state jurisdiction resulting from the UNCLOS III negotiations and the *1982 UNCLOS* that emerged from them. For the UK, in its own *maritime domain*, such tasks performed by maritime and other military forces fall under the heading of MACA and are discussed under that heading below. Suffice it to say here, that any such operations within coastal states' relevant zones of maritime jurisdiction (be they UK, UK Overseas Territories' or foreign states') have to be conducted in accordance with the laws and other relevant legal rules and procedures enacted by the coastal state.

THE BENIGN APPLICATION OF MARITIME POWER

Benign tasks are those such as humanitarian aid, disaster relief, search and rescue or ordnance disposal for which military forces contribute organized and self-supporting formations with specific capabilities and specialist knowledge. The tasks are benign because violence has no part to play in their execution, nor is the potential to apply force a necessary backdrop.

As part of our overall security policy, Britain's armed forces have a history of contributing to regional stability by participating in **humanitarian aid** and **disaster relief operations** around the world. The flexibility of maritime forces and their independent logistic support makes them particularly effective in disaster relief operations following hurricanes and tropical cyclones, local unrest or infrastructure collapse. The armed forces may in particular be required to provide disaster relief to the Overseas Territories, several of which are in the Caribbean where there is frequent hurricane damage. Maritime forces can provide a comprehensive logistics base and refuge offshore for humanitarian operations in support of peace initiatives, with shipborne helicopters providing a versatile means of transport. Maritime forces are especially important in the very early stages of disaster relief when they may well be the only assistance available to provide 'first-aid' while other agencies, including NGOs, mobilise longer term assistance. However, it is important to recognise that military forces are not well placed to provide long-term assistance; they are neither equipped for it nor very cost-effective over time.

THE APPLICATION OF MARITIME POWER

All vessels on the *high seas* are required under international law to assist in **search and rescue**, and **salvage operations** may also prove appropriate in some circumstances. In some circumstances, it may be necessary to carry out some degree of **marine pollution control**. This is also a particularly specialist task that military forces cannot cope with over extended periods or if the level of pollution is high - as it often is if it emanates from a striken oil tanker, for example. Again, maritime forces may be extremely useful in the early stages of a crisis (carrying out initial surveillance or providing early command and control) and in some instances may even be able to provide specialised 'first-aid' equipment (the RN's offshore patrol vessels carry spraying equipment). After the initial stages of a crisis, however, military forces will need to make way for other agencies once the latter have arrived on-scene.

4/8. Disaster Relief

In early November 1998, Hurricane Mitch caused great disruption and enormous loss of life in the Central American area, particularly in the Honduras and Nicaraguan regions. Mounting Operation TELLAR, HM Ships SHEFFIELD and OCEAN, carrying a mix of SEAKING support and LYNX helicopters and accompanied by RFAs BLACK ROVER and SIR TRISTRAM, 45 Commando and Dutch Marines, became fully involved in humanitarian relief operations in conjunction with other international military units. This involved moving up to 150 miles inland to stabilise the population until other international relief organizations arrived to take over.

Many of these benign operations are both manpower and specialised equipment intensive. Disaster relief and salvage operations in particular may involve the entire ship's company of a frigate or destroyer and require a good deal of specialist equipment. Ships deploying to the West Indies, where such operations occur frequently, receive additional training and equipment prior to their deployment.

Two types of operations which represent important contributions to the well-being of the broader maritime community made by the UK's maritime forces, but which have so far not been mentioned, are **ordnance disposal** and **hydrographic surveying**. There is a substantial amount of unexploded ordnance left in the waters around northern Europe. This dates back to both World Wars and frequently results in RN mine countermeasures vessels and clearance diving teams responding to calls from the general public, particularly from fishermen. On a more routine basis is the hydrographic surveying effort contributed by the Hydrographic Surveying Squadron, which consists of set amounts of surveying conducted in accordance with formal inter-departmental agreements.

As in the case of *constabulary* tasks undertaken within the UK, the military involvement in benign tasks at home falls under the heading of MACA and is discussed in more detail below.

THE FRAMEWORK FOR MARITIME PEACE SUPPORT OPERATIONS

Peace Support Operations (PSOs) are carried out in support of efforts to achieve or maintain peace, in most cases with the consent of at least one of the belligerent parties. PSO forces should invariably attempt to act impartially, although during higher intensity peace enforcement activity (Operation DESERT STORM being a pertinent example) the concept of impartiality may appear singularly inappropriate, especially from the perspective of those directly involved in warfighting activities. Maritime forces can contribute a variety of tasks in PSOs, all of which will fall under one of the *military, constabulary* and *benign* headings discussed already above. However, there is a vocabulary associated with PSOs that can be confusing and which doctrinally we must superimpose on the categorisation employed above.

PSOs are defined as multi-functional operations involving military forces and diplomatic and humanitarian agencies. They are designed to achieve humanitarian goals or a long-term political settlement, and are conducted impartially, usually today in support of a UN or regional organization mandate. The complete range of PSOs and their definitions, as agreed by NATO and reflected in the UK's own doctrinal publication (*JWP 3-50 Peace Support Operations*) is as follows:

Peacekeeping

Peacekeeping operations are generally undertaken under Chapter VI of the *UN Charter* with the consent of all the major parties to a conflict, to monitor and facilitate the implementation of a peace agreement. A long running example is the UN operation in Cyprus (known as UNFICYP) that, since 1974, has patrolled the line dividing the Greek and Turkish Cypriot areas of the island, for which the Royal Marines have frequently provided forces since the operation commenced, in somewhat different circumstances, in the early 1960s. By their nature, such operations are principally engaged ashore, although there may be maritime aspects at the margins or involving the patrolling of rivers and other internal waterways, as in Cambodia in the early 1990s.

Peace Enforcement

Peace Enforcement operations have the potential to be coercive in nature and are undertaken under Chapter VII of the *UN Charter*, when the consent of any of the major parties to a conflict is uncertain. They are designed to maintain and re-establish peace or enforce the terms specified in the mandate. Some aspects of the operations in and around the Former Republic of Yugoslavia and Adriatic have been peace enforcement.

Conflict Prevention

Conflict prevention activities are normally conducted under Chapter VI of the *UN Charter*. They range from diplomatic initiatives to preventative deployments of forces intended to prevent disputes from escalating into armed conflicts or from spreading. Conflict prevention can also include fact-finding missions, consultations, warnings, inspections and monitoring. Preventative deployment within the framework of conflict prevention is the deployment of operational forces possessing sufficient deterrent capability to avoid a conflict.

Peacemaking

Peacemaking covers the diplomatic activities conducted after the commencement of a conflict aimed at establishing a ceasefire or a rapid peaceful settlement. They can include the provision of good offices, mediation, conciliation, diplomatic pressure, isolation and sanctions. Such activities were necessary in the brokering of the Dayton Agreement in 1995. Military support to add weight to the diplomatic process may well be required. This was the case in the autumn of 1995, when aircraft from HMS INVINCIBLE flew sorties over Bosnia as an important part of the process of persuading parties to accept the Dayton Agreement.

Peace Building

Peace building covers actions which support political, economic social and military measures and structures, aiming to strengthen and solidify political settlements in order to redress the causes of conflict. This includes mechanisms to identify and support structures which tend to consolidate peace, advance a sense of confidence and well being, and support economic reconstruction.

4/9. Yugoslavia - Maritime Peace Support Operations

The Royal Navy's contribution to UNPROFOR in the former Yugoslavia has included:

- fighter aircraft patrols (supported by shore based AWACS aircraft and air-to-air refuelling) in support of the No Fly Zone from a carrier in the Adriatic.

- reconnaissance and *close air support* to troops ashore.

- support helicopters based ashore for casualty evacuation.

- combat service support to the British UNPROFOR contingent.

- embargo operations.

In addition to the value as a command and control and staging platform, the carrier's ability to position herself close to the operational area and minimise the effects of adverse weather makes her organic aircraft ideal for short notice tasking together with her ability to position herself in the most favourable tactical situation. RN destroyers and frigates, acting under NATO and WEU command have enforced the UN embargoes, and in the first two and a half years NATO and WEU vessels boarded over 3,345 ships and diverted more than 653 suspected violators.

Ch 4
THE APPLICATION OF MARITIME POWER

> Heavy equipment was moved to the theatre by sea and a Royal Fleet Auxiliary ship alongside in Split provided accommodation and ammunition and stores support. On two occasions RN ships were used as neutral territory to host meetings between warring factions; in one case this resulted in the lifting of the siege of Dubrovnik.

Humanitarian Operations

Humanitarian operations are conducted to relieve human suffering. Military humanitarian activities may accompany, or be in support of, humanitarian operations conducted by specialised civilian organizations. Recent humanitarian operations include those conducted in the Former Republic of Yugoslavia and in Northern Iraq, in both of which there was a military dimension - in contrast to the benign involvement of UK armed forces personnel and equipment in Central America in late-1998.

FA2/GR7s- Peace Support Operations in the Gulf 1998

The activities of forces involved in PSOs are conditioned by the diplomatic environment and complicated command and control arrangements that often apply. Operations will typically be carried out under the auspices of the United Nations or the OSCE, although NATO, the WEU, European Union and other regional organizations may also be involved. UK forces may be operating under the aegis of the UN, under national command in co-ordination with other UN forces or under NATO or other coalition auspices. The hierarchy of military activity will not be clearly defined during PSOs. The presence of civilian UN authorities, civilian staff of non-governmental organizations (NGOs) such as the Red Cross, the multiplicity of national and international *operational* and *tactical* headquarters in theatre, and the intricate and frequently ad hoc co-ordination arrangements between them will all serve to complicate the situation.

4/10. Peace Support Operations - Maritime Tasks

- Active monitoring of a sea area for infringement of sanctions/embargo.

- Patrolling and monitoring a maritime cease fire line or demilitarized zone.

- Enforcement of sanctions/embargo.

- Supervising cantonment of vessels.

- Contribution of *organic aircraft* to enforcement of a *no fly zone* and *combat air support*.

- Contribution of organic helicopters for in theatre movement of peacekeeping forces and humanitarian aid, and casualty evacuation.

- Contribution of forces to ground peace support operations.

- Maintenance of an integral amphibious capability in theatre to permit withdrawal of peacekeeping forces, aid workers and other civilians.

- Provision of seaborne medical and other logistic and humanitarian resources where access by land is difficult.

- Environmental monitoring and patrol.

- Assistance to seaborne refugees.

- Provision of a neutral platform for peace negotiations.

- Mine countermeasures to provide access or contribute to a new peace.

DOMESTIC APPLICATIONS OF MARITIME POWER

Since 1964, the waters adjacent to the UK have fallen progressively under extended and enhanced forms of domestic jurisdiction. In 1964 the UK established jurisdiction over its continental shelf and passed legislation creating safety zones around offshore oil and gas installations. These zones had the effect of extending criminal jurisdiction to the many exploration and production platforms operating today, principally in the North Sea. In the same year, inshore fisheries jurisdiction was extended to 12 nautical miles. In 1977, a 200 nautical mile extended fisheries zone (EFZ) was established and, in 1987, the UK extended its territorial jurisdiction from 3 to 12 nautical miles. The extension and enhancement of domestic jurisdiction within the UK's *maritime domain* has also had the effect of extending constitutional and administrative law principles and conventions to the same area. This has meant that those principles governing the use of the armed forces in providing assistance to civil authorities in the UK itself, are also extended to the maritime domain.

In the UK, as in any well established liberal democratic polity, there are strict legal controls imposed on the domestic activities of the armed forces. Whenever they operate they must do so in accordance with the law and in support, or at the behest of, the appropriate civil authority. The constitutional convention and administrative doctrine that governs the domestic use of the UK's armed forces is known under the general heading of Military Assistance to Civil Authorities

(MACA). MACA as a legal concept is sub-divided into three quite distinct categories. Military Aid to the Civil Power (MACP) is assistance provided for law enforcement and internal security purposes. Activities under this heading may necessitate the armed forces personnel involved carrying weapons and using authorised violence to achieve their objectives. Indeed, only armed forces personnel involved in legitimate and correctly authorised MACP operations are permitted to use arms within the UK's domestic jurisdiction. Military Assistance to Civil Ministries (MACM) is the use of the armed forces to ensure the provision of essential services during industrial disputes. Armed forces personnel used for MACM tasks are emphatically not to be armed and MACM operations must never be confused with MACP operations for that reason. Finally, Military Assistance to the Civil Community (MACC) is any form of *benign* assistance provided to the community at large, either directly or at the request of appropriate civil authorities, including other Government departments. All legitimate military activity having a domestic impact must fall under one of those three well established legally significant headings. (The MACA sub-headings and their constitutional and administrative law meanings are not necessarily synonymous with the headings of relevant Military Tasks listed in Government policy documents and which serve internal MOD accounting and force allocation purposes.)

All maritime MACP functions are, by definition, *constabulary* operations. They include: RN and RM patrols around the coast of Northern Ireland in support of the civil power in the province; any military reaction to terrorist attacks on shipping or offshore installations within *territorial waters* or on the UK *continental shelf* (maritime counter-terrorism or MCT); any drug interdiction operations conducted at the request of HM Customs and Excise; and fishery protection patrols that are conducted to enforce fisheries legislation within the UK's EFZ.

MACM has only very limited potential application in the maritime domain. However, there is a very wide range of activities that falls under the MACC heading conducted by the armed forces in the UK's maritime domain. The list includes: maritime search and rescue, salvage, ordnance disposal, support for pollution control operations, hydrographic surveying operations and the provision of vessel traffic services in Dockyard Ports under the auspices of Queen's Harbourmasters.

CONCLUDING COMMENTS

The mission of forces engaged in a particular *campaign* or *operation* may entail the use of force in more than one of the three ways (*military, constabulary* or *benign*) simultaneously or consecutively. For instance, benign disaster relief may require constabulary or military protection, depending on the nature and scale of any threat (such as looting or attempts to exploit civil disorder to seize power). Similarly, *constabulary* use may escalate into military use if there is a challenge of sufficient magnitude to the regime that is being enforced. For example, what may begin as a constabulary task, may deteriorate into peace enforcement or evacuation operations, which are military or combat governed tasks. If a situation has deteriorated to the extent that terrorism or combat is being conducted by well armed groups or irregular forces, the task of restoring order will clearly be one requiring the military use of force. However, this is not to suggest that these distinctions in the use of military force are in any sense arbitrary or a matter of degree. The legal basis for each of the three uses is different. *Specific doctrine* must be developed for each use and distinct attitudes of mind are required of the command and military personnel involved.

Furthermore, the perceptions of any potential or real opposition and of non-combatant civilians in theatre will to some extent drive decisions about whether a particular operation can be restricted to *benign* or *constabulary* use. As a result there are very real problems for military forces in a theatre in which forces from the same nation, coalition or agency are simultaneously engaged in different uses of force. For instance, it may be necessary for personnel and operational units from the same maritime *task group* in a single theatre to carry out combat operations against insurgents (*military* use) while enforcing a UN Security Council Resolution through embargo operations (*constabulary* use) at the same time as providing humanitarian assistance (*benign* use). The maritime commander in such circumstances will have to remain conscious of the distinctions, consider the ROE appropriate to each task and ensure that the conduct of each remains within the limits imposed by international law and the law of the country and coastal waters in which the operations are taking place. In such circumstances it may be that the military opposition will take action against those elements of the task group conducting constabulary or benign tasks. These are the sorts of complexities with which those who have operated in and around the Former Republic of Yugoslavia in recent years will be only too aware.

THE APPLICATION OF MARITIME POWER

APPLICATION OF MARITIME POWER

MILITARY

- **FROM THE SEA**
  Power Projection
  - Nuclear Deterrence
  - Combat Operations Against the Land
  - Combat Operations in Defence of Land Forces
  - Evacuation Operations
  - Naval Force in Support of Diplomacy
  - Peace Support Operations

- **AT SEA**
  Sea Control
  - Operations Against Enemy Forces
  - Protection of Maritime Trade

CONSTABULARY
- Embargo, Sanctions & Quarantine Enforcement
- Peacekeeping
- Anti-piracy Operations
- Fishery Protection
- Drug Interdiction
- Contraband Operations
- Oil and Gas Field Patrols
- Maritime Counter-Terrorism
- Support to Counter-Insurgency Operations
- Enforcement of Maritime Agreements

BENIGN
- Disaster Relief
- Assistance to Refugees
- Peace Building Operations
- Search and Rescue
- Salvage
- Ordnance Disposal
- Pollution Control
- Hydrographic Surveying
- Vessel Traffic Services
- Military Assistance to Foreign and Commonwealth Governments

Fig. 4/1

Ch 5

RFA INDULGENCE sails for the Gulf 1998

MARITIME LOGISTICS AND SUPPORT

Chapter 5

The purpose of logistic support is to ensure the provision, sustainment and recovery of forces, thus enabling the maintenance of combat capability and allowing the operational commander to deploy forces at the time and place of his choosing. Logistic support includes medical and repair facilities, movement of personnel, and the transport of the fuel, lubricants, ordnance, spare parts, food and other provisions, and the many stores required for missions. The sea will remain the principal transport medium for large, heavy and bulky items. Ships are, therefore, important joint *logistics* assets. The availability of shipping and the ability to transfer ashore may ultimately govern whether, where and when military operations can take place. However, as a corollary the use of *sea lines of support* to a campaign may be considered a critical vulnerability, and shipping may require protection. Similarly, at the *tactical* level, a formation's *organic* logistic shipping will invariably be essential to its mission and thus require special effort to be devoted to its protection.

The ability of ships to carry and transfer stores and fuel allows *maritime forces* to conduct self-sustained operations at considerable distances from fixed bases. Indeed the sailor is so used to the level of organic logistics support that is provided routinely in a ship and its tactical formation that logistic considerations are intrinsic to maritime doctrine. For the operational commander, maritime and land logistics are not conceptually dissimilar, because the ability to use lines of support along which a maritime force is *consolidated*, is comparable with tasks relating to seaborne support of land operations and to land *lines of support*. In any event, logistic support is a fundamental activity in which resources and facilities must be pooled and focused to sustain a joint campaign in all its phases and environments. It is a tenet of joint *doctrine* that administrative services of common usage in the three Services can be provided by one Service for the use of others. At the operational level, logistic policy, planning and execution will be jointly co-ordinated.

Maritime logistics support to joint operations comes with two important advantages. *Sea basing* of logistics support leaves very little in the way of a 'footprint' ashore and allows that support to be landed in sufficient quantities as required without necessarily placing it all in a vulnerable and essentially immobile location. Sea basing also allows for the protection of logistics support, especially important in operational environments that may be affected by WMD.

LOGISTICS AT THE STRATEGIC LEVEL

At the *grand-strategic level*, the logistics process provides the link between the resources of the nation and the military operations of combat forces. The creation of logistic resources (or *production logistics*) is almost entirely a civilian commercial process. Once they are manufactured, the employment of these resources in support of military operations (*consumer logistics*) becomes a military function, albeit one heavily dependent on civilian support. The integration of production and consumer logistic systems takes place at the *military-strategic level* and is the responsibility of the Chief of Defence Logistics (CDL). The determination of strategic requirements, procurement, planning of logistic aspects of *regeneration* capability, central storage and bulk distribution are all *military-strategic* logistic functions.

LOGISTICS AT THE OPERATIONAL LEVEL

Maritime operational logistic functions are:

- the movement of logistics into, within and out of theatre;

- the establishment of logistic bases;

- the apportionment and allocation of logistics between subordinate commands; and

- the protection of logistics bases, on land, and along *sea lines of communication.*

RFA FORT GEORGE

For the *Naval Service* this function is carried out by CINCFLEET. In war, protection and distribution of logistics may constitute a major operation in its own right as a commander will want to ensure that his logistic plan is adequate to support his concept of operations. Logistic feasibility will frequently be the deciding factor in choosing a course of action. For this reason logistic planning will require the same attention as planning for warfighting, and must underpin all envisaged contingencies during each phase of the campaign plan. Detailed logistic planning is vital particularly during amphibious operations to ensure that manpower and equipment are integrated, accessible and flexible to match the tempo of operations set by the operational commander without the delays caused by the need to restow ships. This process is aided if the commander at each level has control over the allocation of the logistic support to the forces under his command. Complete unity of logistic command is desirable but difficult to achieve for two principal reasons. First, the harmonization of production and consumer logistics is a continuous process involving a large number of organizations most of whom will not be under the control of the operational commander. He may therefore have little control of the supply side of his logistics. Second, there are particular problems associated with the control of logistics during joint and, especially, multinational operations. The establishment of the Joint Task Force Logistics Component under the Joint Task Force Commander (JTFC) with responsibility for logistic support, enhances unity of logistic command in national joint operations.

MULTI-NATIONAL LOGISTICS

Logistics during multinational operations have traditionally been, and remain, a national responsibility. This will inevitably be the case within an ad hoc coalition where there is little standardization between nations' equipments. However, NATO and the WEU have developed a principle of collective responsibility between member nations and Allied authorities, although specific national requirements, especially in ammunition resupply and the maintenance and repair of weapon systems, still limit the effectiveness of multinational logistics. Allied maritime contingency planning includes the establishment of a *Multinational Logistic Commander* (MNLC) to plan, co-ordinate and control all maritime logistic shore support. Additionally, both NATO and the WEU have developed Joint Logistics Doctrine, encompassing a Multinational Joint Logistics Centre (MJLC) similar to the MNLC concept. Interoperability within an alliance is a prerequisite if one nation's logistic resources are to support another's, and considerable work in NATO's standardization agencies is devoted to this end. Standardization of fuel grades, replenishment rigs and connections allow for regular transfer of fuel between NATO nations and, indeed, between other nations who have adopted NATO standards. Medical support, supply of provisions and general stores, and non-specialist transport can generally be treated as common resources.

LOGISTIC PRINCIPLES

The principles of joint logistics are: foresight, economy, flexibility, simplicity and co-operation. The need for foresight in logistic planning has been discussed earlier in this chapter, as has the requirement for co-operation between Services, nations and commands, particularly where control of logistics is not unified. Economy, flexibility and simplicity deserve special mention:

Economy

Logistics resources will usually be in short supply and sufficiency should be the objective of the logistician. It is possible to overplan as well as to underplan logistic requirements. Over-planning can consume resources that could be devoted to combat forces. Furthermore, an over-large logistic organization may require additional logistics staff who, in turn, will need logistic support, and the whole may draw forces for protection away from the main effort.

Flexibility

A logistic plan must be capable of responding to the inevitable changes in any operational plan. Equally, the logistic system that executes the plan must be capable of adapting to rapid changes of requirement. A large logistics organization geared to supporting a major campaign can acquire a momentum of its own and generate wasteful stockpiles of materiel, if it is not sensitive to change. It may also be necessary for an operational commander to take a calculated risk over logistic sufficiency, in particular where there are opportunities to exploit success or to maintain tempo. For example, he may allow the fuel and ammunition levels of a *naval force* that is exploiting success to fall below prudent norms in the expectation that consolidation forces will arrive. A flexible logistic system will minimize differences between operational and logistic tempo and therefore the attendant risk. It is relevant that a principal reason for the planning of *operational pauses* in a campaign is to allow the consolidation of logistics and to avoid reaching *culmination* before success is achieved.

Simplicity

Any unnecessarily complicated aspect of operational planning will be prone to disruption. Logistic planning is in large part carried out by experts and can appear intractable to non-experts charged with assessment and execution. The principal non-expert may be the operational commander. A comprehensive, but simple, plan that accords with the direction given by the operational commander is more likely to gain approval and be correctly interpreted and executed.

ROULEMENT

Consideration must be given at an early stage in strategic and operational planning to relieving maritime forces and personnel in an operational theatre for an extended period. Although ships, given sufficient logistic support, can remain on station almost indefinitely, the efficiency of personnel can be expected to decline during deployment. Furthermore, some aspects of maintenance may suffer if the tempo of operations is high. The rotation of ships and personnel on station to maintain a high state of *readiness* is known as *roulement* and is an important feature of the maritime component of a campaign plan.

SHORE SUPPORT

Shore support, whether at home or abroad, provides the starting point for any maritime logistic chain. The home base will provide the main supply depots and dockyard facilities. Most supplies and repairs are obtained from the private sector under contract. Procurement of materiel must be carefully monitored both to ensure that adequate stocks of equipment and stores are available for transfer to the fleet and to avoid wasting resources in the production and retention of unnecessarily large stocks. When *Host Nation Support* (HNS) is available, it may supplement afloat support by providing useful forward airheads and seaports for logistic and personnel movements to and from the theatre of operations, and forward operating bases for replenishment, maintenance and repair. HNS may help to economize on the need for logistics, but such support is not an essential feature of purely maritime operations. Indeed, a forward operating base may be no more than a sheltered anchorage for a support or repair ship. However once troops are ashore, the significance and dimensions of the organization to co-ordinate and take advantage of HNS can increase substantially. HNS arrangements are often pre-planned in outline and formalised by inter-governmental Memoranda of Understanding (MOU). They are, nevertheless, not guaranteed to remain in force as the situation changes. Lack of HNS may cause the emphasis of an operation to remain with maritime logistics support.

> **5/1. Field Marshal Viscount Alanbrooke's Appreciation of Sea Transport's Importance in the Second World War**
>
> "Brooke's strategy, like that of all Britain's greatest commanders, depended on salt water. With his grasp of essentials, he saw that sea transport was the key to the offensive. Without it nothing could be done to take the pressure off Russia or deprive the enemy, with his central land position, of the initiative".
>
> (Sir Arthur Bryant, **The Turn of the tide 1939-1943**, a study based on the diaries and autobiographical notes of Field Marshal The Viscount Alanbrooke KG OM. (1883-1963), Chief of the Imperial General Staff and Chairman of the Chiefs of Staff Committee from 1941 to 1945.
>
> Churchill endorsed Alanbrooke's view when he wrote: "Shipping was at once the stranglehold and sole foundation of our war strategy". (**The Second World War** *Volume IV*.)

SUSTAINED REACH

No maritime force is complete without support vessels to provide fuel and other essential stores. An integral part of the Fleet, the Royal Navy's logistic shipping is organised as the *Royal Fleet Auxiliary* (RFA), manned by personnel employed under Merchant Navy articles, and whose officers provide afloat support expertise on Command staffs. Replenishment at Sea (RAS) from auxiliary ships enables naval forces to extend their reach world wide without the need to enter port. The RFA, supplemented where necessary by chartered vessels or Ships Taken Up From Trade (STUFT), gives British maritime forces a unique capability to carry out sustained operations at considerable distances from their home base, and as such, the UK continues to maintain considerable investment in these ships; the effort is enhanced by in-theatre consolidation and the provision of air based supply. The mechanism for taking ships up from trade is well established and, in crisis, early identification of the need for STUFT is important if forces containing such vessels are to be formed in a timely fashion.

THE MARITIME OPERATIONAL LOGISTICS PIPELINE

The sustained reach of maritime forces and the reach which they in turn provide to other forces are key components of maritime power. However military and RFA support shipping form only a part of the maritime logistic system. Figure 5.1 shows the extent of the Operational Logistics Pipeline from the UK bases to the furthest forward fighting unit. The Pipeline includes an Initial Handling Point (IHP), possibly an *Advanced Logistic Support Site* (ALSS) and, potentially, several *Forward Logistics Sites* (FLS) within the operational theatre. The establishment and maintenance of these sites, together with the provision of transport between them, will, in most cases, be a joint and frequently multinational requirement. The locations of the ALSS and FLS would be chosen to provide optimal support to the campaign and may need to move if the situation changes.

The pipeline must handle the movement of materiel and people into, within and from the operational area. Personnel may include casualties, refugees, displaced persons and prisoners of war. Segments of the pipeline may consist of air, land or sea transport, which could be supporting all three Services as well as multinational requirements. Priorities across commodities, services and nations will need to be established to cater for constraints on transport capacity.

SEA CENTURION Ro-Con Strategic Sea Lift

CONCLUDING COMMENTS

The accurate preparation, sequencing and positioning of logistics in peacetime, and the seamless understanding between logisticians and warfare specialists at each level of command, are fundamental to the success of operations throughout the spectrum of likely tasks. Modern *joint* operations will only retain their effect when complemented by flexible, mission focused logistics drawing together single-Service, joint and civilian elements.

Ch 5
MARITIME LOGISTICS AND SUPPORT

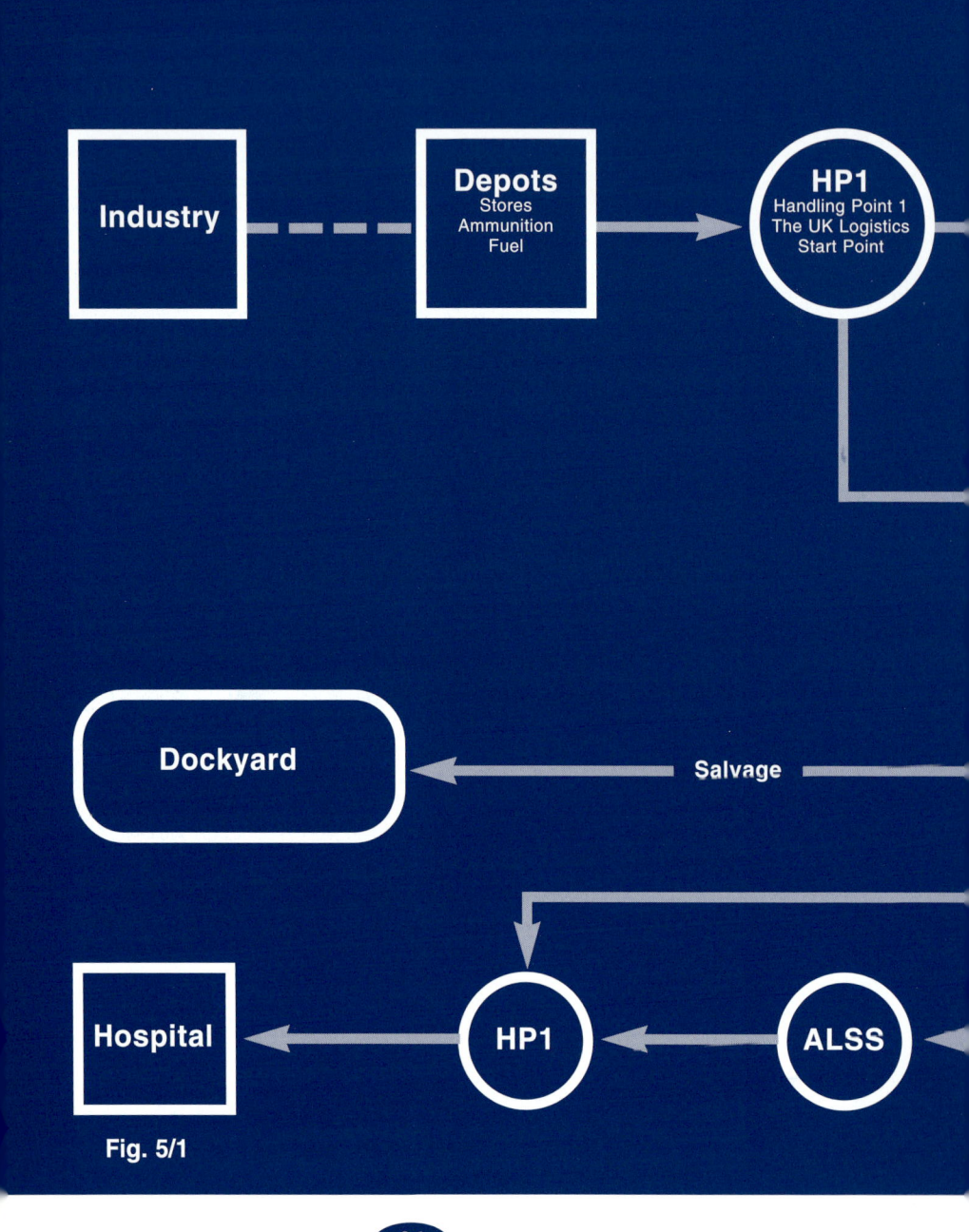

```
Industry -------- Depots ───────▶ HP1
                  Stores           Handling Point 1
                  Ammunition       The UK Logistics
                  Fuel             Start Point


Dockyard ◀────────── Salvage ──────────


Hospital ◀── HP1 ◀─────── ALSS ◀──
```

Fig. 5/1

Ch 5
MARITIME LOGISTICS AND SUPPORT

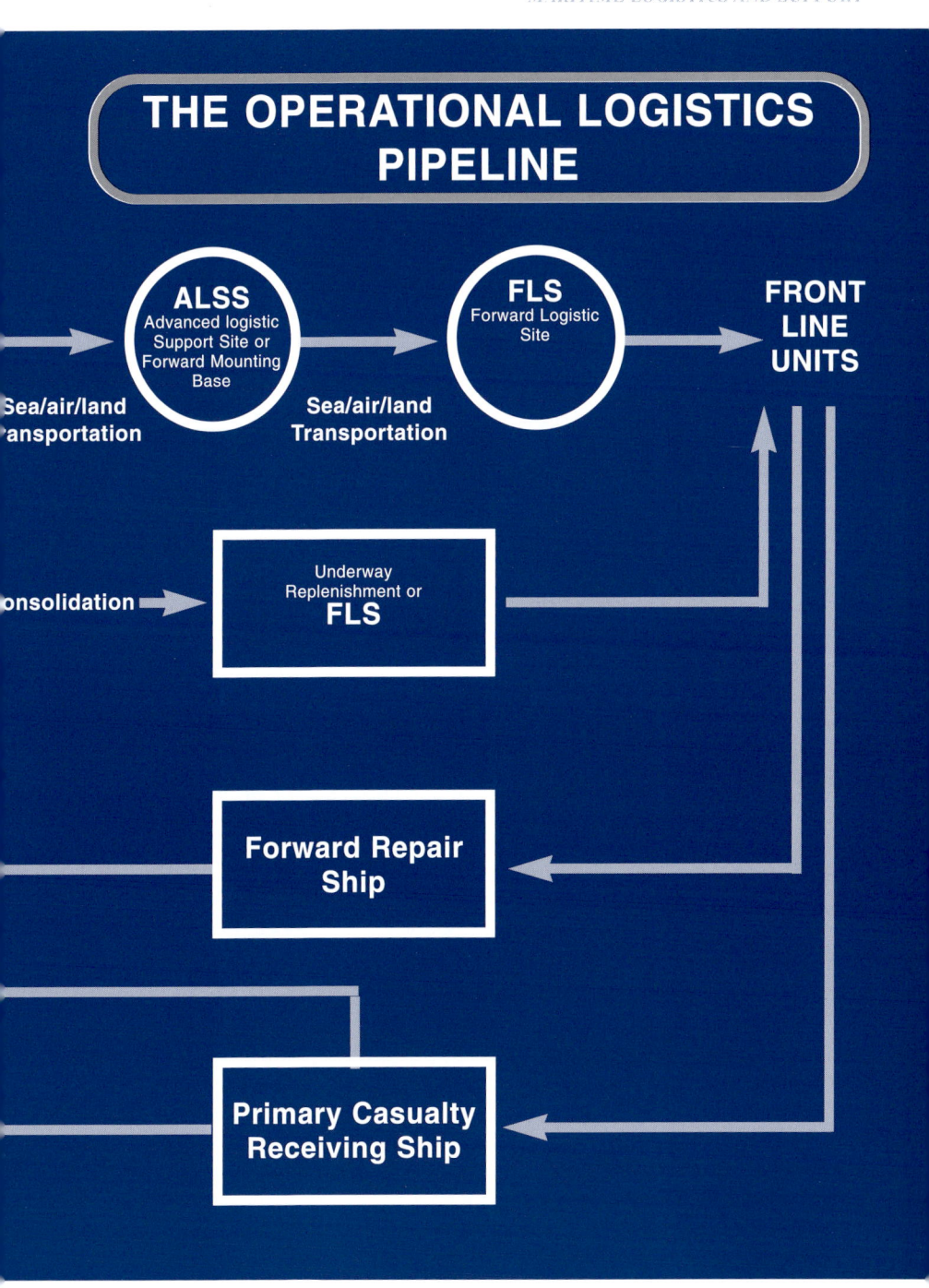

THE OPERATIONAL LOGISTICS PIPELINE

ALSS
Advanced logistic Support Site or Forward Mounting Base

Sea/air/land Transportation

FLS
Forward Logistic Site

Sea/air/land Transportation

FRONT LINE UNITS

Consolidation

Underway Replenishment or **FLS**

Forward Repair Ship

Primary Casualty Receiving Ship

87

Ch 6

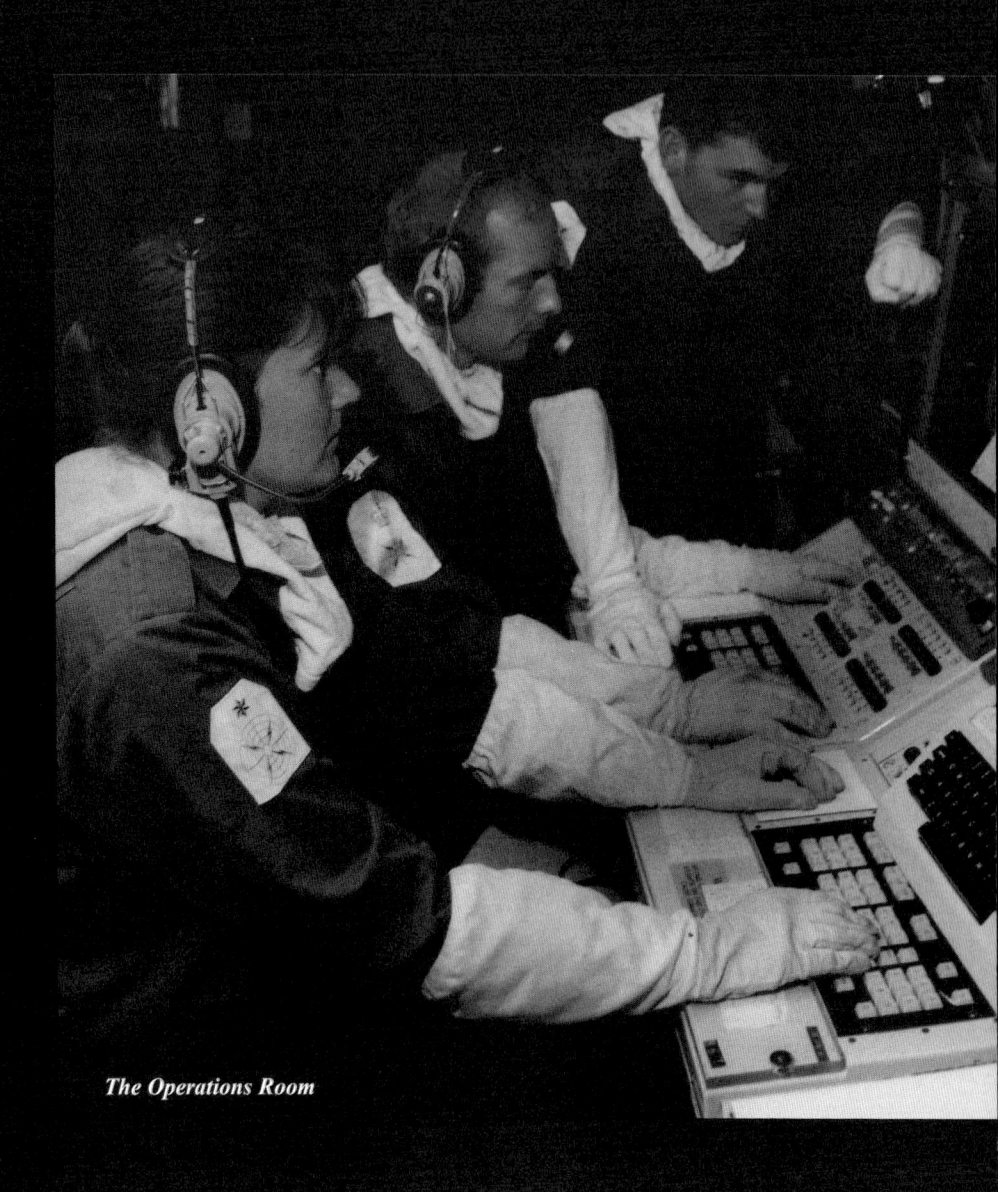

The Operations Room

MARITIME COMMAND AND CONTROL

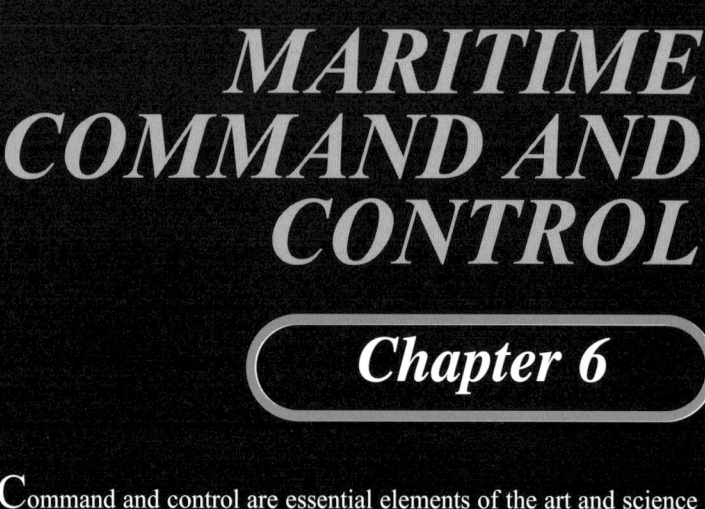

Chapter 6

Command and control are essential elements of the art and science of maritime warfare. *Command* is the authority granted to an individual to direct, co-ordinate and control military forces. *Control* is the actual process through which the commander organizes, directs and co-ordinates the activities of forces allocated to him. Command and control, supported by a system of people, information, and technology, enable the maritime force commander to cope with the uncertainties of combat and to employ military force efficiently. Command and control governs all areas of maritime operations and new technology is broadening its scope and increasing its complexity. Nevertheless, its foundations remain constant: professional competence born of a high level of training and a thorough understanding of relevant doctrine, and an effective means of communicating information and directions through the operational chain of command.

Ch 6

MARITIME COMMAND AND CONTROL

To be fully effective, commanders need to have a thorough understanding of the nature and conduct of military operations, the leadership attributes required, and the command and control processes through which they will direct operations. The latter requires an appreciation of the vulnerabilities and weaknesses in one's own command and control process and systems, as well as insight into the nature of one's opponent's command and control.

The maritime command and control system encompasses all personnel, systems and resources throughout the maritime force, that support the flow and processing of information. It includes the functions of: intelligence, surveillance, target acquisition and reconnaissance (ISTAR); information processing; intelligence; decision-making and display; communications; electronic warfare; cryptology; and information operations, including command and control warfare. The requirement to exercise effective command and control in today's environment extends to all levels of warfare and across the full range of military operations.

HIGHER COMMAND OF THE ARMED FORCES

The command of each of the UK's fighting Services is vested in the Sovereign. The Secretary of State for Defence is appointed by the Crown after nomination by the Prime Minister and is accountable to Parliament. He is responsible for the defence of the realm, is supported by the Defence Council and is advised by the Chief of the Defence Staff (CDS). The Service Chiefs of Staff are members of the Defence Council and are individually responsible for the fighting effectiveness, management, overall efficiency and morale of their respective Services. They report to the Secretary of State through CDS, but retain the right of direct access to the Secretary of State and the Prime Minister.

OPERATIONAL AND TACTICAL ORGANIZATION

For operations mounted by the UK alone, overall command is exercised by CDS. Future *campaigns* and operations are likely to be joint. If they are, CDS will appoint a *Joint Commander* who will exercise Operational Command (OPCOM), from the Permanent Joint Headquarters (PJHQ), over the forces assigned to him. In theatre, a *Joint Task Force Commander* (JTFC) will be nominated, and he will exercise *Operational Control* (OPCON) through individual component commanders. Component commanders straddle the dividing line between the operational and tactical levels. They have a planning function within the JTFHQ that they discharge at the operational level. In executing their component of the plan, they command at the tactical level.

This organization provides the essential unity of command required at the operational level. It also ensures that authority and responsibility for an operation are clearly defined, and appropriate expertise and experience is in place to provide effective command and control of assigned forces. This structure requires a trained and experienced joint staff drawn from the participating Services. This in turn necessitates regular exercises in joint command and control. Levels of command are illustrated in Figure 6.1.

Maritime forces are organized *functionally* for operations into a *task organization* consisting of a maximum of four levels of *echelonment: task forces, task groups, task units* and *task elements* (see Figure 6.2). The use of these levels is flexible and they bear no direct relationship to levels of command or levels of planning.

COMMUNICATIONS

Communications is one of the two fundamental means by which effective command is exercised (the second is through the promulgation of sound doctrine). Modern communications present commanders with two challenges. The first of these is a consequence of effective communications and is the possibility of superior levels of command 'micro-managing' operations at lower levels. This is a tendency that is increasing, with tactical decisions having, at times, strategic effect and with even the political leadership being tempted to interfere in tactical decision-making. The second challenge comes as a consequence of too heavy a reliance on communications followed by subordinate levels lacking necessary initiative when communications links are severed.

Micro-management undermines subordinate commanders' ability to seize the initiative when the opportunities arise. The ability to seize the initiative is fundamental to the application of a manoeuvrist approach to operations. However, the desire of superior commanders to apply a manoeuvrist approach, in which a range of disparate activities require co-ordination if effective systemic disruption is to be achieved, may lead them towards micro-management of forces under their command. The main message here is that commanders, in applying a manoeuvrist approach should beware of an instinctive tendency to interfere, only doing so when not to do so would undermine the overall objective; balance, as ever, is the key.

Continuous superior interference in subordinate level decision-making will also have the effect of rendering subordinate commanders inexperienced in dealing with the challenges that arise when communications links are severed. The assumption that communications will be effective may also lead to complacency as far as doctrine is concerned. If communications were invariably effective, allowing superior commanders to micro-manage effectively, there would be no necessity for developing robust doctrine for the guidance of subordinate commanders in a position to exercise initiative. In brief, the danger is that the promise of communications may foster a neglect of doctrine. Needless to say, such a tendency should be avoided.

PJHQ and JHQ

The only response to these two opposing but connected challenges is to achieve a responsible degree of balance in command and control and for superior levels of command not to interfere routinely in the conduct of operations at subordinate levels. The balance should be somewhere between the contrasting approaches of Beatty and Jellicoe, allowing initiative to be taken by subordinates but with a responsible superior hand able to convey guidance when appropriate. Given the immediate impact that tactical decisions can have on strategic outcomes, achieving the right balance will not always be easy, but that will never be an excuse for over-bearing command and control.

6/1. The Failure to Delegate

The history of the Royal Navy in the Twentieth Century is littered with officers who perverted their natural instincts for hard work into gross over centralization. This led to such disasters as the scattering and subsequent massacre of Convoy PQ17 on the personal orders of a First Sea Lord who did not have a clear understanding of the tactical situation. Similarly officers have worked themselves to premature deaths. The other side of this coin, an unwillingness to act on initiative in an over-centralised Grand Fleet, was a major factor in the escape of the Germans from almost certain destruction after the Battle of Jutland in 1916.

A sound philosophy of command has three enduring tenets: timely decision-making; understanding a superior commander's intention; and a clear responsibility on the part of subordinates to fulfil the superior's intention. This requires a style of command which promotes: decentralized command; freedom and speed of action; and initiative. The overall concept of *Mission Command* developed within the British Army is also applicable within maritime forces and will be applied in joint operations. Mission command has the following key elements:

- A commander gives his orders in a manner that ensures his subordinates understand his intentions, their own missions, and the context of those missions;

- Subordinates are told what effect they are to achieve and the reason why it needs to be achieved;

- Subordinates are allocated sufficient resources to carry out their missions;

- A commander uses a minimum of control in order not to limit unnecessarily the freedom of action of his subordinates;

- Subordinates decide within their delegated freedom of action how best to achieve their missions.

Too great an emphasis on delegation in applying the principle of Mission Command could jeopardise manoeuvrist operations just as surely as will too great an emphasis on micro-management. Decentralized command and the application of too much initiative by subordinates will make co-ordination of effective manoeuvre difficult. Again, it is stressed that the key to success is achieving the right balance between control by superiors and subordinate freedom. An experienced and skilled commander will be one who recognises this command and control dilemma and achieves the necessary balance in his style of command that allows him adequate control while endowing his subordinates with sufficient freedom to use initiative. One should never underestimate the difficulties of achieving this balance; it is a fundamentally important skill for commanders to develop and will require a good deal of serious thought to get right.

Effective communication links that are secure and invulnerable to supression, manipulation or degradation, are an essential means of effecting proper command and control. However, in some situations, certain ships may not be fitted with the necessary communications to meet the wider command and control needs of the force. This needs to be taken into consideration during the planning process and allowed for when assessing the degree of control and tempo possible within an operation.

No commander should be, or will wish to be, wholly dependent on umbilical communications links with higher command ashore or afloat. It is essential, therefore, that commanders and their staffs have a clear understanding of the higher commanders' intentions so that they can take appropriate action in the absence of timely direction. This requirement reinforces the importance of decentralized execution. At the operational level, such understanding should include appreciation of national policy and the diplomatic and political environment in which operations are being conducted. As a general rule a commander and his staff should understand their immediate superior's detailed intentions, and the broad intentions of the commander two levels above him.

The command and control systems of a command ship together with the intelligence systems and communications connectivity supporting them are elaborate and comprehensive. They allow joint operational control to be exercised over a large theatre of operations from a platform which is self sufficient, mobile and flexible. However, the implications of the loss of such a capable unit needs to be addressed and contingencies arranged.

6/2. Command and Control and Doctrine in the Pacific

"The sum total of the American naval forces in the Philippine Sea area constituted the greatest assembly of naval might the world has ever seen or may ever see again - far greater than the strength that the Japanese Navy could muster in that area. And yet, mark you, there was no effective single command agency which could weld all our naval forces into a single fleet under single command; Admiral Nimitz did not have that authority, nor did General MacArthur; and no higher echelon could or would step into the breach. The details of the second battle of the Philippine Sea (usually referred to as the Battle of Leyte Gulf) will keep students occupied for decades to come. Obviously there were many things done which could have been done differently in the light of hindsight; obviously there were things left undone which could have been undertaken to great advantage. But to me, in retrospect, the vital and important thing is that, although not unified under a single authoritative command, all of those separated commanders were thinking in sufficiently like terms to construct a mosaic of tactical victories fitting together into a greater mural of strategic victory which effectively terminated Japanese seapower. There were gaps in communications and gaps in mutual understandings among the commanders, but the great principles of seapower had been inculcated in all of those commanders and were literally second

> nature to them, so that even without authoritative co-ordinated command, they instinctively moved in directions which were basically sound."
>
> Vice Admiral Robert B Carney *US Navy, US Naval War College Review,* October 1948.

RULES OF ENGAGEMENT

Rules of Engagement (ROE) are issued to provide political direction, authorisation, guidance and instruction to commanders. ROE are the primary means of defining political limits to the use of military force and take the form of general policy indicators and directives, prohibitions and permissions. They can be instruments of *escalation, de-escalation* and the *maintenance* of the status quo. They are formulated and sought by military staffs at the operational and tactical levels and authorized at the political (grand-strategic) level following military and legal advice at the military-strategic level. ROE must be under constant review in order to ensure that they reflect changing military and political circumstances. Dormant ROE may be prepared and authorized for immediate use if certain contingencies arise. It is a military-strategic level function of the very greatest importance to ensure that ROE are crafted to allow effective use of military force, while providing proper protection. The operational commander in turn must ensure that he fully understands these rules, promulgates them throughout his force and is willing to make a robust case for alterations when circumstances change. It is a major challenge to create, in a few words, a vivid and succinct description of the changing situation, possible outcomes, and precise reasons for seeking new or amended rules. ROE are the basic tool for ensuring coherence between the political and military process, and should fit the mission as well as the capability of a force to ensure survivability. As a consequence, adequate time and training will be needed for ROE at all levels of military planning. Rules of Engagement are likely to be major planning constraints and may shape significantly courses of action. During multinational operations variations in national ROE may be a principal constraint on the tasking of forces (See Multinational Operations below).

NAVAL COMMAND, CONTROL, COMMUNICATIONS, COMPUTERS AND INFORMATION (C4I) SYSTEMS

Naval C4I systems are the information systems, equipment, software, and infrastructure that enable the commander to exercise authority and direction over assigned forces. C4I systems also help the commander monitor and influence the actions of the maritime force through the chain of command. These systems support the following five basic functions:

- **Collecting** Gathering and formatting data for processing.

- **Processing** Filtering, correlating, fusing and evaluating data to produce a picture required for the commander to take appropriate action.

- **Disseminating** Distributing information for use or further processing, and distributing orders and instructions.

- **Displaying** Presenting information to the user in the most effective and efficient manner.

- **Protecting** Guarding information from an adversary's attempts to exploit, corrupt, or destroy it.

C4I systems encompass the hardware structure supporting the command and control process. Although highly automated, this structure should be designed very much with the 'user' in mind, giving them access to information and helping them make effective use of it. In modern warfare, advanced technology is essential for automating the collection, processing, dissemination, and protection of vast quantities of information. However, technology is not a means of taking the man out of the command and control process; instead it is used to enhance overall performance. Technology automates routine functions that machines can accomplish more efficiently, freeing commanders to focus on the aspects of command and control that require their experience, judgement, and intuition. It must be remembered, however, that while enhancements to C4I systems should upgrade the quality of the commander's information, more information is not always better information. C4I systems should:

- support all aspects of the commander's decision making process, from initial observation and orientation, to ultimate execution and validation.

- enable maritime forces to integrate their efforts with those of others when appropriate.

- monitor and exploit all dimensions of the battlespace, using all available sensors.

- provide a coherent, accurate, and timely picture of the situation, scaled to the needs of the user.

- allow information flow throughout the force: not just up and down the chain of command, but laterally as well.

- be designed as part of an architecture that can integrate with other operational systems, software, and databases quickly.

- support the maritime commander's efforts to exploit or attack the adversary's information systems and disrupt his ability to co-ordinate his forces.

C4I systems are vital for planning, executing, and sustaining a successful naval, joint, or multinational operation. All aspects of naval warfare operations, logistics, planning, and intelligence depend on responsive command and control. Integrating command and control requirements and plans with those for operations, logistics, and intelligence is essential. Experience has repeatedly demonstrated that command and control support staff should be brought in at the beginning of the operational planning process, and they must liaise continuously with those who will execute the operation.

CHARACTERISTICS OF NAVAL C4I SYSTEMS

Depending on the operational situation, maritime commanders may attach greater importance to some areas at the expense of others. Consequently, the order in which the characteristics of naval C4I systems are listed below is not intended to indicate their relative importance.

Reliability Systems must be available when needed and perform as intended with low failure rates and few errors. Reliability is also assisted by: standardisation in equipment, procedures and training; the provision of appropriate levels of redundancy; availability of effective logistics support; and protection against computer virus attack, electronic jamming, deception and manipulation. Systems should perform reliably, even in the most austere and demanding conditions.

Security Security, commensurate with the operator's requirements and the perceived threat from interception and exploitation, is essential. This may be achieved by employing appropriate security protection, including: cryptographic systems; using transmission security techniques; and educating and training personnel in security procedures. These measures must be kept under continuous review in order to counter any evolving threat.

Timeliness Information must be processed and disseminated between and within commands rapidly enough to maintain a high tempo of operations and ensure that the decision-making process remains faster than that of any opponent.

Flexibility Systems must be capable of being reconfigured quickly so that they can respond to any rapidly changing environment. This can be enhanced by intelligent system design and the sensible use of a diverse mix of fixed, mobile and transportable facilities, owned by both military and commercial organizations.

Interoperability In order to ensure that information can be exchanged amongst all commanders and forces involved in an operation, maritime C4I systems should be able to operate in joint and multi-national environments, integrating with other government departments and civilian organizations in theatre.

Survivability Survivability can be attained by dispersal and protection of key nodes, physical and electromagnetic hardening, and redundancy of communications paths and information processing nodes.

INFORMATION OPERATIONS

Effective command and control are essential to success in modern operations. Protection and maintenance of command and control facilities is of paramount importance since the whole system can be degraded through the loss or malfunctioning of one, or a small number of, components. Consequently operations conducted against an opponent's command and control infrastructure and decision-making process play a key part in modern *conflict*. In recognition of the importance of the battle for control of information, the term Information Operations has been devised to embrace Command and Control Warfare (C2W), Media Operations, CIMIC, and strategic Psychological Operations. C2W is the term used to embrace aspects of *electronic warfare*, physical destruction, *operational deception*, *psychological operations* and *operational security*. It aims at gaining information superiority by exploiting, influencing, degrading confusing or destroying the enemy's command and control capabilities, while protecting friendly systems against such actions. Good intelligence and co-ordination between various elements in joint and combined forces are essential to its success.

SPACE

Modern command and control makes extensive use of space systems for communications and navigational accuracy; they are also a medium for critical, strategic and operational surveillance assets. The United States is a principal contributor of space systems to Alliance and coalition operations. Space is one of the five *warfare environments*, along with the sea, the air, the land and the electromagnetic spectrum. It can be an important enabler which may not only be exploited by a sophisticated opponent but also by an increasing number of nations and interests serving, in part, proxy and commercial sources.

MULTINATIONAL AND COALITION MARITIME OPERATIONS

In multinational operations there will be an additional dimension to the command and control organization. Multinational operations are conducted by *integrated* multinational forces and, by their nature, are complex. They involve forces with different national equipment and *doctrine*, often with specific political constraints on their employment. Close liaison between the various governments and their own individual services is required to ensure the achievement of common objectives. When national forces are assigned to a NATO operation, OPCOM and OPCON will normally be given to a *Major NATO Commander* (MNC). The NATO chain of command has traditionally passed from MNC through a *Major Subordinate Commander* (MSC) and *Principal Subordinate Commander* (PSC) to the operational formations. Following the introduction of the *Combined Joint Task Force* (CJTF) Concept, a CJTF Commander may be appointed under the command of an MNC or MSC. He will normally have OPCON of all the different participating national units. The CJTF Concept can also be used for purely European operations under WEU command, and for operations in which other nations participate alongside NATO or WEU forces. (Note: during the currency of this edition of *BR1806*, NATO terminology is due to change and it is intended that MNCs, MSCs, and PSCs will be replaced/retitled as Strategic Commands, Regional Commands and Joint Sub-Regional Commands/Component Commands)

Multinational Co-operation

Multinational military co-operation offers nations and coalitions both political and military advantages in the pursuit of their interests. National contributions must be judged by the full range of benefits they bring to a coalition, not solely by the capability of military forces provided. These operations also present a number of challenges which must be resolved if they are to be effective. These include: different national security policies, force structures, and force capabilities, as well as a wide range of equipment and procedural interoperability issues. Nations can prepare for multinational operations through: political interaction; exercises and war games; personnel exchanges; port visits; cultural, legal and language training; and equipment standardization programmes with potential partners. This preparation serves routine peacetime political and military purposes and provides a framework within which a multinational force could operate during a crisis or war.

Principles for Multinational Operations

Multinational operations must be directed toward a well understood and agreed-upon *objective*, and all partners must strive for *unity of effort* in its achievement. Adherence to these principles is vital for success.

Command and Control Organization

Organization plays a crucial role in the conduct of multinational maritime operations. It determines how the constituents of a multinational maritime force will interact with each other and with other non-maritime forces involved. Command and control terminology must be agreed and understood by the participants before a command structure is developed to meet the needs, political realities, constraints, and objectives of the participating nations. Command structures may range from highly to loosely centralised. In highly centralised command structures, the degree of command and control may approach that existing in individual nations. In looser command structures, the command relationship is more accurately described in terms of co-operation and co-ordination. There are three basic organizational structures, which may be used in combination:

- **Parallel Command** Forces operate under national command in the co-operative pursuit of coalition objectives.

- **Lead Nation Command** One partner is designated the overall commander and the other participants follow the concepts and direction of the lead nation, which may rotate among the partners.

- **Integrated Command** A single commander with a staff composed of representatives from all member nations commands the operation.

Key Factors in Multinational Operations

Multinational operations will require maritime commanders to consider a wide range of factors that may have a decisive impact on the cohesiveness and effectiveness of the force. The factors listed below are not placed in any particular order, although the need for shared doctrine must be considered of prime significance, as also must be awareness of differences of meaning or interpretation in ROE.

Commanders In all but the parallel structure, a Multinational Maritime Force Commander may be appointed. His authority is determined by the participating nations, and is often substantially limited. In any event he will have to establish unity of effort through consensus building and extensive liaison with the National Maritime Component Commanders designated by each participating nation. Achieving and maintaining a sufficient degree of interoperability

Multinational MCM operations

will be a primary objective of the multinational command regardless of the structure chosen.

Shared Doctrine and Publications Shared doctrine and publications are fundamental to any successful multinational maritime operation. With the assistance of a broad range of maritime nations, including Russia and other former Soviet and Warsaw Pact states, the US Navy's Doctrine Command has developed a set of multinational maritime operations publications. Based on a series of unclassified tactical publications worked up under NATO auspices for use by Partnership for Peace nations, the **Multinational Maritime Operations** capping document and associated **Multinational Maritime Manuals** (**MMMs**) (previously known as **1000 Series EXTACs**) are under constant development to provide a common body of multinational maritime doctrine.

Language In the earliest stages of a multinational operation, agreement on a common language and terminology to co-ordinate coalition activity must be reached.

Liaison Officers Liaison officers improve the flow of information and act as bridges between cultures, languages, doctrine, and procedures. They are vital to the effective conduct of multinational operations.

Information Exchange A multinational maritime force must have common situational awareness based on the effective exchange of intelligence and tactical data. This must include the location, disposition and movement of friendly, neutral and opposing forces, supplemented by information on the environment. In order to facilitate this exchange of information, communications planners must consider the need for equipment interoperability common protocols and procedures, and the necessary levels of security required to protect information without hindering operations.

Force Co-ordination Weapons safety, collision avoidance and air and water space management procedures are essential to prevent mutual interference between ships, aircraft, and submarines, and to avoid friendly fire incidents. Multinational air operations are likely to require a particularly high level of co-ordination and the appointment of an overall commander for air operations may be necessary.

Ch 6
MARITIME COMMAND AND CONTROL

Rules of Engagement ROE differences within a force may reduce operational effectiveness. Common or harmonized ROE should be sought as early as possible. All partners must, as a minimum, understand how each will apply force in support of the mission or in self defence. This will avoid units being placed in situations in which differences in their ROE prevent them conducting properly co-ordinated responses.

Safety Issues The ability to conduct a variety of seamanship evolutions, operate and support helicopters, and conduct co-ordinated search and rescue operations are all important to the safe conduct of a multinational maritime operation.

Planning Planning for multinational maritime operations focuses on developing and maintaining the ability of the elements composing the force to work together toward the objective. It commences with a directive from the authorizing organization detailing the mission, resources, and general command and control arrangements. The commander and his staff then analyze the mission and prepare an estimate of the situation that will address all aspects of the operation, including mission, situation analysis, and friendly and opposing courses of action. A best course of action is then selected and expressed in the commander's concept of operations that describes how and why he intends to employ his forces to achieve the desired end state. Once the concept of operations has been produced, the staff will develop the operation order, which gives detailed directives and guidance on all aspects of the operation.

Logistics A clear logistics plan will be required to support the operations plan. It must resolve national differences in logistical doctrine and capabilities, establish the responsibilities of each nation and the multinational maritime force commander, and detail a logistics organization.

Concluding Operations The success or failure of any multinational operation will largely be determined by the decisions made at the very beginning of the planning process. The objectives and desired end-state must be clearly stated and acceptable to all participants. Moreover, the perception of progress toward achievement of the desired end-state is important to prevent premature dissolution of the coalition. Establishing realistic measures of effectiveness will help maintain focus on the mission, and prevent mission creep as the situation evolves. Nations will decide individually when their participation in a multinational operation should end, and some may wish to terminate their participation earlier than others. Ideally, nations should inform partners of their intentions to end their participation as far in advance as possible. Before withdrawing, they should clean up the area of operations, meet all financial obligations, and provide a comprehensive turn over to follow-on forces or civil authorities. Finally, the lessons learned from the operation should be recorded and published for future reference and the relationships formed in the conduct of the operation should be maintained to ease future co-operation.

6/3. Failures of Command and Control at Antwerp

The problems which failures of command and control can bring are well illustrated by the history of British maritime operations against Antwerp. In 1809, in the greatest amphibious operation carried out by Britain to that date, almost 40,000 troops were sent primarily to capture the city and destroy the large French fleet and dockyard and, secondly, to divert Napoleon from his attack on Austria. The Naval commander, Sir Richard Strachan, did not have the intelligence or doctrinal grasp to operate effectively with the lethargic land force commander Lord Chatham. This resulted in the occupation and eventual evacuation of the island of Walcheren at the mouth of the Scheldt with little else to show for the loss of over 4,000 men, all but 106 to illness. 135 years later, in 1944, ineffective operational direction saw the capture of the city of Antwerp totally neutralized by German retention of the Scheldt estuary. Only after a properly carried out maritime operation under effective joint command was Walcheren captured and access to a port, vital to the logistics of the Allied armies, obtained.

CONCLUDING COMMENTS

It matters not how effective all other aspects of a maritime force's capabilities happen to be, if the command and control arrangements, including communications and doctrine, are inadequate or lacking in some way, an operation may be undermined and an entire mission placed in jeopardy. While an operation will never succeed by effective command and control alone, it will undoubtedly fail if the command and control arrangements break down completely. Command and control arrangements are, therefore, a very high priority when planning an operation.

Ch 6
MARITIME COMMAND AND CONTROL

NATIONAL LEVELS OF COMMAND

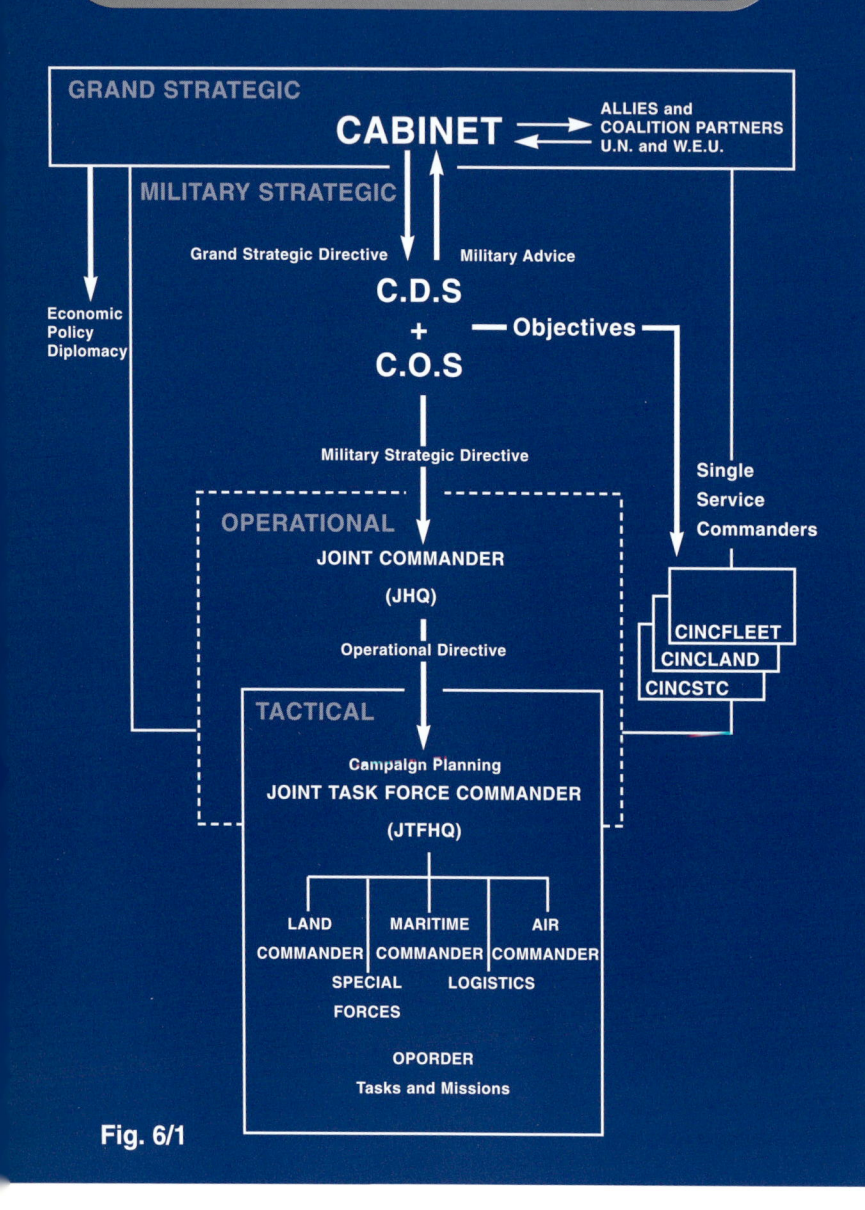

GRAND STRATEGIC

CABINET ⇌ ALLIES and COALITION PARTNERS U.N. and W.E.U.

MILITARY STRATEGIC

Grand Strategic Directive → ← Military Advice

C.D.S + C.O.S — Objectives —

Economic Policy Diplomacy

Military Strategic Directive

OPERATIONAL

JOINT COMMANDER

(JHQ)

Single Service Commanders

CINCFLEET
CINCLAND
CINCSTC

Operational Directive

TACTICAL

Campaign Planning

JOINT TASK FORCE COMMANDER

(JTFHQ)

LAND COMMANDER — MARITIME COMMANDER — AIR COMMANDER

SPECIAL FORCES   LOGISTICS

OPORDER
Tasks and Missions

Fig. 6/1

ILLUSTRATIVE TASK ORGANISATION

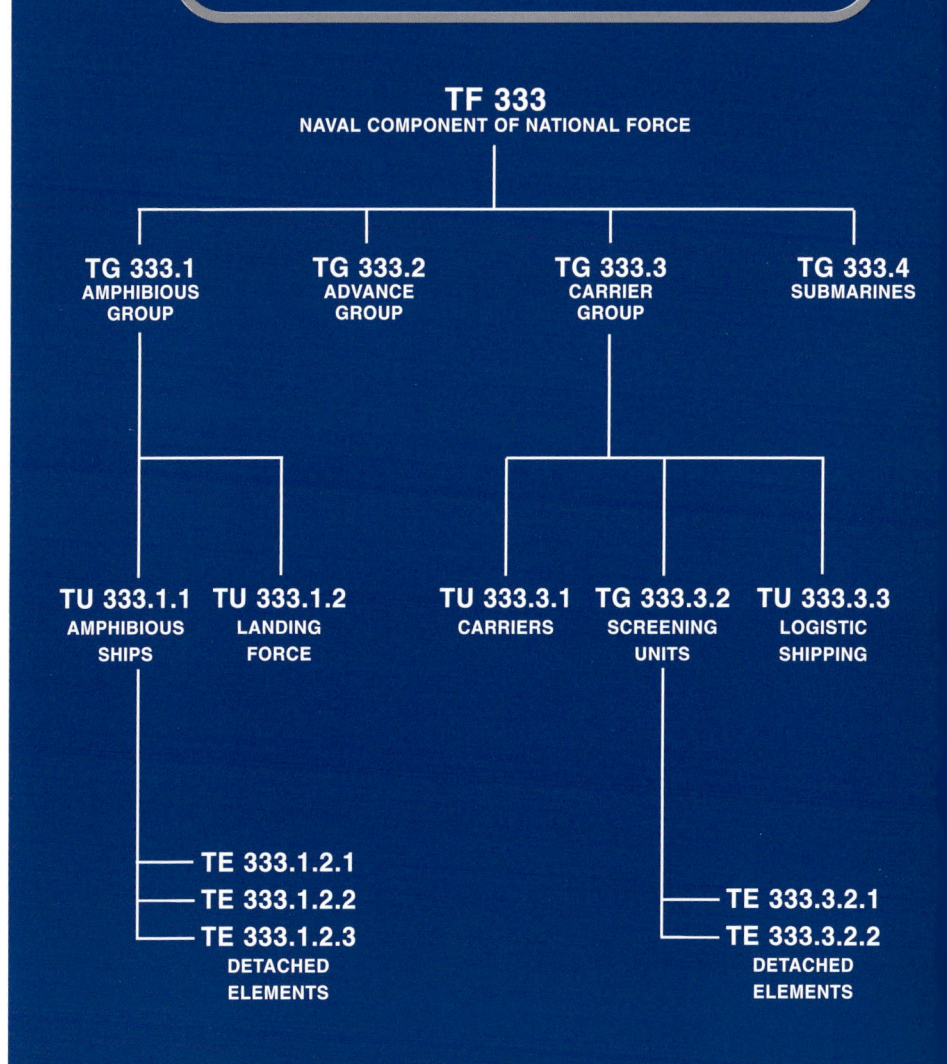

TF 333
NAVAL COMPONENT OF NATIONAL FORCE

- **TG 333.1** AMPHIBIOUS GROUP
  - **TU 333.1.1** AMPHIBIOUS SHIPS
  - **TU 333.1.2** LANDING FORCE
    - TE 333.1.2.1
    - TE 333.1.2.2
    - TE 333.1.2.3
    - DETACHED ELEMENTS
- **TG 333.2** ADVANCE GROUP
- **TG 333.3** CARRIER GROUP
  - **TU 333.3.1** CARRIERS
  - **TG 333.3.2** SCREENING UNITS
    - TE 333.3.2.1
    - TE 333.3.2.2
    - DETACHED ELEMENTS
  - **TU 333.3.3** LOGISTIC SHIPPING
- **TG 333.4** SUBMARINES

Fig. 6/2

Ch 6

HMS FEARLESS - amphibious operations

PLANNING AND CONDUCTING A MARITIME CAMPAIGN OR OPERATION

Chapter 7

The emphasis in this chapter is on the operational level of military planning and the conduct of maritime operations. As such, it deals with the sorts of issues with which the *Maritime Component Commander* (MCC) will be concerned and provides a link to operational and tactical level doctrinal publications, in particular **Fighting Instructions**. The MCC straddles the divide between the operational and tactical levels, fulfilling a planning function on the *Joint Task Force Commander's* (JTFC) command team and commanding the activities of the maritime component of the force. In the former function he is working at the operational level and in the latter at the tactical. This chapter will concentrate on operational level planning considerations. However, it is not intended to provide detailed guidance on operational planning, nor to describe in detail planning tools such as *The Joint Task Force Commander's Estimate*. What it does is set the principles discussed in earlier chapters in a practical context. The relative importance of these will vary during the different stages of a campaign.

THE MILITARY-STRATEGIC AIM

The policy objectives of military action will be decided at the *grand-strategic* level by the Cabinet. In the context of major *war* these are often known as the nation's war objectives. The strategic *mission* for a particular campaign in a particular theatre will be formed at the *military-strategic level* in the Ministry of Defence and passed to the *operational commander* usually in the form of a directive from the Chief of the Defence Staff. In the UK command system, the recipient and implementer of the military-strategic directive is the *Joint Commander*, who is an operational commander in his capacity as implementer of a military-strategic directive. For a NATO campaign the *grand-strategic* level is the Military Committee supported by the International Staff. The military-strategic level is the Military Committee supported by the International Military Staff. The Major NATO Commanders are the top tier of the operational level. A UK JTFC or Allied Commander may operate at the operational or tactical level, depending on the scale and strategic significance of his mission.

In the majority of cases, the nominated UK Joint Commander will be the Chief of Joint Operations (CJO) at the PJHQ. Having received his directive from CDS, he will in turn issue his own directive (agreed by the Ministry of Defence) to the JTFC who will, in turn, normally be supported by a MCC. These in-theatre commanders may operate at the *operational* or *tactical levels*, depending on the scale and significance of their operations. The maritime, ground and air components of a campaign must be integrated fully to execute a single joint *concept of operations* to fulfil the military-strategic aim.

A mission may not in itself be identical to a strategic aim. A mission statement may be fairly broad and brief and may spawn a number of objectives. The operational commander will need to sort these into a principal *aim* and a number of subordinate objectives. Conceivably, at first glance, one or more of these may be incompatible with the principal strategic aim or with one another. In such cases, clarification must be sought from the strategic level.

Although maintenance of the aim is a Principle of War, a particular feature of maritime operations is that certain preventive, precautionary or pre-emptive tasks may be carried out when political and military-strategic objectives are unrefined and immature (see, in particular, the discussions about naval diplomacy in Chapter 4). Commanders should also be alert to the fact that political objectives can change during the course of a campaign. Indeed, once actual *hostilities* begin, a train of unpredictable events may occur with bewildering rapidity and may reshape and alter political objectives. Defining the aim and associated objectives are part of an iterative process as the results of specific operations and new intelligence are fed into the decision-making chain.

Conditions for Success and the End-State

In establishing his aim, a commander must consider what constitutes success. Certain types of task, such as many *constabulary* tasks, are a continuous process and there will be no easily measurable conditions for success, except perhaps the integrity of the environment or area to be covered. The same is true for some tasks of *naval diplomacy* such as *presence*, where the effects and success are rarely obvious except in retrospect and in the context of a larger political or military campaign. Indeed the only reliable measure of *deterrence* is evidence of its failure to deter. However, for most *military* (or combat governed) applications of force, success can be defined as meeting certain specific conditions. These conditions are referred to in **UKOPSDOC** as the desired *end-state*. In classic military operations or in war, there are usually clear *military conditions*, such as control of territory, the sea and airspace, that can constitute military success. That said, success is more usually defined in terms of the elimination of the enemy's physical means of resistance and/or the collapse of his will. For *coercive* operations, military conditions often cannot be specified, and success is measured by compliance or acquiescence by the target government, power or regime.

In thinking and planning the maritime component of the campaign there are several issues the MCC and his staff need to take into account, using the Estimate Process as the basis for planning. There will have to be some thought put into the nature of the campaign and the concepts of operational art that have relevance to it. The MCC will need to consider whether the campaign is to be *cumulative* or *sequential* or both. There will also need to be consideration of which operational functions will be relevant and how they should best be applied in the prevailing circumstances. This chapter deals with all these issues, concluding with a description of the phases and stages of the campaign.

CONCEPTS OF OPERATIONAL ART

There are several concepts that are common within the lexicon developed around the conduct of land operations, but which are recent additions to the vocabulary associated with maritime operations. Although one should guard against assuming that concepts associated with land operations can be used in relation to maritime tactics, at the operational level some can have relevance and prove to be useful as planning aids. They are particularly useful when looking at joint operations and will certainly have relevance in any major operation involving maritime and other forces in a *joint* campaign in the *littorals*. Those of particular relevance are discussed below.

Centre of Gravity

This expression is used extensively in joint doctrine. The *centre of gravity* can be defined as those characteristics, capabilities or localities from which enemy and friendly forces derive their freedom of action, physical strength or will to fight. Examples that are frequently given include: the mass of an enemy army, the enemy's command structure, public opinion and national will, or an alliance or coalition structure. There may be both strategic and operational centres of gravity. Success at both the strategic and operational levels is achieved through identifying and controlling or destroying the enemy's centre of gravity and protecting one's own. The concept is central to modern interpretations of *manoeuvre warfare*, discussed in Chapter 3. A measure of caution is appropriate, however: it is often easier for military historians to identify where a centre of gravity *was* than for a military commander to identify where the centre of gravity actually *is* at any given time.

Decisive Events and Decisive Points

Military use of force is combat, or the threat or possibility of combat, to bring about decisions that will define the subsequent progress of a campaign. The term, *decisive point*, is used in joint warfare for intermediate objectives, the prosecution of which lead

Ch 7

PLANNING AND CONDUCTING A MARITIME CAMPAIGN OR OPERATION

TLAM from launch...

.....to TARGET

ultimately to the enemy's centre of gravity. They are frequently geographic locations to be seized but may be characteristics or capabilities of the enemy. They may be multiple and are distinct from the centre of gravity, although they may provide an avenue to it. The successful pursuit of decisive points is a central feature of the *manoeuvrist* approach to warfare which seeks to shatter the enemy's cohesion and will to fight.

The Culminating Point

This is the point in time and location when an attacker's *combat power* no longer exceeds that of a defender and the attacker risks both effective counter-attack and the failure of his own operation. To be successful, an attack must achieve its objective before reaching a culminating point. Successful defence may involve luring an attacker beyond his culminating point and then counter-attacking. During *linear operations*, the further an attacker advances, the larger the number of forces he requires to protect his lengthened *lines of support*, while the defender may be correspondingly closer to his own logistic bases. *Attrition* and combat fatigue may also take their toll and contribute to culmination. Another factor that can bring a force to a culminating point is time.

> **7/1. Risk of Culmination in the Falklands Campaign**
>
> During the Falklands Campaign it was important for British forces to have completed the re-occupation before the combined effects of extended lines of support, attrition of forces, possible dwindling of national will, cumulative material defects and the onset of winter might have brought about culmination.

CUMULATIVE AND SEQUENTIAL CAMPAIGNS

Campaigns and operations are of two broad types: cumulative and sequential.

Cumulative Campaigns

A *cumulative campaign* is one in which the entire pattern of the campaign consists of a collection of lesser actions, usually independent of each other, offering individual outcomes which together influence the overall outcome of the campaign. The effect is therefore an aggregation or accumulation of these discrete actions. Examples of cumulative campaigns are *guerre de course*, a strategic bombing campaign, and some forms of *insurgency*. Cumulative operations may exist within or in parallel to a sequential campaign; for instance, a submarine cumulative operation against the seaborne support of a phased ground campaign. However it is often difficult to predict the timing of success in cumulative campaigns and therefore the timing of the onset of subsequent events.

7/2. Cumulative Campaign in the Second World War

The German and American offensives against merchant shipping in the Second Word War were two examples of cumulative campaigns. In both campaigns, submarines and aircraft tried to inflict sufficient attrition on the enemy merchant fleets so that the vital maritime lines of communication of the Anglo-American alliance and the Japanese Empire would be severed for lack of sufficient ships. Success would be determined by the cumulative effect of a number of otherwise unrelated events. The Germans called this 'tonnage warfare'. They were unsuccessful in their aim because the introduction and improvement of the convoy system kept Allied losses to bearable levels and eventually led to the defeat of the U-boats. The Japanese only introduced convoys belatedly and did not develop the concept properly. They thus paid the penalty and lost eighty per cent of their mercantile marine to submarine and air attack. It was a most successful guerre de course and it is a matter of debate whether Japan could have continued resistance for long even if nuclear bombs had not been dropped in August 1945.

Sequential Campaigns

A *Sequential Campaign* can be considered as a series of discrete phases, each a natural progression, and therefore dependent upon the one preceding it. In constructing his plan, a commander will normally define certain phases of his campaign that will ultimately lead to the desired end-state. As it is not possible to predict in detail the course of events from start to finish, the first phase of a campaign will be subject to the most detailed planning, with subsequent phases addressed in outline and with allowance for the unexpected. Phases may be planned to lead up to a decisive event. Careful consideration of the 'what ifs' associated with each phase will greatly enhance the flexibility of a campaign plan. Alternative plans for a particular phase should be considered (*branches*), and planning should be conducted for the possible outcomes of a phase (*sequels*). A campaign may consist of a series of consecutive phases or simultaneous operations or a mixture of both. *Operational pause* may occur between phases, during which logistics can be accumulated, forces rested and reinforcements introduced. Operational pauses may be necessary to avoid reaching a *culminating point*.

7/3. A Sequential Campaign - The Gulf War 1990-91

A good example of a sequential maritime campaign was the maritime contribution to operations against Iraq in 1990-91. The Royal Navy Task Group 321.1, part of Operation GRANBY, formed the maritime component of the overall UK Joint Force contribution to Operations DESERT SHIELD and DESERT STORM. First, the Group was closely integrated into the coalition embargo effort as it worked itself up for the expected hostilities. The maritime campaign plan was in three phases:

1. A progressive sea control campaign consisting of the neutralization of the Iraqi surface fleet and maritime air forces. Sustained sea control, which included RN Type 42 destroyers providing Anti Air Warfare (AAW) protection well up threat at the northern end of the Gulf, was a prerequisite for subsequent phases. Sea control operations continued during phases 2 and 3 below.

2. A maritime contribution to a joint air campaign against Iraq provided by US carriers and cruise missile equipped surface ships and submarines. In this phase the Type 42 destroyers were an integral part of the US/UK AAW barrier for the coalition maritime forces.

3. A move inshore to the Kuwaiti coast with MCM forces completing the sea control task by clearing the way, both for battleships to provide naval gunfire support and amphibious forces to carry out an assault, should it have been required. The Type 42 destroyers provided local area AAW protection to the force and this phase included the shooting down of a SILKWORM missile by SEADART. The war began with an air campaign that was itself initiated with a 72 hour surge (600 carrier sorties per 24 hours) and then continued at a reduced but still rapid tempo (400 sorties per 24 hours). Sea control operations continued with the destruction of an initial Iraqi air attack on coalition maritime forces and continued with attacks on Iraqi vessels, both in port and at sea. Royal Navy shipborne helicopters were especially successful against Iraqi FAC. Lastly, the third phase, the advance to Kuwait, could be initiated. With the threat to them largely neutralized,

> MCM forces were able to clear the way for bombardment and amphibious forces up to the shores of Kuwait. Surface escorts provided protection from the residual threat posed by coastal defence missiles. Fighting ceased before an amphibious landing could take place but the threat of such a landing had an important operational effect.

THE PLANNING PROCESS

Doctrine does not supplant the need for good planning, but it aids the process of thought and eases the dissemination and understanding of the resulting plan. In maritime terms, doctrine is the safe sea shore from which to launch into the sea of initiative. Furthermore, doctrine, coupled with a clear statement of a commander's intentions, allows subordinate commanders to adapt their missions in response to a changing situation. In developing his concept of operations the commander must analyze the enemy's situation, vulnerabilities, vital and critical interests and likely courses of action. The situation of his own and friendly forces should be examined along similar lines to that of the enemy. Any restrictions imposed upon the use of force, ROE, assumptions made and deductions drawn from the analysis must be noted.

The Commander's Estimate

This analytical process is formalized in the Commander's Estimate, which reviews several courses of action to accomplish a mission, and from which the operational plan can be developed. But such an estimate is only a tool aiding the commander to orchestrate the conduct of his campaign or operation. It is not an end in itself.

The estimate process is central to the formulation and modification of the campaign plan. here are four key stages of an estimate process for every type of operation. These are: mission analysis, evaluation of factors, consideration of courses of action (COA), and, finally, the commander's decision. A more detailed description of this process and the production of the operation order is contained in Chapter 7 of **UKOPSDOC**.

The Operational Functions

The commander's concept of operations or 'design for battle' should serve to exploit his strengths to advantage and ensure that he seizes and maintains the initiative. He should always seek to limit enemy activity to reaction to his own actions, thereby ensuring that battles and engagements are fought in the manner, and at the place and time of his choosing. All these areas are pre-eminent in shaping the battlespace for subsequent exploitation. In orchestrating his campaign and designing his battles, the commander must also consider the maritime *Operational Functions*. These are not ends in themselves. Rather, they assist the commander by allowing him to design his campaign and then execute his concept of operations. The operational functions cannot be viewed separately. They are interdependent and produce a synergy greater than the sum of their individual worth.

Command and Control A maritime operation involves the direction and co-ordination of many activities in all *warfare environments* in what may be a hostile or potentially hostile situation. Command and control must be robust, flexible and capable of dealing with a rapidly changing situation. It must permit swift decision making so that opportunities can be exploited as they are provided. Additionally, it must support the principle of centralized direction and decentralized execution, thus allowing and encouraging freedom of action within the overall concept of operations. (Command and control is discussed in detail above, in Chapter 6.)

Intelligence and Surveillance Success in a campaign is often heavily dependent on the maintenance of a clear picture of the disposition of forces, known at sea as the *Recognized Maritime Picture* (RMP). Intelligence is an important contributor to this picture, particularly during the early stages of an operation when it may be necessary to seek political clearance for reconnaissance and intelligence gathering activities. Intelligence is not just a matter of information gathering over the duration of a campaign or operation. Strategic intelligence, which is of more long term significance than operational or tactical intelligence, is the product of continuous in-depth analysis of the political, economic, industrial and social characteristics of potential adversaries, as well as the military capabilities of any adversary and the characteristics of their armed forces and military leadership. Strategic intelligence is derived from a variety of sources and is used to inform and educate operational intelligence, which is more military in focus and specific to the theatre of operations. Operational intelligence needs the political, economic and psychological context for interpretation. Tactical intelligence mainly comprises the RMP, and has the narrowest and most detailed military focus. Strategic intelligence, collected over time, enables a commander to use judgement in planning a campaign in the absence of operational intelligence or tactical information, and allows subordinate commanders to act appropriately even when the RMP is sketchy. A commander should nonetheless seek to obtain as much intelligence and information as possible to inform his decision-making. This will require the optimum employment of his intelligence gathering assets. On the other hand he should not become a slave to intelligence gathering. There will always be gaps in a commander's knowledge, particularly in the matter of enemy intent, and a commander must be prepared to take decisions in situations of incomplete intelligence. Information that is available must be analysed, but commanders must be aware of the tendency, present in everyone, to make information fit any preconceptions.

E3D AWACS

Tactical Exploitation of the Environment A tactically exploitable knowledge of the environment based on superior technology is essential to the JTFC's dominance of the JOA. The blurring of the sea, land, air and space boundaries demands a cohesive environmental overlay. Maritime commanders must understand the maritime environment and its impact on operations. Joint forces require organic military Environmental Assessment (EA), Rapid Environmental Assessment (REA) and combat hydrographic capability for expeditionary warfare. EA and REA enhance operational capabilities by providing increased options for positioning forces to advantage and for entry operations. Direction of effort, including targeting and transit of Precision Guided Munitions (PGMs), TOMAHAWK Land Attack Missile (TLAM) and other systems coming into service, demands highly detailed environmental information. Weapon delivery platforms also rely on information in the launch zone, particularly in the *littoral*.

Protection The protection of maritime forces as an operational function is concerned specifically with preserving the combat power of the force. This can take a variety of forms: layered defence shielding of high value targets; routeing to avoid enemy capabilities; deception to prevent successful enemy attack; and, of course, the destruction or neutralisation of the enemy's combat power. The aim is to preserve one's own power so that it can be used to advantage in the manner, and at the place and time of one's choosing.

Application of Combat Power The combat power of a maritime force is a combination of its combat systems and its ability to bring firepower to bear effectively. Individual units must be given suitable tasks, and commanders the necessary direction so that they can co-ordinate their efforts to execute the concept of operations. All in the command chain must share a common purpose, and personnel must be imbued with the will to fight. Thus leadership and morale, are critical elements of the combat power of a maritime force. A commander should seek to maximize the combat power of his force and then use it to advantage against his enemy. Crucial to success are an accurate assessment of the enemy's strengths and weaknesses, and a correct judgement as to how his own combat power can most effectively be brought to bear against the enemy's critical vulnerability to cause incapacitation or systemic disruption.

Logistic Support The operational function of Logistics is the planning and carrying out of the movement and maintenance of

Ch 7

PLANNING AND CONDUCTING A MARITIME CAMPAIGN OR OPERATION

forces. It is both an enabler and a constraint and the logistic tempo should at least match the operational tempo. Good logistic planning is the art of the possible and must be an integral part of operational planning. Logistic considerations pervade all aspects of a campaign from deployment, to employment, and withdrawal. Operational *tempo* cannot be achieved without responsive and reliable logistic resupply. During a campaign, logistic support will usually be limited to some degree. Logistic priority must be given to support the *main effort* yet all elements of the force must be adequately provisioned including those engaged *in holding or economy of force operations*. A commander may require to surge his logistic support when the situation demands. Conversely the need to consolidate logistics may be a major factor in planning an operational pause. (Logistics are the subject of Chapter 5.)

Influence over the Battlespace There is risk associated with any military combat operation. To minimize this risk and to ensure success, it is necessary to define and shape the situation in and around the operating area in order to prevent enemy action or other circumstances from disrupting the operation. This *influence over the battlespace* is achieved by a combination of *command and control warfare* (C2W), control of the electromagnetic spectrum, situational awareness, *interdiction* of enemy forces, and a responsive and agile force capable of acting faster than the enemy. Using these instruments the commander can create the conditions that will allow his operation to succeed and reduce risk and the operation of chance to a minimum. Influence over the *battlespace* can permit deception, distraction, *disruption*, preemption and *dislocation*. It allows a force to attack the enemy's cohesion and ability to react, whilst simultaneously carrying out operations at a tempo that the enemy cannot match.

7/4. Gallipoli - How not to Structure a Campaign

The Allied maritime operations in 1915-16 to exploit the possibilities of strategic *leverage* and pass through the Dardanelles with a fleet that would force Turkey out of the war, were a case study in how not to mount a joint operation. The initial plan, to carry out the operation with ships alone, reflected the lack of a joint approach at the *military-strategic level*. The original campaign plan underestimated the power of the mutually supporting gun and mine defences, and was finally abandoned because of a failure at the tactical level to neutralize them sufficiently. When amphibious landings on the Gallipoli peninsula eventually took place, inadequacies in command and control resulted in failure to achieve their objectives. Although the Army had produced doctrinal publications for amphibious operations from about 1904 onward, they were largely unread and tactical commanders did not realize what was expected of them. A second wave of landings failed for the same reasons. The result was stalemate on the ground and the landing forces were eventually withdrawn in a meticulously planned evacuation that was the most successful part of the whole affair. A campaign imaginatively conceived at the *grand-strategic* level failed because of strategic, operational and tactical errors.

Additional Planning Considerations

What follows is a collection of additional issues to be taken into account when planning an operation. They are not in any particular order of priority, nor is the list necessarily exhaustive.

Flexibility Plans must be flexible to take account of the unexpected, especially in the light of enemy response. It is a truism to state that no operation ever goes strictly according to plan, which is why the planning process does not stop the moment the operation starts. The estimate process in support of the plan is a continuous one and will require frequent updating as events unfold.

Exploitation The commander must plan to enhance the strengths of his force and work with the environment to exploit the opposition's weaknesses and his own success. The MCC, in the context of a joint operation, must be aware of his force's strengths and weaknesses, as well as those of the other components, in order that he can keep the JTFC aware of all possible options, remembering that the real value of joint operations is the extent to which each component can be played to its strengths as an effective element of a *manoeuvrist* campaign.

A Favourable Balance of Advantage The destruction of an enemy's forces will be a deciding factor during combat. In the process own losses must be considered. Society has become less tolerant of the loss of people in combat, both friendly and enemy, and large losses may not be politically acceptable. Furthermore warships are costly, may take weeks to repair and years to replace, while crews take time to train. Preservation of forces will be a factor in planning and restricting acceptable risk. To minimize risk, a plan should create the conditions for a highly favourable *balance of advantage* at the decisive event. Calculation of exchange ratios should consider both quantitative and qualitative factors.

Termination Termination of a campaign must be considered at the outset of planning. Planning must consider the conditions and the mechanism for withdrawal. Termination of an independent naval operation may be a relatively simple matter compared with that of a fully joint campaign involving extensive *sealift*.

Organization The *task organization* for a campaign must be appropriate to the mission, properly reflect command relationships, and preserve unity of command at the operational and tactical levels (see Chapter 6). Consideration must be given to the scale and experience of staffs and the capacity of headquarters facilities. Multinational operations bring particular problems as mechanisms must exist for senior officers of national elements to exercise appropriate influence, to consult with political and non-governmental authorities, and to provide advice on national capabilities and political constraints.

Liaison with Civil Authorities and Non-Governmental Organizations Close liaison and co-operation must be maintained with civil authorities in theatre to arrange use of port facilities, diplomatic clearance for passage through *internal waters* and *territorial seas*, staging of aircraft and overflight, control of aircraft movements for the safety of civil aircraft and activation of *Regional Naval Control of Shipping*. NGOs will also be important in a great many situations, especially those with a humanitarian aid dimension.

Public Information Images of *conflict* can be brought directly into homes through television, radio and newspapers almost as events are unfolding. The media are a powerful influence on public opinion at home, on an opponent and within the international community. A democratic government can only engage in combat while it has public support and the endorsement or acquiescence of the international community. Although it is possible to exercise some control over the news media at sea, this option must be taken advisedly. Unbalanced reporting can be a consequence of strict control afloat and free reporting from ashore. A commander must treat public information as an important element of his campaign plan so that he can benefit from opportunities and manage negative aspects. A careful balance must be struck between the needs of security and the advantages of candour. However, in all cases, the commander should establish and disseminate his strategic aim and operational objectives with regard to the media so that it is not, in the worst case, to his detriment.

Biological and Chemical Warfare If the use of biological and chemical weapons is anticipated then the planning process will need to take account of any constraints this may place on maritime forces, especially in the littoral region. The psychological effects on personnel and public perceptions need consideration, as well as the provision and timing of prophylactics. In particular it will determine the balance of concentration and dispersal, as well as the need for a greater stand-off range and remote sensors and weapons.

Preparation Although ships and submarines are stored and manned for combat during peacetime, they are likely to require some additional reprovisioning before they deploy to ensure full stocks are carried. Preparation time will depend on the *readiness* of the unit. Some naval units may require to be brought forward from longer readiness, both to provide front line forces and to service any *roulement*. Preparation includes training, both specialist training for a particular environment or task, and group and force training in company. The period of passage into theatre may be used for some *shakedown* and limited *work up* training. However, experience has shown that ships' collective performance can only be honed effectively by appropriately structured staff-covered *operational sea training* in a realistic tactical environment.

Deployment Effective crisis *management* usually demands a rapid response. Force deployment times will vary with the distances involved and speed of transit. Speed and time are not, however, the only considerations in selecting methods of transport. Lead elements of ground forces may be able to deploy into theatre most rapidly by air if suitable airfields and ramp space are available and overflight rights granted, but seaborne transport will usually provide the quickest and invariably the cheapest movement of a substantial force of personnel and equipment.

HMS FEARLESS deployed with SK4s embarked

Sustainability A sustained and tailored logistic train will be needed to support a campaign and forces using sea lines of support and communication (and may need protection) together with those forces deploying by air over oceanic and other littoral regions. See Chapter 5.

Unity of Effort Resources must be concentrated on achieving the aim and should not be squandered on secondary objectives. To achieve this focus, a clear statement of the mission and commander's intentions is essential. It may be necessary to designate some operations within a campaign as holding operations. Ideally there should be unity of command over all resources including logistics. Where command and control is complex, especially likely in joint and combined operations, there must be co-operation and co-ordination of activities to this end.

Tempo Tempo is the rate at which events are driven in relation to the enemy and the situation. Forces that can maintain high tempo, with fast decision-making cycles, can seize the initiative, take advantage of uncertainty, and exploit the weaknesses of the enemy. To achieve high tempo and keep the initiative, and to exploit success an operational commander must be prepared to devolve decision-making. This can be achieved by use of what are sometimes known as *mission orders* that tell a subordinate commander what his task is and its purpose, without dictating how it should be done.

Simultaneity Simultaneity seeks to disrupt the decision making process of the enemy commander by confronting him with a number of problems simultaneously, such as attack or the threat of attack from several directions. He is denied the ability to concentrate on one problem at a time or establish priorities between problems. If simultaneity can be achieved, the enemy's decision making may be delayed or incoherent, allowing the operational commander to seize or maintain the initiative.

Iterative Planning It is rarely possible to plan in great detail beyond the first phase of a campaign because the outcome of that phase will shape subsequent phases. Part of the planning process must be a consideration of the "what ifs" or branches and sequels. Once the plan has been set in motion, the commander must constantly study the unfolding situation, and revise and reorder the plan as necessary.

STAGES OF A MARITIME CAMPAIGN

As a gross simplification there are typically seven stages of a maritime campaign: identification of a crisis; force generation; deployment; sea control operations; power projection; support to operations ashore; and withdrawal. In reality these stages will not be easily distinguishable; nor will they necessarily coincide with the *phases* of a specific campaign plan.

Identification of a Crisis

Initial indications that a crisis is developing will probably come from a variety of sources including strategic intelligence, wide area *surveillance* systems, and open sources such as the news media. Intelligence gathering and analysis can provide warning of changes in operating patterns, exercise and *work-up* programmes and communications volume, and allow for *strategic level* identification and evaluation of potential crises. Intelligence recovery is now a global science which involves close co-operation with allies, swift dissemination of assessed data, clear presentation and early background advice to commanders. Early assessment of the military capability of any potential adversary will play a significant part in assessment of the size and composition of forces needed to address a crisis.

Maritime forces operating in international waters can gather a wide variety of useful intelligence and provide a significant surveillance capability. Information gathered in this way is sometimes the only reliable source of evidence and, as such, is a critical element in identification and assessment of a crisis. Monitoring of shipping or air activity may be a preliminary phase to embargo or sanctions enforcement, or may support other constabulary tasks such as drug interdiction. Intelligence gathering and surveillance will continue throughout a campaign, although its focus will shift from the strategic and general in the early stages to the operational and tactical, and hence become more specifically military as the campaign develops.

Force Generation

The size and composition of the forces required to respond to a developing crisis will be shaped by:

- the policy objectives and strategic concept - what the Government wants to achieve, how it wishes to act and, in a multinational operation, what the UK contribution should be;

- understanding of the military *conditions for success* or *end-state* - what the military commander must achieve to be successful;

- assessment of the threat - and therefore the combat power and levels of protection that may be required to achieve the aim;

- the forces available and their readiness - which will depend in part on the priority given by Government to the policy objectives;

- the time available to respond.

Among the factors that must be considered is the requirement for a robust, flexible, and responsive command and control system able to adapt to changing force levels and threat. In multinational operations, it must be able to integrate with the coalition command and control structure whilst meeting any national requirements. The potential duration of the campaign, the need to sustain or increase force levels, and logistic support requirements throughout the campaign will also have a profound influence on force generation.

Deployment

Deployment to a theatre of operations involves: mounting and sailing the force from home bases (although maritime forces can often be diverted directly from their current locations); passage to the area of operations; transit; and arrival in the theatre of operations in a posture appropriate to the threat and mission. Co-ordination of the deployment will require detailed planning, close liaison with diplomatic posts, other civil authorities, Allied military authorities and probably foreign government agencies. Consideration must be given to the legal position of the forces, selection of ROE and the use of civil transport such as chartered ships and STUFT. The routeing of forces must be carefully considered to ensure their security.

The protection of shipping forming a part of a maritime force and providing strategic lift into theatre may take on the characteristics traditionally associated with the wider wartime task of protecting maritime trade and strategic SLOCs. This can take different forms and depends upon whether the aim is to deter attacks, or to defend against them. If the threat to shipping is sufficiently great, protection will require sea control methods (discussed below). Merchant shipping may benefit from a wider sea control campaign that will offer protection in the waters through which it will pass, or a specific sea control operation may be devoted to the shipping under threat using **Convoying**. Both concepts can be used within a wider sea control campaign if resources permit. When there is a severe risk to maritime trade, convoying is a method of reducing the scale of the sea control problem that has, in the past, proved effective. If shipping is gathered into convoys, the area and time over which sea control must be exercised for their protection is reduced to a minimum. Convoying complicates the attacker's task and concentrates escorting forces to enhance the effectiveness of protection. However convoying is less likely to deceive the enemy or deny him intelligence about the position of friendly shipping. It is also disruptive to trade. The strategic or operational decision to convoy requires a careful weighing of the balance of advantage and the opportunities for drawing the enemy into decisive action.

If there is regional tension or where there is a threat of *piracy* or attack by irregular forces, maritime forces can be in theatre, demonstrating presence to deter attack. When the threat is greater, **Distant or Close Escort Operations** provide more specific protection. Maritime forces can provide surveillance against threats, be positioned in the vicinity of concentrations of merchant shipping (distant escort), or remain in direct proximity to selected ships (close escort). While conducting both close and distant escort, naval forces offer a measure of defence, but the concept is to deter attack through the threat of reprisals. In looser coalition operations, **Accompanying** may be adopted, with warships ready to react depending on emerging circumstances. It will rarely be possible to escort and, thus, to defend every vessel, in which case measures must be taken to enhance the defensive capability of individual merchant ships.

Sea Control Operations

Wherever the freedom of action of the maritime force is challenged and, in particular, as it approaches the area of operations, there will be a requirement to establish levels of sea control that will be sufficient to ensure its protection and to enable subsequent operations. Without sea control, the ability of maritime forces to manoeuvre, concentrate for offensive action, apply *leverage*, project power ashore, and deny the same to an opponent, will be adversely constrained. Sea control is synonymous with dominance of the maritime battlespace, which allows the force's strengths to be used to advantage, while at the same time, protecting its combat power. All maritime operations will require sea control and all the types of operations discussed in the chapter are either so much a part of sea control operations as to be indistinguishable from them, or are themselves dependent on sea control operations as a preparation for their conduct.

In open ocean, there is rarely, if ever, a precise geographical area of sea to defend in the way that distinct areas of land may be defended over time by ground forces ashore; maritime forces at sea do not 'hold ground' in that way. Rather, they take measures to protect themselves, in both their immediate vicinity and over wider areas which, since they are themselves moving, means that the areas over which sea control operations are concentrated will be ambulatory.

Notwithstanding this, **Area Sea Control Operations** are essentially geographic and are conducted using long range surveillance and weapon systems over extended areas of sea. Targets are principally enemy aircraft, ships and submarines which are transiting to attack positions. However, area sea control operations may also include defining and shaping operations. It is important that commanders responsible for area sea control take necessary measures to ensure that their activities do not conflict with those of other units and task groups that are passing through their area and which may well be conducting their own sea control operations in their immediate vicinity. Careful co-ordination of command and control is required to integrate a mobile force, to deconflict operations and to avoid mutual interference or *fratricide*.

Fleet submarine sails for patrol

Blockade can be used as a method of achieving sea control through sea denial by preventing access to and from enemy ports and harbours. To be recognised under international law, a blockade must have been declared and notified to all concerned, it must be effective, and it must be applied impartially to ships of all nations. The term 'blockade' has a clear legal meaning, therefore, which very definitely does not include embargo operations in support of economic sanctions of the sort approved by the UN Security Council (see the discussion of *constabulary* operations in Chapter 4). A blockading force has the legal right to seize in prize any merchant ship, either enemy or neutral, which attempts to run the blockade either inwards or outwards. The blockade can be either close, denying an enemy access to or from his ports, or distant, denying access to a sea area through which all ships must pass in order to reach the enemy's territory.

Containment Using their high transit speed, nuclear powered submarines can be despatched covertly ahead into theatre to pose a threat to enemy surface and submarine forces and valued land targets, and to tie down enemy forces in defence. Offensive mine-laying might be used to enhance containment, if available and if ROE allow. If friendly shore based and *organic* attack aircraft are within range and the ROE allows, they might *interdict* port facilities, airfields and command and control installations and enemy surface shipping.

Area and Barrier Operations In the past, attempts to defend sea lanes directly have always failed because the available sensors and weapons were not able to prevent attacking forces from penetrating the defences. However, there are some defined areas of water which may need to be cleared of hostile forces and subsequently protected against incursion. These might include straits, approaches, convoy assembly and dispersal areas, and the area selected for an amphibious assault or joint entry into theatre. Submarines and maritime patrol aircraft conduct surveillance of the sea areas through which friendly naval surface forces and logistic shipping will in due course pass, locating and tracking submarine and surface targets and interdicting these as ROE allow. Helicopters from the carrier group might assist with prosecution of submarine and surface contacts when within range.

Force Protection A maritime force, most of the elements of which will have a multi-role capability, will not only require self protection but will inevitably contribute to the overall protection of the Joint

Ch 7
PLANNING AND CONDUCTING A MARITIME CAMPAIGN OR OPERATION

Force itself. To achieve this, maritime assets can be employed against the threat according to their individual and corporate capability creating a moving area of battle space control, thereby protecting power projection forces and support. Force protection is achieved through the warfare disciplines:

Anti-Air Warfare (AAW) The protection of friendly forces from the air threat, irrespective of the launch platform, is achieved through the principles of: denying intelligence to the enemy; obtaining warning; applying defence in depth; and co-

Lynx HMA Mk 8

ordinating air defence activity. The maritime force will contribute to and benefit from the Joint Air Defence plan, using shore-based and organic Airborne Early Warning (AEW) and fighter aircraft and ships armed with surface to air missiles supported by Electronic Warfare (EW) systems. The inner layer of defence for a maritime force is provided by a combination of point defence missile/close in weapon systems and the use of EW and decoys.

Anti-Surface Warfare (ASuW) Protecting the force from the enemy surface threat is achieved through the same principles articulated above in AAW. Establishing a good surface picture, normally through the use of shore based Maritime Patrol Aircraft (MPA) and organic helicopters, will enable the MCC to deploy his ASuW assets to best effect, keeping the enemy at arm's length. A wide range of attack assets can be used: submarines with missiles or torpedoes; attack aircraft and organic helicopters armed with air to surface missiles, bombs, rockets and cannon; ships and fast attack craft (FAC) armed with surface to surface missiles, guns and torpedoes.

Anti-Submarine Warfare (ASW) The best form of ASW is for vulnerable platforms within a force to operate in a different time and space from enemy submarines. Within an operational level approach to the problem which includes neutralisation of all aspects of submarine operations, such as their infrastructure, communications and support, continuous efforts must be made to evaluate the location of all enemy submarines so that they can be avoided, through intelligence and sensible routeing. If vulnerable assets must enter an area of submarine threat, then a co-ordinated all arms approach must be taken. Space, air, surface and subsurface assets would be co-ordinated to deceive, distract, detect and destroy submarines. Nuclear powered attack submarines and MPA in support of the force provide the outermost layer of anti-submarine and anti-surface defence. The next layer of anti-submarine defence is composed of frigates with long range sonar, together with supporting MPA and organic helicopters, which also assist in the location and prosecution of submarine contacts. The innermost layers of anti-submarine defence are provided by helicopters, using passive and active sonar, and then surface ships using hull mounted sonars.

Mine Countermeasures (MCM) The most effective MCM is to avoid mined areas. Exploratory MCM will be required by dedicated MCM vessels to determine the extent to which mines have altered the geography of the area. Once the size and shape of the minefields have been established, task groups may either avoid the area or dedicated mine clearance tasks may be conducted. However, it must be assumed that mine clearance operations rarely match the pace and tempo of modern campaigns and emphasis necessarily has to be on exploratory operations.

Advance Sea Control Operations (Shaping Operations) During the transit phase, an advance sea control group may be despatched to complement anti-submarine and anti-surface static area operations. These forces may also be used to establish elements of sea control in any *holding areas* to be used by power projection forces as they poise offshore. Before an amphibious operation it may be necessary to conduct prolonged littoral sea control operations to eliminate any threat from FAC and shore batteries and to reduce the risk from mines and conventional submarines to an acceptable level. During these operations MCM vessels are vulnerable to enemy attack and their protection will be an important consideration. In preparation for an amphibious landing *advance force operations* may involve the submarine insertion of special forces for *reconnaissance* and possibly interdiction and the landing of SF, beach control parties and *naval support* controllers.

Sea Lines of Communication (SLOC) Although mentioned already above (under Deployment), it is worth stressing that sea control operations must provide for the protection of reinforcement and resupply shipping, providing support to the entire national intervention force. Once the maritime task force is on station, this protection may require a separate operation involving the *escort* or *screening* of important units and, perhaps, full convoying.

Afloat Support Forces engaged in sea control operations will need afloat support which will either benefit from the wider sea control regime or will require its own layered defence. This support need not necessarily be independent of that provided to power projection operations. The replenishment of forces that are operating in outer layers of defence or on area operations need careful planning as time off task while in transit and during replenishment must be minimized for both combat units and auxiliaries. For operations of long duration organic afloat support must be *consolidated*. The routes for consolidation shipping constitute campaign *lines of support*, and the ability to use them must be safeguarded.

Power Projection Operations

With the establishment of appropriate levels of sea control, maritime forces are able to project power ashore. Power projection can take a number of forms, for example: NEOs, amphibious operations, maritime air support, and surface and sub-surface land attack. A robust command and control system that, in the case of amphibious operations must be capable of deploying ashore, gathering intelligence, concentrating combat power, and generating influence over the battlespace, are critical functions for power projection operations. Co-ordination and *synchronization* with land and air operations will be required.

Non-Combatant Evacuation Operations (NEOs) An early concern once forces have started to arrive in theatre may be the protection of UK and other uninvolved citizens. NEOs can involve maritime forces, either alone or as a part of a joint force. When airfields and commercial ports are not available, an independent naval operation may be necessary. Maritime forces may also be used to poise in theatre as a precaution should an evacuation become necessary as a result of local instability. The host nation may be able to provide for the security of the evacuation, in which case the UK or coalition forces would provide assistance to the process. In extreme cases an evacuation may be effected through the mounting of an amphibious raid. Maritime based forces will land, secure and defend beachheads and airheads, establish mustering points for evacuees and the routes linking them, move the evacuees to safety and, finally, withdraw. Maritime forces are well suited for NEOs in that they are self-sustaining, require little or no in-country or host nation support, and have the capability to respond rapidly to any deterioration in the situation. The decision to evacuate nationals is the responsibility of the local British Ambassador, or other Head of Mission, whose staff will normally give instructions to evacuees. Command and control arrangements must integrate that Mission and any SF contribution. National and NATO *Joint Theatre Plans* include contingency plans for evacuation.

Amphibious Operations The Amphibious Task Group (ATG) is the focus for the projection of amphibious power ashore, normally operating in conjunction with a Carrier Task Group. The full campaign may include operations to secure initial *access* to territory, manoeuvre from the sea, raids, feints, demonstrations, withdrawal and redeployment of the Landing Force, adjacent operations and subsidiary landings. Amphibious operations are arguably the most complex of all military activities, co-ordinating, as they do, many units across all the operational environmental boundaries. The four principal types of amphibious operation are:

Amphibious Demonstration This is an operation conducted to deceive an enemy or illustrate capability. They must pose a credible threat to a land commander which then requires him to allocate sufficient forces to counter that contingent risk. Demonstrations can be used as components of shaping operations and exploiting operations, prior to or during an amphibious assault. The demonstration is perhaps the most elegant expression of amphibious capability. The limited liability offered by poising at sea, both in a military and political context, provides a unique form of leverage which can easily and rapidly be converted into combat action ashore.

Amphibious Raiding These are operations that are limited by time, space and resources and conducted in order to destroy or disrupt part of an enemy's infrastructure. Raids involve the temporary occupancy of an objective followed by a pre-planned withdrawal. As with all amphibious operations, raids can be used to increase the tempo of a campaign, shape the battlefield or create opportunities for subsequent operations. In many circumstances, the raid will be the method of choice for the joint, maritime or amphibious commander. Raids offer precision violence, minimal risk, and avoid the requirement to invest substantial combat power ashore for extended periods.

Amphibious Assault This is the principal type of amphibious operation. It is distinguished from other types in that it involves establishing, with some permanence, a force on a hostile or potentially hostile shore. The purpose of such an assault is to secure operational objectives in support of the campaign's main effort, or in preparation for subsequent operations ashore such as the introduction of follow-on forces.

Amphibious assaults exploit the full effects of maritime combat power and can be conducted across the full depth and breadth of the littoral battlespace, to find, fix or strike an enemy. They are most effective when the landing force can have a disproportionate impact on heavier forces which are impeded by local conditions such as adverse terrain, climate or infrastructure.

Withdrawal phase

Amphibious Withdrawal These occur when the amphibious force re-embarks onto parent shipping, either in preparation for re-deployment after the seizure of amphibious objectives, or as part of a pre-planned evacuation operation from a hostile or potentially hostile shore. Withdrawals are complicated by the necessary requirement to reload tactically and reconfigure the landing force in its parent shipping, often when time and space is at a premium. The amphibious withdrawal is the principal means of reconstituting the amphibious force at sea, thus bestowing operational level capability.

All amphibious operations will consist of a number of separate activities, some of which will run concurrently. These include:

- planning to establish the most suitable time and place to conduct the operation;

- advance force operations to gain intelligence, survey potential landing sites, deceive the enemy and disrupt his activities;

- establishment, if required, of an *amphibious objective area* (AOA) including, if necessary, mine countermeasures operations;

- the landing of up to brigade size designed to establish the necessary combat power, logistic support and command and control capability ashore to carry out the task;

- and subsequent operations such as withdrawal for other tasks, the maintenance of a *lodgement area* to allow the introduction of follow-on forces, or military operations as part of a land campaign.

Support by Organic Air Aircraft from a carrier task group will contribute air defence of the battlespace (*counter air*), *anti-surface force*, and *combat support* air operations in association with land based aircraft when available. Maritime aircraft should be integrated into joint air forces and have their activities co-ordinated by the *Joint Task Force Air Component Commander's* (JFACC) HQ when it is established in theatre. The carriers may also embark RAF aircraft if the operations require their assets. Air launched *land attack missiles* can complement *air interdiction* forces against a range of important targets.

Surface and Sub-Surface Land Attack Surface and sub-surface land attack missiles will also provide the primary means of organic long range attack, particularly in the early stages of a conflict, and have particular utility for coercion. They will subsequently complement other air interdiction forces. Naval fire support may conduct advance bombardment and will complement landing force artillery once this is landed. It is also available to other ground units operating in the littoral region.

Sustainment of Operations

Once the focus of an intervention campaign moves ashore, the emphasis of maritime force operations will shift from being enabling to being supportive. That is not to say that the tasks assigned to maritime forces will necessarily alter significantly, but the wider purpose to which those tasks will contribute will change. Maritime forces can continue to provide aspects of all the principal operational functions during this stage of the campaign. Expressed in the most appropriate doctrinal terms, maritime power can contribute to all the components of capability required for the conduct of operations ashore. In particular, the focus will be on enhancing the manoeuvrist characteristics of the land campaign by intelligent application of the principal attributes of maritime power, in particular its ability to enhance manoeuvre and apply force where it is least expected. Additional tasks are likely to be protection and logistic support: protection of units using the sea lines of communication, of the maritime flank, and of logistic support to forces ashore and afloat, sustainment by *sealift*, and an alternative supply to *Host Nation Support* (HNS).

Withdrawal

The withdrawal of forces at the end of a successful campaign will need to be planned as carefully as the deployment to the area of operations. Indeed there may be the added complication of recovering unusable equipment, and a political requirement for a speedy extraction and return. Moreover, if conditions for success have not been achieved, and withdrawal is to be made in the face of continuing or escalating conflict, it will be even more problematical. There may be a need to increase combat power ashore to stabilize the situation before withdrawal can take place. Command and control will be difficult and fragmented. A JTFHQ(Afloat) may provide the most secure and capable communications to assist in this respect, and there will be a requirement to provide protection, both for the maritime forces supporting withdrawal and for the forces being withdrawn. Protection of a withdrawal, like a landing but in reverse, requires the establishment of necessary levels of sea control.

Ch 8

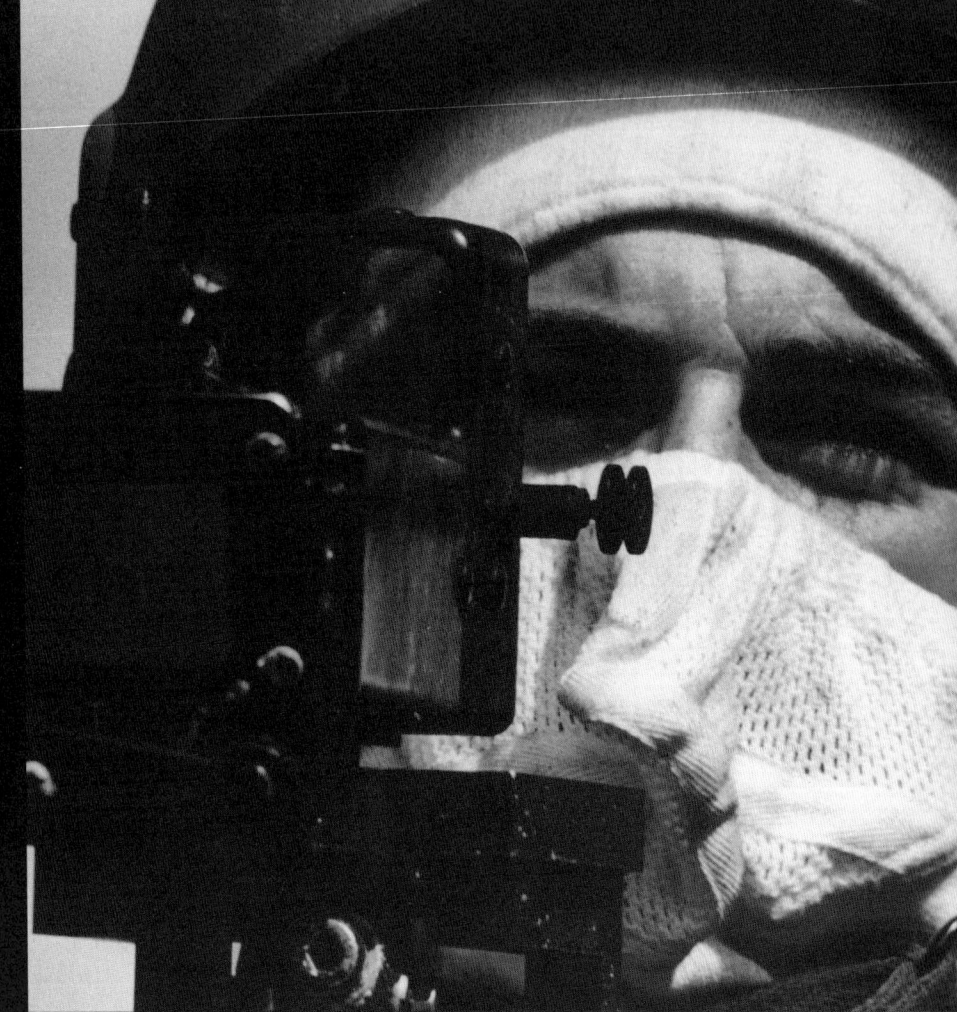

MARITIME OPERATIONAL CAPABILITY

Chapter 8

The applications of maritime power (discussed in Chapter 4) encompass a wide range of operational situations from peacetime and benign activities to full *hostilities* in high intensity situations. The majority of possible applications are *military* (combat governed), even though the actual pattern of employment of the UK's maritime forces may seem to suggest that it is either *constabulary* or *benign* operations that tend to dominate the Fleet programme. No apology is necessary for this because it is the ability to continue action through to combat if necessary, and the message maritime forces convey as a consequence, that confers upon them their effectiveness in a very broad range of peacetime activities. Not least, of course, is their effectiveness in applying naval diplomacy as a means of keeping the peace and thereby avoiding the actual use of the full range of their military capabilities.

Ch 8
MARITIME OPERATIONAL CAPABILITY

It is vitally important that the UK's maritime forces maintain an appropriate level of operational capability (OC) in order that, should the need arise, their military attributes can be brought into effective play in support of UK national interests. Operational capability means more than simply the ships, aircraft, their weapons systems and other equipments that exist on the 'inventory'.

The Chiefs of Staff are responsible for delivering to the Secretary of State, through CDS, the overall Military Capability of their respective Services. In turn, the Commanders in Chief are responsible for delivering OC. For the bulk of the UK's maritime capability, the responsibility for delivering OC rests with the Commander in Chief Fleet. There are five elements of capability: manpower, equipment, collective performance, deployability and sustainability. Maritime OC is, therefore, a combination of the ships, aircraft and other equipments, the people that man them, and the training that they undergo, both as individuals and as members of operational units, in order that our maritime forces are able to meet the readiness states necessary to deploy and to achieve and sustain the Military Tasks identified in Government policy. This chapter discusses each of the components of maritime OC in turn, concentrating on those aspects that have a direct bearing on the conduct of operations.

PEOPLE

Ultimately it is people that realise the level of capability that ships and other equipments can provide. The UK has fully professional regular armed forces with a long history of excellence in leadership, training and motivation. These are world recognized strengths that require time, effort and resources if they are to be developed, maintained and exploited to the nation's advantage. As a component of OC, manpower has to be available at appropriate levels, people must be individually and collectively trained and practised to meet the demands placed upon them, and they must be well motivated and fully committed with a high level of morale.

Life at Sea

Within our maritime forces, large numbers of sailors, marines, airmen, soldiers and, indeed, civilians have to live and work in very close proximity to each other. The ship, which is their home for extended periods in peace and conflict, is a cramped and often uncomfortable space. The maritime environment is featureless, tiring and demanding. Patterns of life during peacetime exercises differ little from those during hostilities. Historically, maritime warfare has been characterised by long periods of inactivity, surveillance and search followed by short bursts of intense combat. Concentration and alertness must not be allowed to drop during quieter periods. People, weapon systems and sensors must be integrated together into a composite team.

Leadership

It is the Commanding Officer who must stamp a leadership style on the ship. But he is not the only person onboard who must be trained to lead. A ship's company is divided into departments, sub-departments and sections. At each level, strong leadership will contribute to the effectiveness of the team and the smooth functioning of the ship. Leadership at all levels is a principal element in the maintenance of morale.

Effective command depends on effective leadership. Born leaders are rare, but leadership potential can be developed by training, experience, study of the methods of great leaders in the past, and a knowledge of military doctrine. Through this process, individuals must develop their own style of leadership and no two people can, or should, lead in exactly the same way.

The development of leadership potential involves study of the qualities of others and must start with self-discipline. It is a continuous process throughout training and daily life. It is the prime responsibility of all leaders to promote this process amongst their subordinates by:

- decisive action;

- precept and example;

- advice, encouragement and admonishment;

- giving subordinates every opportunity of contributing to operational and tactical success.

An outstanding characteristic of all great commanders is their refusal to be dominated by circumstances. While not challenging the inevitable, they use events around them to achieve their own ends, rather than modify their ends to keep pace with the tide of events. Personal qualities present in a successful commander are:

- an open mind which is receptive to all possibilities;

- the ability to grasp the essentials important to success;

- firmness and speed in decision, largely acquired by thinking out during quiet periods what action should be taken if different circumstances arise;

- calmness in crisis; the courage to withstand mental stress and strain, and the refusal to be distracted by bad tidings;

- the ability to explain clearly what he wants to achieve and why, so that he can be effectively and appropriately supported by his peers and subordinates;

- boldness; a good leader must be successful to retain the confidence of his subordinates, and success will not come from faintheartedness;

- a readiness to accept and discharge responsibility at all times; the mere acceptance of responsibility without the determination to fulfil it by executive action is useless;

- the ability to generate mutual trust, respect and confidence between himself and subordinates, peers and superiors.

- the ability to convince subordinates at all levels that he has their best interests at heart by a mixture of wide and sympathetic understanding of human nature (supported by a sense of humour), an understanding of the strengths and weaknesses of individuals, and meticulous and impartial care in dealing with their affairs.

- the confidence to delegate in the knowledge that his intentions have been clearly expressed and well promulgated.

- capacity for accurate risk assessment.

Stand easy

Morale

The maintenance of good morale is one of the *Principles of War*. It is based on recognition of the needs of the individuals who collectively form the team, and it manifests itself in the will to win. Morale promotes the offensive spirit and determination to achieve the aim. Good morale is based on: a shared sense of purpose; clear understanding of, and belief in, the aim; discipline and self-respect; confidence in equipment; training; and well merited mutual trust and respect between those in and under command. The naval systems of command and its long standing Divisional System provide a clear framework for effective leadership and support for the individual within the ship, or unit.

Supportive public opinion at home is also vital to the maintenance of morale. The presentation, by the media, of the conduct of an operation and of the personalities involved, can assume great significance. The ability of the operational commander to provide a clear, confident and credible message to those at home is crucial, but he must balance the need for security with that of accurate reporting from the operational area. Operational success provides the quickest and most effective boost to morale for those at war but outstanding leadership will sustain high morale when all other factors are against it.

Discipline

Military training instils discipline from the outset. Ideally, rather than being imposed from above, discipline rests within the individual. From self-discipline stems the spirit of teamwork and the willingness to be led. Many of those who have no personal experience of the modern, professional armed forces tend to assume that their efficiency and ability to achieve their success is due to a rigid, disciplinarian's approach to getting things done. Nothing could be further from the truth. Ultimately, in the tightest and most demanding operational circumstances, orders need to be given and carried out with a sense of urgency and without question. However, those circumstances are few and far between and the essence of sound military organization is achieved by instilling in people a discipline based on co-operation and teamwork. This must involve a willingness to: challenge superiors when appropriate and to accept such challenge from subordinates; to maintain an open mind and to apply free thought responsibly; and to accept also the need to act with others in a co-ordinated fashion by subordinating one's own personal desires to the higher needs of the Service.

Combat Stress and Fatigue

Every commander must know how hard to drive his force. It must not be spurred beyond the limits at which people lose their powers of recovery. Undue mental strain often leads to physical exhaustion and undue physical strain to mental eccentricities. Combat stress is inherent in warfare but it can be tempered by an individual's physical and moral courage and by his confidence in a sound and well-expressed plan. A commander must have a firm knowledge of the dangers and warning signs of unrelieved combat stress. Effective leadership, self-control and confidence in the team all combine to help limit the natural fear of violence.

A commander must also consider his own fatigue, for it is essential that his energy, mental and physical, should be conserved for crucial periods. He must ensure he has adequate and regular periods of rest and reflection, avoid over immersion in matters of detail that are the job of his staff and delegate as much as possible to subordinates. He should issue clear and concise orders and leave his staff to work out the details. This creates a more responsive force, gives subordinates vital experience essential for their own development, and preserves the vital force of the commander for when it is most required.

EQUIPMENT

Operational capability depends on the availability of an appropriate range of equipment for those tasks that maritime forces are likely to have to meet. The ships, aircraft, weapon systems and sensors need to be of a suitable mix, available in sufficient quantities, and endowed with reliability, given the conditions in which they are likely to be employed. There are both national and multinational reasons for the UK to possess a spread of maritime assets with a range of combat capabilities; what has traditionally been referred to as a balanced *fleet*. Independent national operations require the complete suite of maritime warfare capabilities, at both the operational and tactical levels.

It is not possible to create robust coalition formations capable of high intensity combat at short notice from an assembly of disparate national capabilities. Although *maritime forces* can easily be brought together to form a multinational force for tasks in which there is a low risk of combat, a fully integrated fighting force requires a period to work up from basic levels of inter-operability to full OC under the direction of an experienced commander and afloat staff. Within NATO the problem of creating major multinational fighting formations is simplified because it is probable that the United States will provide the core capabilities for a *NATO Task Force* or *NATO Expanded Task Force.* For a WEU or other coalition operation, in which the US has chosen not to participate with combat forces, these core capabilities must be provided by other nations. The UK, as the leading European maritime nation, would be able to make a significant contribution in the allocation of forces to such an operation. It is one of very few nations that is able to provide the core building blocks, such as a carrier task group and amphibious force, to a multinational maritime formation. It can also contribute a tried and tested, comprehensive, afloat command and control facility. This range of capabilities enables the UK to make an effective contribution to multinational operations, giving it the authority significantly to influence decision-making within any maritime coalition, be it allied or ad hoc.

The principal platforms and units that are available within the UK's maritime forces represent a well balanced and independently capable collection of capabilities. That collection consists of the following.

Nuclear Powered Ballistic Missile Submarines

Nuclear powered ballistic missile carrying submarines (SSBNs) deploy the TRIDENT missile system that provides *strategic* and *sub-strategic nuclear deterrence* for the UK and NATO.

Aircraft Carriers and Their Organic Air

The RN's aircraft carriers (CVS) are substantial contributors to sea control, power projection and to the overall command and control of maritime operations. They operate a mixed and flexible air group consisting of *short take-off and vertical landing* (STOVL) jet fighter attack, reconnaissance and *close air support* aircraft, as well as anti-submarine and AEW helicopters. They can also embark STOVL ground attack aircraft from the RAF. The exact composition of the carrier air group (CAG) will be tailored to the mission of the force. Organic air provides the ability to conduct independent air operations when it may not be possible to use bases ashore, coupled with the mobility to find clear flying conditions and to react rapidly when the force is close to the combat zone. CVSs provide essential command and control capabilities for a Maritime Component Commander (MCC) at the tactical level. At the operational level, when suitably augmented, they can provide a *Joint Task Force Headquarters* for a national JTFC, or embark a NATO/WEU *Combined Joint Task Force* (CJTF) Commander. If required, a carrier can also be used to carry units of a Landing Force for operations of limited duration as an LPH (see the section on Specialist Amphibious Shipping below) in the fast dash role. Operating as an LPH, aircraft carriers can embark a carrier air group (CAG) made up entirely of helicopters for support of land operations.

Nuclear Powered Attack Submarines

Nuclear powered attack submarines (SSNs) are capable of high transit speeds and sustained underwater operations. They constitute

HMS ILLUSTRIOUS in the LPH role

a principal sea denial system having excellent anti-submarine capabilities and an anti-ship capability using torpedoes and anti-surface missiles. When fitted with land attack missiles, SSNs have a power projection capability of considerable range and penetrability, with important uses for *naval diplomacy*. SSNs can gather intelligence and insert special forces. They can operate independently or in support of surface forces and contribute to the protection of the strategic nuclear deterrent.

Specialist Amphibious Forces

The UK's specialist amphibious forces represent a comprehensive range of capabilities, fully able to operate independently if required, but also eminently suitable for integration with other UK forces and those of other nations. There are three essential elements to this amphibious package.

3 Commando Brigade The principal essential element of an amphibious capability is a Landing Force organised, trained and equipped for amphibious operations. This is provided primarily by 3 Commando Brigade Royal Marines and consists of three *Commandos*, a light artillery regiment (Royal Artillery), an air defence battery, a combat engineer squadron (Royal Engineers), a logistic regiment, a light helicopter squadron, a landing craft squadron, a headquarters and signal squadron with integral air defence, an EW capability, strategic communications and a long range patrol capability.

Amphibious Shipping The specialist shipping provided to transport the landing force consists of:

   Landing Platforms Dock (LPDs), equipped with both landing craft and a flight deck;

   Landing Platform Helicopter (LPH) Although the RN now has a specialist LPH in service, if required a CVS can also be operated as an LPH;

   Landing Ships Logistic (LSLs).

In a potentially hostile environment these vessels can provide the transport and initial offload of the lead elements of a landing force, in a tactical posture without recourse to harbours and airfields. They provide the launch platforms for assault landing and raids by landing craft and support helicopters. LPDs have the necessary command and control facilities for a brigade size operation, and are capable of landing a two company group surface assault, as well as heavy battle winning equipment (such as *armour*) and landing force vehicles and equipment. The LPH can accommodate a full commando and deploy half the helicopters required for a two company group assault landing. LSLs provide *lift* for personnel and *materiel* additional to that provided by other specialist amphibious shipping. They also have helicopter spots, stern offload ramps and carry *Mexeflotes*, which are large, powered pontoons capable of offloading heavy stores and materiel from amphibious shipping and Ships Taken up From Trade (see discussion of STUFT below). Given satisfactory topography, some LSLs can also beach for rapid bow offload.

Landing Force Movement Assets The process of landing amphibious forces from the specialist shipping involves the use of aircraft and landing craft. The facilities available within the maritime force includes raiding craft, landing craft, Landing Craft Air Cushion (LCACs), Mexeflotes, and support helicopters that are indigenous to the amphibious shipping. These assets can be transferred to the landing force on completion of a landing, thus providing it with tactical mobility in the absence of amphibious shipping. Helicopters enhance *tempo*, increase the Landing Force Commander's options, contribute to the tactical mobility of the force and, in particular, improve the force's ability to achieve depth in the initial phases of a landing.

Destroyers and Frigates

In many senses the workhorses of the fleet, frigates and destroyers (FF/DD) are multi-purpose combatants with an emphasis on AAW or ASW, but with capabilities in many disciplines, including the ability to provide fire support to forces ashore. They are the smallest units that are deployed autonomously for extended periods for military tasks, and their numbers and capabilities allow them individually to cover a wide range of *military, constabulary* and *benign* tasks. They are particularly useful in establishing maritime presence. They are also versatile building blocks for larger formations, essential defensive elements of task groups, and contributors of organic helicopters to a force.

Mine Countermeasures Vessels

Mine countermeasures vessels (MMs) include vessels capable of minesweeping and minehunting. They operate in support of the home base in critical waters. These include the approaches to friendly harbours and choke points where they are used to maintain the flow of shipping and access to the open ocean for SSBNs. When operating in support of power projection, they are an important element of task groups, particularly in advanced sea control operations prior to an amphibious landing. MMs are used to establish the presence and extent of mining. They then provide mine clearance if required to enable other maritime operations to take place. MMs require a measure of forward support, a tasking authority and a degree of protection when operating in a surface or air threat environment, if they are to be deployed effectively for an extended period.

HMS SCOTT

Hydrographic Vessels

Hydrographic survey vessels (SVs) provide the surveying, charting, oceanographic and meteorological capability on which ships and submarines rely to navigate the seas safely and to exploit the environment to the full. *Rapid Environmental Assessment* (REA) involves the mission specific collection of essential environmental data, which is then provided to the databases of many weapon systems allowing them to achieve optimum performance standards. It also encompasses real time tactical measurement and exploitation of the environment. SVs also provide direct specialist support for amphibious and mine clearance operations, by conducting tactical surveys and providing logistics and command platforms.

Patrol Vessels

Patrol vessels are deployed routinely around the UK, principally on *constabulary* tasks, to protect economic interests and ensure the good order and security of the *maritime domain*. They include units of the Fishery Protection and the Northern Ireland Squadrons. For fishery protection, the ships are operated under contract to the Ministry of Agriculture and Fisheries to patrol UK waters to protect UK fishing vessels and to enforce fisheries regulations. The Northern Ireland Squadron is the maritime contribution to counter terrorism in that Province. The Ice Patrol Ship makes annual deployments to Antarctic waters to demonstrate British interest in the region and to provide assistance to the British Antarctic Survey; it also undertakes hydrographic survey and meteorological work.

Nimrod MPA takes off on patrol

Maritime Patrol Aircraft

The speed of transit, wide sensor and communications fit, ability to cover large areas, substantial capacity for weapons, and their recourse to shore supply, make maritime patrol aircraft (MPAs) important contributors to both ASW and AsuW. They are particularly useful for area ASW operations, surveillance and reconnaissance, if they can be based and supported within range of operations.

Afloat Logistic Support

Afloat logistics support provides for the direct organic replenishment of fighting units and is required for any operation where a self reliant naval force must be sustained at distance from shore bases. Ships of the *Royal Fleet Auxiliary* provide fuel, stores and ordnance while maintenance can be carried out by a Forward Maintenance and Repair Organization (FMRO) often deployed in a Forward Repair Ship (FRS). Many auxiliaries carry helicopters which can be integrated into the air assets of a formation. Specially equipped ships may be required to receive casualties if extensive combat is envisaged. Freighting support is required to move supplies from the main support area (usually the UK) to *Forward Logistics Sites* and to consolidate organic logistic shipping (see Chapter 5). Ships taken up from trade (STUFT) are also used for this task and can be modified to carry helicopters.

Ships Taken Up From Trade (STUFT)

An Amphibious Task Group will normally include STUFT to complement the lift provided by specialist amphibious shipping. STUFT may include transports for personnel (passenger vessels), vehicles (*RO-RO ferries*), hospital ships, container ships, water ships, tankers and specialist lift shipping, such as semi-submersibles to transport additional landing craft.

COLLECTIVE PERFORMANCE

Collective performance is the ability to apply current tactical and operational doctrine in the full range of maritime operations. It requires the possession of a body of doctrine for maritime operations that allows for the effective employment of the force. There also needs to be a range of operational contingency plans. Ultimately, there must be a level of collective competence specific to the role of maritime forces, for the full range of operations required to meet

Ch 8
MARITIME OPERATIONAL CAPABILITY

those tasks listed in Government policy. It is important to recognise that collective competence in maritime forces encompasses more than just that which the term 'maritime doctrine' implies. It includes the competencies necessary to power a warship and run it and its weapon systems, none of which are the business of maritime doctrine, which is to do with maritime tactics and operations. The warship is, in general, the smallest tactically relevant element of a maritime force; collective performance is about how that warship floats, moves and fights. A ship's company is a cohesive body of men and women, all of whom have a vital function to perform in delivering combat power. Essentially, collective performance is achieved through training; not just that training associated with maritime tactical doctrine but also that to do with maintaining weapons systems and power plants and personnel support services.

The quality of the UK's military training is respected worldwide and is one of its armed forces' greatest strengths. Training builds proficiency, cohesion and teamwork. It ranges from individual training for each member of the maritime force, to the conduct of large exercises involving full maritime task forces which test command and control and the application of doctrine.

In the Fleet all ships are expected to achieve a level of OC laid down by Fleet Staff. Each ship must have a high proportion of its personnel at or above the standard laid down in the Operational Performance Statement OPS. To achieve that, individuals must have achieved the standards laid down in the Training Performance Statement (TPS) for the billet they fill on the ship's Scheme of Complement (SOC). This will depend on their own career training and development and those elements of Pre-Joining Training (PJT) deemed necessary for the billet they are filling. Once they have joined their ships, individuals will require an amount of On Job Training (OJT) to raise their level of competence to that of the OPS.

As individuals, the men and women filling the billets on the SOC will need to be trained to function as a team in order that the ship operates as a whole effectively. The ship's departments will have training programmes and serials to complete, including Command Team Training (CTT) for those responsible for applying tactical doctrine in the operational environment. Each ship will undergo Operational Sea Training (OST), on successful completion of which it will become a fully operational unit within the Fleet, available for all appropriate tasking. Further training for the ship will include Area Capability Training (ACT) which will enhance its ability to perform its primary warfare function (an ASW frigate, for example, will spend time on ASW training in deep water). Finally there are Joint Maritime Courses (JMCs) and major exercises that involve ships operating as an integral part of a maritime task group.

Training enables operations to continue effectively in the confusion and stress of combat. The maintenance and demonstration of operational effectiveness through exercising is an essential part of the deterrent value of our armed forces. Teamwork is essential within a ship if it is to be efficient and effective in combat. But the requirement for good teamwork extends beyond the individual ship. It is also crucial within a force, where each unit must understand its contribution. If the task group has an international dimension, the task of developing interoperability and forging corporate team spirit is equally important but more difficult to achieve. One of the basic building blocks is the establishment of standard tactical and operating procedures. Ships must continually hone their skills in these procedures to maximize their contribution to the force.

Realistic training maintains fleet operational effectiveness by preparing ships, task groups and task forces for war. Maritime task group and individual crew training specific to the scenario and threat should continue during passage to a theatre of operations, thereby ensuring a high state of readiness on arrival. This may be invaluable for a multinational force, whose individual units have little or no experience of operating together. Military training on passage is less easy to achieve; the landing force and the individuals within it must be fully trained before deployment to theatre.

Commanders must have a clear grasp of current *doctrine* so that they can fully comprehend their orders and execute them effectively. A knowledge of doctrine will also allow commanders to take decisions in accordance with the intentions of their superiors even when they are out of contact with higher levels of command. Commanders must use judgement. They must not follow doctrine slavishly but must learn from the lessons of their own experience and be prepared to deviate from established doctrine when required, explaining their reasons for doing so to their subordinates.

SUSTAINABILITY

Sustainability is about:

- the holding of sufficient combat supplies, equipment, spares and other essential stores;

- the ability to deploy with the levels of stores needed for an operation and within acceptable time scales;

- the ability to deliver re-supplies to required locations in good time;

- the ability to treat and evacuate casualties; and

- the ability to provide sufficient reserves of manpower and materiel to allow a force to sustain operations, if necessary for extended periods.

The military-strategic and operational aspects of logistics support have already been discussed in detail in Chapter 5; the importance of sustainability is at the core of the UK armed forces' approach to logistics. In manpower terms, sustainability is achieved by having a pool of trained, professional, regular servicemen and servicewomen capable of meeting the tasks laid down by Government, and by having well trained and prepared Reserve Forces capable of supplementing their regular colleagues if operations are mounted for extended periods or if specialist skills are needed in specific circumstances.

CONCLUSIONS

At first sight it might appear strange to link system capabilities and personnel matters in a single chapter but this is precisely the association that typifies combat at and from the sea. High technology equipment, complex command, control and information systems and highly trained and motivated personnel must function in complete harmony under conditions of stress and battle damage if maritime power is to be applied effectively. Individual vessels and aircraft are partners in the business of sea control and power projection whose capabilities must be meshed to bring success. Similar partnerships must exist between force, group and unit commanders, and, within each unit, between the people and the equipment they operate.

Operational capability, the four essential components that go to make it up and the detailed means by which those components are delivered, all constitute the real effectiveness of military forces. A military force may have the most advanced and sophisticated technology at its disposal, but if it has badly motivated people, an inadequate approach to teamwork and an inability to maintain operations over time, it will fail to achieve its potential. The UK's maritime forces are of a high quality and are capable of delivering because they have achieved a balance of all the components of operational capability.

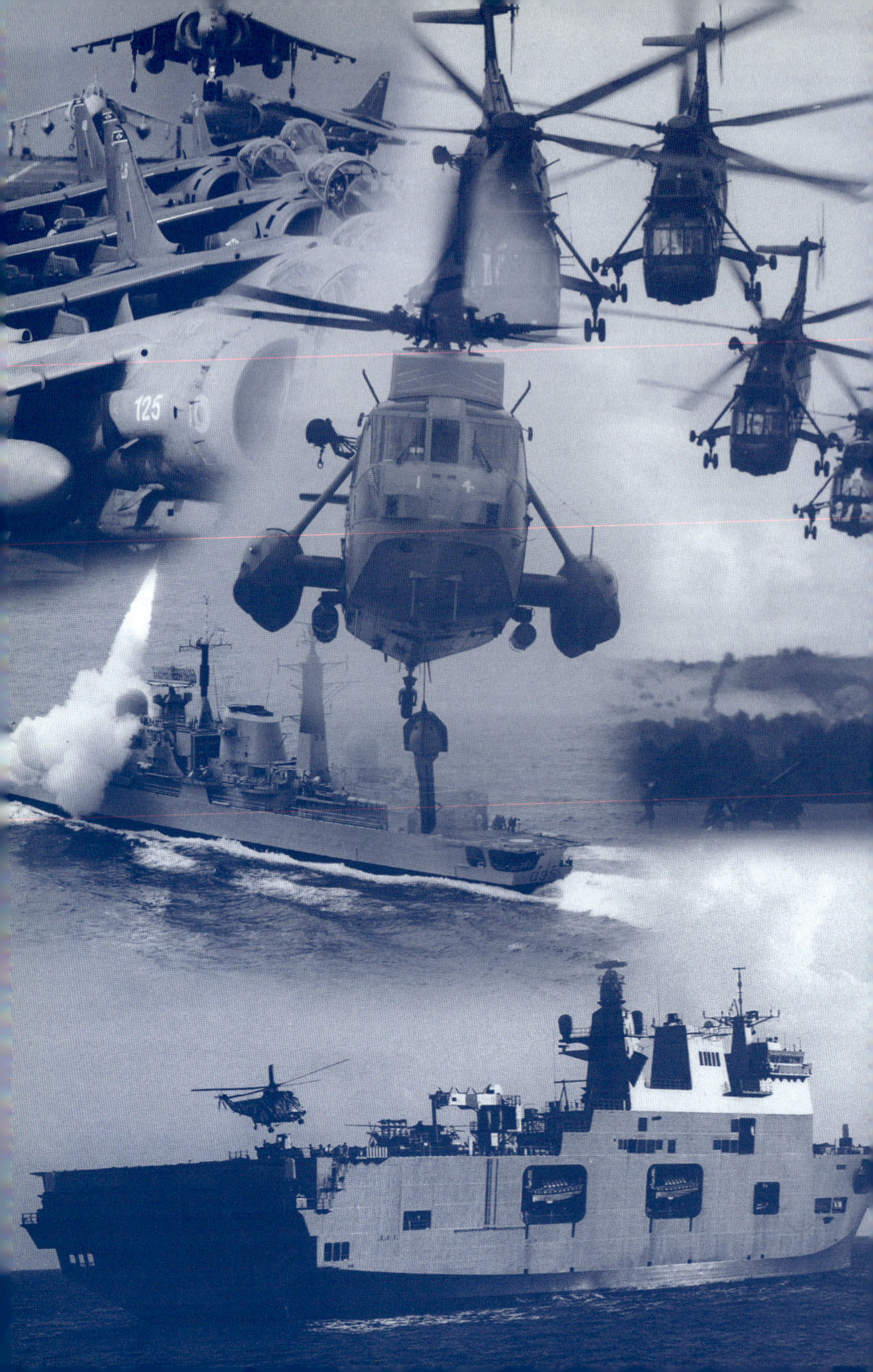

SUMMARISING THE MARITIME CONTRIBUTION TO JOINT OPERATIONS

Chapter 9

The maritime environment consists of the sea, the land in those areas known as the littoral, and the airspace above both. It was stressed in Chapter 1 that modern maritime operations are by definition joint because they involve activities in all those dimensions. This book also reflects the belief that modern military activities at the *operational* and *military-strategic* levels are inherently *joint* and frequently multinational. Nevertheless, despite acknowledging those imperatives, the bulk of this book has been discussing the doctrinal foundations of what would have been known, until a few years ago, as 'naval' operations.

Ch 9
SUMMARISING THE MARITIME CONTRIBUTION TO JOINT OPERATIONS

While the use of the word 'naval' has been kept to a minimum, it is inevitable that the 'naval' elements of maritime operations have emerged with the profile they have in a book of this sort. **BR1806** is, after all, principally concerned with educating members of the Naval Service about the attributes and operational potential of the forces in which they will spend most, if not all, of their formative professional years. However, of equal importance is the need to inform others about the military potential that maritime forces represent. Maritime forces are of little practical moment unless their potential is fully appreciated and their influence brought to bear with skill and sound judgement to help shape military and political circumstances ashore. That will not be possible unless the characteristics of maritime power are understood by those in overall command, who must have a clear idea how maritime forces are to be used as an integrated component of the joint force.

So, the maritime doctrine articulated in this book has to be regarded as sitting in a much broader context. For example, when describing the utility of a naval platform - an aircraft carrier, an amphibious unit, a submarine, a frigate or a destroyer - it is not possible to do justice to it without making reference to its operational relationship to both air and land forces. Both air power and land doctrine provide pointers to the full potential of maritime forces.

With that point firmly in mind, this final chapter is, essentially, an essay describing in general terms the ways in which maritime forces can contribute to joint operations. It draws on doctrine, in particular when relating the capabilities of a maritime Task Group to the combat capabilities required to conduct operations ashore. However, it is more conceptual in its pitch than the earlier chapters and moves the discussion on, from pure and enduring doctrine to the new operational concept of Maritime Manoeuvre.

CURRENT STRATEGIC CIRCUMSTANCES

The collapse of the Berlin Wall ended a 40 year rift across Europe. It also marked the end of a rather longer period of strategic inertia. For the first time in over 200 years the UK is in a position to think about politico-strategic issues freed from the immediate need to defend its own territory. The persistence of a major immediate threat on the continent of Europe has been a constant worry for defence planners. However, the recent profound changes in the political landscape of Europe have presented the UK with politico-strategic choice. There is now an opportunity to take full advantage of the potential of maritime power and deploy it in direct support of UK interests wherever in the world they may be engaged.

The shift in security priorities has been but one of the influences on the nature of post-Cold War strategic thinking. A second important consideration is the so-called Revolution in Military Affairs (RMA), which is the supposed imminent transformation of military operations by radical technological developments. More accurately described as evolutionary rather than revolutionary, it is certainly an exciting feature opening up new possibilities, but it can also be a double-edged sword. Technology rarely provides as great or as rapid a benefit as its most enthusiastic supporters claim. Equipment, even the most advanced, can break down. When it does, it can be difficult to repair in combat conditions. Advances in C4I by the wealthiest nations add huge capability but, through their cost, seriously threaten interoperability with the not so rich. Cruise missile precision provides a dramatic coercive capability but technology also gives potential adversaries the prospect of deploying weapons of mass destruction, the proliferation of which, in the Middle East and Asia, seems set to be a factor in the first part of the 21st century.

If technology needed a showcase, it got it during the Gulf War of 1990-91. However, it was an unusual set of circumstances that provided coalition forces with the recipe for success:

- There was wide consensus that Iraq had violated international law and should be forced to withdraw.

- The sea lines of communications, on which so much depended, particularly during the mounting phase, were unchallenged.

- There were guaranteed and relatively secure points of entry.

- There was almost unlimited host nation support.

- There was time to build up forces, develop political and military pressure, and choose the moment of attack.

While the provision of HNS and the security of deployment routes into the theatre of operations did not create insurmountable problems during the crisis in the Gulf in 1990-91, we can no longer rely on that experience, even in the Gulf itself. This is particularly the case during the early stages of crisis response, as experience during the period of tension in the Gulf in the winter of 1997/98 demonstrated. And it is vital that we do not forget the sea denial potential of mines, conventional submarines and shore based missiles. Iraqi minefields did, of course, create significant problems for coalition maritime forces, effectively preventing the engagement of amphibious forces. Moreover, one or two submarines, with relatively modest capabilities, deployed in the Mediterranean by Iraqi supporting Maghreb states, for example, would have complicated the Gulf deployment considerably. The number of states with submarines is increasing and, while most of these do not pose an immediate threat there is no guarantee that some will not do so in the future.

So, while the Gulf War was certainly a milestone in terms of international diplomatic and military co-operation, there are dangers in seeing it as a paradigm for all future military activity. It was also a full military campaign involving two adversarial sides in what most people would regard as a war and what is often referred to today as a *symmetric* campaign, albeit one with *asymmetric* aspects at the tactical level. Lower intensity peace support operations, for example, generate quite different challenges at all levels. The complexities of both high and low intensity operations can be made even more difficult when the forces involved are engaged in an asymmetric campaign.

Just as in the mid-1980s it was dangerous to use the Falklands War as a template for future military thinking, so today it is unwise to rely on the experiences of 1990-91 to fashion our approaches to security crises in the wider world. While the Gulf War provided an impressive display of the advantages of high technology warfighting, there is plenty of additional evidence to stop us from becoming sanguine; given the speed with which disputes can flare up and spread, complacency is not an option.

Looking as far ahead as we reasonably can, there are at least some probabilities. As a given, operations seem certain to be at some distance from the UK and probably to be multinational in character. This means deployability and strategic lift and it means access to entry points. These operations will be to a large extent discretionary. Even low casualty rates will be politically difficult to accept and media attention will continue to increase the degree to which military operations are exposed to public scrutiny. Operations may well be difficult to terminate and withdrawal may become as much, and as difficult, a part of our operational vocabulary as entry.

It would be far better if the need to conduct combat operations could be obviated. There is wisdom in deploying forces early to stop a crisis developing, to apply influence in its very early stages or to have a decisive impact in the opening phase of a campaign. Maritime forces can be very useful in this way provided, of course, there is sufficient public support and political will for such initiatives to be taken.

The changed military and political world is one for which the inherent flexibility of maritime power might have been designed. But it is important to stress again that maritime power does not mean naval power in the narrow sense. It means the use of the sea to deliver sea, land and air power to where it can most usefully be applied; to provide transport, mounting bases, airfields for all comers, stores depots, barracks, fire support, and refugee havens. It is a thoroughly joint contribution to a necessarily joint endeavour.

OPERATIONS IN THE LITTORAL

Not all operations will directly involve maritime forces. However, a significant proportion are likely to be conducted around the periphery of land masses, where centres of population, resources, industrial production, political control and trade are concentrated, and where crises involving UK interests may occur. Effective operations in these *littoral* areas, which straddle the boundary between land and sea, are potentially of crucial importance, either as the scene of an operation itself or as the focus for deploying and sustaining forces deeper inland.

The Oxford English Dictionary defines the 'littoral' as "of or on the shore; the region lying along the shore". However, the term has in recent years developed a broader meaning in the military-strategic context. This book employs the following definition: "The area from the open ocean which must be controlled to support operations ashore, and the area inland from shore that can be supported directly from the sea". By this definition, the littoral is a flexible concept, the geographical extent of which will depend very much on the particular circumstances to which the term is applied. In one sense the 'littoral region' can be described as a product of a coastal operational state of mind: one instinctively knows when one is in it because of the range and nature of operational challenges and opportunities one has to confront. These are, understandably, most readily apparent to those who operate routinely in the maritime environment. For those whose joint awareness is limited, the complexities of operations in the littoral and the opportunities for applying military force across environmental boundaries are not always so easily appreciated.

MARITIME MANOEUVRE

Military planners, now a long way from the certainties and clearly drawn scenarios of the Cold War, are dealing with a daunting range of variables. In prudent response to these challenges, the UK armed forces have adopted the *manoeuvrist approach* to operations. *Manoeuvre* is defined as force which comprises movement plus fire, or fire potential, to achieve advantage. *Manoeuvre warfare* is defined as a style of warfare which seeks to collapse an enemy's cohesion and effectiveness through a series of rapid, violent and unexpected actions that create a turbulent and rapidly deteriorating situation with which he cannot cope.

As an element of joint operations, use of the sea offers unique access, in terms of movement, concentration of fire-power, surprise or overt presence, to gain an advantageous position - the central precept of *manoeuvre warfare*. There are numerous examples of the ways in which maritime capabilities can contribute to joint manoeuvre, and to the projection of force to bring about the resolution of a problem on land, where it must, ultimately, be resolved. Some examples of how they can make a significant contribution to each phase of an operation or campaign, even when adequate host nation support is available, will give a flavour of their usefulness and flexibility.

Before the build up of friendly forces in theatre, their presence can be used to deter further escalation, especially against a friendly and adjacent host nation. Maritime forces can be used to deter an aggressor by deploying into a region at an early stage, at relatively low political risk and, if necessary, in considerable strength. This is the principal reason why the UK has always aimed to deploy its navy widely rather than keep it at home. It is not by accident alone that

British warships are so often in an area of interest, ready to make their impact at a time and precise point of political choice. Indeed, the freedom of the seas, freedom for use, freedom from boundaries and frontiers is why the sea is so valuable an arena for joint force manoeuvre. In preparation for subsequent operations, maritime forces can be employed to both gather intelligence and mount non-combatant evacuation operations, withdrawing civilians from a potentially hostile combat zone. As forces build up in theatre, they can demonstrate further resolve, if necessary, for example, by launching discrete amounts of mixed land, air or sea force against key enemy targets, to prevent or impede a potential aggressor from using force. Importantly, they can do this with a measure of control over factors that might otherwise lead to major escalation. In other words, as well as supporting operations on shore, maritime power can stop crises ever happening or nip them in the bud.

Prior to the main offensive, maritime forces can help to shift the emphasis from defensive to offensive operations by disrupting enemy activity, especially by the use of *raiding* techniques into enemy territory. Developing techniques for inserting forces from their sea bases directly to their operational objective is an important way of enhancing this capability. During the main combat phase of an operation the maritime component's full range of capabilities, in particular its ability to engage in precision attack against designated targets, can be brought to bear in support of forces ashore. Finally, when it comes to withdrawal, the ability of maritime forces to transport large numbers of personnel and heavy items of equipment out of theatre, and protect them in the process, could be a vital function. It would be dangerous to assume that military operations will necessarily be successful. The problem of force extraction is a demanding one, particularly when under attack and especially so if a force has to rely solely on its own assets deployed with it and under its control.

MARITIME TASK GROUPS AND FORCE PACKAGES

Aircraft carriers, amphibious and logistic shipping, submarines, and frigates and destroyers are all able to provide combat capabilities to whichever commander has need of them. All can operate independently but will normally be grouped with other forces in an appropriately packaged Task Group. There is no precise definition of a Task Group, nor the number of vessels that will go to make it up. It is, rather, a generic expression to describe a group of warships and other shipping capable of operating together in pursuit of a unified aim. The operations of a single Task Group will usually be concentrated geographically. However, if maritime operations within a campaign are geographically dispersed, they may require either the single Task Group to split or the deployment of more than one Task Group, with different capabilities. It may be necessary, for example, to have one concentrating on the security of sea lines of communication for deployment into theatre, where a second will be operating in direct support of ground forces ashore.

A Task Group's size and its mix of vessels will depend on the scale and the nature of the tasks it might need to undertake and the functions required to meet those tasks. However, a key asset that would have a profound impact on its the overall ability to influence joint operations would be an aircraft carrier. An amphibious element, including an LPH, together with a balanced range of frigates, destroyers and submarines, including a TLAM fitted SSN, would together represent a comprehensive and highly capable range of maritime power projection capabilities. Other forces, including MCM and hydrographic surveying units, can be added to a Task Group to ensure its ability to conduct entry operations. The key to success is to put together a force package, tailored for the needs of the operations in which it will be required to perform. The reconfiguring of an aircraft carrier's air group, by flying aircraft independently out to meet it when it is already forward deployed, is an excellent example of how this can be achieved.

An appropriately constituted maritime Task Group will be able to provide support for operations right through the spectrum, from warfighting to peace support, from high intensity to low and through all seven phases of a campaign. Just as important, it will be able to alter its posture rapidly, moving from low intensity to high intensity with relative ease. Indeed, because of the way that maritime forces deploy fully worked up and with their full suite of capabilities, they can even switch from ceremonial diplomatic activity during a formal port visit, to intense military activity - and all in the time it would take to sail and settle into Defence Watches; a matter of hours not days. This means that their presence anywhere in the world, for whatever routine peacetime activity, provides their political masters with a ready source of military leverage that can be brought to bear in a wide range of crisis circumstances.

Ch 9
SUMMARISING THE MARITIME CONTRIBUTION TO JOINT OPERATIONS

THE BROADER DOCTRINAL CONTEXT

As we noted at the beginning of this chapter, this book has concentrated on the maritime environment, on 'naval' operations and on maritime doctrine. However, the point was also made that the full potential of maritime forces cannot be realised without reference to both land and air doctrine. Indeed, we have also noted that the essence of effective joint manoeuvrist operations is to apply force across environmental boundaries, using the strengths of all components to compensate for each of their inherent or situational weaknesses. For these reasons, this chapter's final section will place maritime forces in relation to land and air power doctrine.

British army doctrine identifies the components of capability required to conduct an operation ashore as: Manoeuvre, Fire Support, Protection, Control of the Electro-Magnetic Spectrum, Command and Control, Information and Intelligence, Sustainability and Deployability[1]. Maritime forces can provide elements of all of these.

A maritime force would be able to conduct **manoeuvre**, provide mobility and countermobility and contribute to the control of an area of influence. As we have already stressed above, manoeuvre is, of course, more than just mobility. A maritime Task Group's ability to poise off a coast ready to provide an instant or rapid response to developments ashore is entirely in keeping with manoeuvrist principles and aims, to achieve an opportunistic and unpredictable approach that will confuse the enemy[2]. The ability to apply force in keeping with manoeuvrist principles ranges, for example, from the very overt use of ground attack aircraft (RAF GR7s embarked in a CVS) to the covert insertion of special forces. Included in the range of possibilities is the use of amphibious forces conducting what the US Navy and Marine Corps refer to as 'Operational Manoeuvre From the Sea', applying appropriate capabilities when and where needed.

In the provision of **fire support**, a Task Group can deliver fire using carrier based aircraft, surface and submarine launched long range precision attack missiles, and medium range gun munitions. The intended future combination of the LPH, HMS OCEAN, and attack helicopters will considerably enhance fire support options. In this sense, a maritime Task Group represents what a soldier would refer to as a 'combat support function' which can process and engage ground targets, integrate fire support and even assess its effectiveness using aircraft to conduct battle damage assessment.[3]

The **protection** of forces ashore preserves their fighting potential[4]. A Task Group formed around an aircraft carrier can provide air defence (both offensive and defensive counter-air) and protection for ground forces in the form of both Close Air Support (CAS)[5] and Air Interdiction (AI)[6]. As Army doctrine states: "air defence is a key function in protecting freedom of action........preventing the enemy using a primary means - air power - of breaking our cohesion"[7]. The LPH or an aircraft carrier with a specifically configured CAG, is also, of course, able to extend protection by its ability to withdraw combat personnel quickly if they come under serious threat.[8]

Interdiction operations are usually conducted on a joint basis at the operational level with land doctrine acknowledging the relevance of maritime forces being synchronised with ground, air, C2W and special forces. In this context, maritime Task Groups may be providers of air capability but also have the potential to provide EW support.[9] They can contribute to the **control of the electro-magnetic spectrum** by determining and managing their own use of the spectrum and by taking action to help deny the enemy the use of it. Domination of the spectrum contributes directly to finding the enemy and, through deception, improving the effectiveness of manoeuvre. Of particular value would be CESM fitted SSNs, destroyers and frigates and their ability to link into intelligence support from our allies via satellite. Nevertheless, any warship fitted with an EW capability has a significant ability to support operations ashore.[10]

The **command and control** function for operations ashore can be based at sea. Although not an aircraft carrier's principal role, the UK's CVSs have the facilities for a JTFHQ (Afloat). In principle there is no reason why an essentially land orientated operation should not be commanded by the Joint Task Force Commander entirely from the sea. Instinctively and understandably, the Land Component Commander is likely to feel more comfortable exercising his command from a location ashore. Nevertheless, the JTFHQ(Afloat) may have important advantages, particularly in the early stages of an operation or during withdrawal when its mobility, security, and command and control fit, combined with a collocated source of support helicopters, may make it a compelling and common sense solution.[11]

Closely related to the command and control function, a key feature of maritime forces is their access to sophisticated, high data rate (satellite) communications which represent a powerful capability for receiving **information and intelligence**. This allows them access to shore based information networks and intelligence databases. With an appropriately configured staff, this joint intelligence product can be collated, processed, supplemented by the local picture and disseminated over maritime and land based communications links.[12]

Obviously, a maritime Task Group may be the means by which an intervention force **deploys**, in particular in effecting entry into theatre and conducting movement within it in later stages.[13] This is an important possibility, with a maritime force typically able to move significant quantities of troops and materiel, once embarked, about 400 miles in 24 hours. Finally there is the sea-basing of forces for use ashore when and where required. Support helicopters using an aircraft carrier, an LPH or an LPD as an operating base are able to provide combat service support to **sustain** operations ashore through all stages of a campaign. Sustainability is "the ability of a force to maintain the necessary level of combat power for the duration required to achieve its objectives".[14]

No weapons platform is able to offer universal application. Some, however, offer such a broad range of applications across so many types of operation that their potential value is considerable. Perhaps no other contains so much joint potential as an aircraft carrier. It is of the sea, in the sense that it operates upon it, yet its utility is fully within all three environments; it is a thoroughly joint asset which, if used to maximum advantage is capable of applying a wide range of attributes to an equally wide range of operational circumstances. To quote the UK's operational level joint doctrine, "The operational level commander should command all elements of the force in theatre and be able to switch resources swiftly to seek a decisive result".[15] In this one paragraph alone, the potential value of the mix of capabilities inherent in aircraft carriers is writ large. They have utility in all three environments within the theatre of operations, in both the delivery of combat capability and its command and control. They are emphatically not merely a maritime asset; they are joint, in terms of both the capability they can deliver and the operational environmental impact they have. There has been a tendency in the past to regard aircraft carriers as naval units, purveying naval aircraft almost in competition with the RAF. This is erroneous and blinkered thinking. There can be no doubt at all that aircraft are best and most easily operated from properly equipped land bases. However, they are not always available. That being the case, aircraft carriers should correctly be seen as 'joint airfields' operated by the RN for all three Services, and even other nations - although, of course, the difficulties of achieving such implied multinational interoperability should not be downplayed.

The development of the Joint Force 2000 concept will see RN and RAF Harriers operate as a cohesive whole from the carrier base. Looking into the future, this force will continue with the Future Carrier Based Aircraft (FCBA), which is likely to be the replacement aircraft for both the Sea Harrier FA2 and the RAF's Harrier GR7.

CONCLUSIONS

Britain can play a significant military role in the business of making the world a safer place. In the new strategic circumstances, a theory of the use of military force based principally upon the philosophy of Manoeuvre Warfare is appropriate. This use of force must be four dimensional, integrating air, land, sea and political aims and tools. All of this draws upon the traditional worth of maritime assets - flexibility, low political risk, access, reach, mobility and sustainability - allowing maritime power to be employed across the range of crisis and political activity, and conferring the ability to give an almost infinite range of signals.

Maritime force has to be regarded in a joint context in which naval assets provided are to a large degree the servants of purposes which will frequently and ultimately be executed on shore and by land forces. But *maritime manoeuvre*, the maritime contribution to this venture, offers a sensitive application of force or influence, enabling intervention at a time and place of political choice, and an opportunity to exploit the effect of joint assets.

Maritime power allows the projection of force to be carried out at minimum risk, reducing financial and diplomatic cost and concentrating and easing the protection problem. It allows for the exercise of Joint Task Force Command from offshore unless and until it is more sensible to move ashore, an attribute that the future digitisation of the battle space will further enhance. Maritime power allows the maintenance in theatre and convenient re-supply of all the impedimenta that make up logistic sustainability. Lastly it allows considerable in-theatre tactical manoeuvrability, at any stage in a campaign.

In sum, the sea is a pre-eminent medium because, above all, it provides access at a time and place of political choice. By history, tradition and skill the UK is better placed, certainly than any other European nation, to exploit this medium and to develop a strategic doctrine of warfare based on the joint use of the sea. The resultant theory is rooted in traditional virtues yet highly relevant to, and congruent with, modern needs, operational and tactical doctrine and providing as much strategic choice and operational flexibility as is likely to be possible. Ultimately, maritime forces can only realise their considerable potential when integrated fully into a joint force, through which operational value is increased beyond the mere sum of its constituent parts.

FOOTNOTES
to chapter 9

1. **ADP Vol 1: Operations** contains references to all of these components of capability.
2. **ADP Vol 1: Operations**, p.5-3, Para.0504.
3. **ADP Vol 1: Operations**, p.5-4, Para.0508.
4. **ADP Vol 1: Operations**, pp.5-5 to 5-6, Paras.0511-0515.
5. **AP3000, 2nd Edition**, Para.0616.
6. **AP3000, 2nd Edition**, Para.0615.
7. **ADP Vol 1: Operations**, p.5-5, Para.0512.
8. **AP3000, 2nd Edition**, Paras. 0831-0833.
9. **ADP Vol 1: Operations**, p.5-8, Para.0521.
10. **ADP Vol 1: Operations**, p.5-11, Paras.0529-0532.
11. **UKOPSDOC**, Interim Edition Para.523.
12. **ADP Vol 1: Operations**, Paras.0425-0433.
13. **ADP Vol 1: Operations**, Para.0418.
14. **ADP Vol 3: Logistics**, Para.0201.
15. **UKOPSDOC** Interim Edition, Para.0321.

FROM TRAFALGAR TO TODAY

A bibliographic essay on doctrine and the development of British naval strategic thought

A fine example of empathy between commanders and mutual comprehension working at all levels is the executive order given by Lord Barham, First Lord of the Admiralty, to Lord Nelson for the final phase of the campaign of Trafalgar. The order told Nelson to sail in the *VICTORY*, collecting other ships on passage down the Channel, to take command of the squadrons of Admirals Calder and Collingwood, blockade Cadiz, reinforce Gibraltar and reorganise an enlarged area of command. No where does the order tell Nelson how to perform these tasks. Rather, the order begins, "...as your judgement seem best..." and ends, "...from the opinion we entertain of your conduct and abilities... you will proceed to form the best system of so extensive a command that circumstances may admit of ...". These two phrases are, of course, the key to understanding the order and its successful outcome. Such an order was only possible because Barham and Nelson were each confident that they were following a common strategy and that they shared the same doctrine, that both knew what the other meant and could be relied upon to act accordingly, using judgement and experience. The order was written in less than 250 words.[1]

> **BARHAM'S INSTRUCTIONS TO NELSON**
> **(5th SEPTEMBER 1805)**
>
> "Your Lordship, being already in possession of our several orders for the government of your conduct as commander-in-chief in the Mediterranean, you are, in addition thereto, hereby required and directed to proceed with the VICTORY and the ships named .... whose captains have orders to place themselves under your orders, to the Bay of Cadiz, where you may expect to find Vice-Admiral Collingwood and Vice-Admiral Sir Robert Calder, and the squadron of HM ships under his command. You

> will take such measures for the effectual blockade of the ports of Cadiz and San Lucar, as to your judgement shall seem best.
>
> "After leaving such number of ships under the command of Vice-Admiral Collingwood for the blockade of Cadiz, as that service may require, you will proceed to Gibraltar, and take the most effectual measures for putting that garrison and the port thereof, so far as relates to the naval department, into the best possible state of defence, by alloting such a force thereto as may secure the trade of HM subjects in passing and repassing the Gut.
>
> "And whereas, from the opinion we entertain of your conduct and ablities, we have thought fit to extend your command to Cape St. Vincent, you will proceed to form the best system for the management of so extensive a command that circumstances may admit of at the time."

Similarly, shared doctrine within the fleet enabled Nelson to bring his ships into battle on the morning of Trafalgar with a minimum of signals. Indeed, even the famous signal, "England expects..." was nearly never made because Captain Blackwood of the *EURYALUS* told Nelson it was unnecessary as the whole fleet seemed very clearly to understand what they were about. A mile away in *ROYAL SOVEREIGN* Collingwood, when he saw the signal, remarked that he wished Nelson would stop signalling "...as we all know well enough what we have to do...".

More than 125 years later, on 12th December 1939, two British and a New Zealand cruiser converged in the South Atlantic and Commodore Harwood issued his orders in a terse signal, "My policy with three cruisers in company versus one pocket battleship. Attack at once by day or night. By day act in two divisions ... By night ships will normally remain in company in open order...". At 0616 the next morning, having sighted the German *GRAF SPEE, AJAX* and *ACHILLES* attacked as one division and *EXETER* hauled out of the line to attack from a different bearing. From then until the bitter action was broken off, when *GRAF SPEE* was chased into a neutral harbour, no other tactical signals were made, the three cruisers manoeuvring as necessary to clear their lines of fire on the German. It is a striking proof of the high state of training and understanding within the Royal Navy at the start of the Second World War that one of the first major actions could be fought on the basis of a signal just a few lines long and that nothing needed to be added during the battle.[2] It is clear, whether it was Harwood and his Captains, Barham and Nelson, or Nelson and his band of brothers that they all shared a common purpose and corporate body of knowledge. Today such knowledge is defined as doctrine.

Just as doctrine is about achieving a common level of understanding of tactics, operations and strategy so that commanders and planners will act instinctively and correctly in the wide variety of situations which they are likely to meet, that admirals will know how their captains are likely to act in any given situation, and captains will know what their superiors would wish, so it is also important to realise what doctrine is not. Doctrine, while it is authoritative, is not a substitute for judgement and experience, though the degree of judgement needed or experience available may vary with circumstances. Doctrine is not dogma: as the first edition of **Fundamentals of British Maritime Doctrine** said, it "...must evolve as its political and strategic foundations alter and in the light of new technology, the lessons of experience and the insights of operational analysis ...". The use of doctrine credits the individual, wherever he or she is in the chain or command, with a wide measure of initiative. Doctrine is not absolute, but is derived from first principles, but these principles themselves are not unchanging: for example, the tactics of the Grand Fleet at Jutland were not appropriate to winning the anti-submarine battle in 1917. Similarly, Western naval strategy in the Cold War is no longer useful when general war in Europe seems unlikely.

At the tactical level doctrine does tend to be specific to its context and to consist of a definite list of recommended actions. In the Royal Navy this tactical doctrine is contained in **Fighting**

Instructions, a classified document which might include, for example, a detailed list of defensive measures to be taken in the event of an attack. When tactical doctrine is not understood, ships are lost. For example, in December 1941 Rear Admiral Sir Philip Vian's flag captain hesitated in turning the force to counter a torpedo threat, and the flagship, *NAIAD*, was sunk.[3] At the higher, operational and strategic levels doctrine is much more interpretative. On another occasion Vian, who was one of the greatest British fighting admirals of the Second World War, displayed his understanding of operational level doctrine by disobeying orders. During the hunt for the German battleship *BISMARCK* in May 1941, Vian was ordered to close on the Commander-in-Chief, but realising that his was the only force which could make contact with the enemy before night-fall, Vian chose to shadow and attack the *BISMARCK*.[4]

> THE LOSS OF HMS NAIAD
>
> "Time elapsed before the signal was seen; and almost as it was received I saw a torpedo track approaching Naiad, which was too close to avoid. I say almost, but indeed there were seconds in which the helm could have been put over. As I was on the bridge, Grantham asked me which way to turn the Force, just as the alarm belatedly came through. I momentarily deliberated: fatally. The torpedo exploded in the exact spot in which a single hit could sink a cruiser of the DIDO class, that is, on the bulkhead between the two engine-rooms. A few yards either side, which an immediate alternation of course would have ensured, would have lodged the torpedo in one engine-room only"

In the American war in the Pacific during the Second World War there was no single unified command but the several commanders were all thinking in sufficiently like terms to construct a strategic victory from a mosaic of individual battles.[5]

Clearly, those in command, preparing themselves for command or contemplating a career leading to command need to be well read. British armed forces are apolitical, so while individuals need to be aware of domestic and international politics and of current affairs, a discussion of these subjects is necessarily outside the limits of this essay. They need however to understand the origins of strategy, its development and historic context. However, if doctrine is about achieving a common level of understanding of strategy, operations and tactics, and, if the Royal Navy has been successful for many years in those very activities, do not the senior officers of the Royal Navy already have, and always have had, a thorough understanding of these issues?

Rather surprisingly in 1890 *The Times*, in reviewing Captain Mahan's first book, **The Influence of Sea Power upon History, 1660 to 1793**, was able to thunder that "... the book is almost a pioneer in its class, for, strange to say, the literature of the greatest Naval Power in history has no authoritative treatise on the principles of Naval Warfare...". Mahan gave statesmen and sailors alike, American, British and many others, the first general theory of sea power in modern times. The concept he gave was that being a great power meant being a sea power and that being a sea power meant commercial and naval strength. Mahan was quickly translated into many languages, and in the German navy the Kaiser made it compulsory reading. However, Mahan's elegant, if prolix, theories were traduced into the idea of a decisive battle between opposing fleets after which one side or the other would be left in command of the seas:[6] this is a crude version of Mahanian theory.[7] Mahan's ideas have been tarnished by this interpretation and the value of his work diminished. Today, for example, among the hundreds of titles all available from the US Naval Institute Press, Mahan is out of print. In any case, pure Mahan can be difficult to access, though one way to come to grips with Mahan's theories is through John Hattendorf's edited selections of **Mahan on Naval Strategy**.[8]

The American Mahan, even if he is the best known, is not and was not the only author to formulate a theory of sea power: his British counterpart is Sir Julian S Corbett. In **The Education of a Navy: the development of British naval strategic thought 1867-1914** Donald Schurman gives a more balanced view than *The Times* in 1890 of the development of British thinking about sea power and naval strategy. Schurman analyses the works of the Colomb brothers (one so verbose that Fisher called him "column and a half"!), Sir John Laughton and Admiral Sir Herbert Richmond, as well as Mahan and Corbett. Amongst other ideas Schurman recognises that thinking about warlike activity has been dominated by concepts which give land forces priority over naval forces and that naval personnel who do think about these things have tended to keep their thoughts to themselves. When analysing the works of Corbett,

Schurman extracts two critical points, that "...it was unanimity of purpose and universality of strategic understanding that stamped the English sea moves with success ... naval officers worked from an agreed body of common doctrine..." and "...that a common knowledge of theory opened up channels of communications between leaders in the military forces and their political masters when all had drunk at the same fountain of knowledge ...".[9]

Eric Grove edits the best edition of Corbett's **Principles of Maritime Strategy**. Corbett recognised the primacy of politics in directing war and developing appropriate strategies. He also distinguished between "...maritime strategy, the principles which govern a war in which the sea is a substantial factor ..." and "... naval strategy, that part of it which determines the movements of the fleet when maritime strategy has determined what part the fleet must play in relation to the action of the land forces...". Famously, he went on to say that "... since men live upon the land and not upon the sea, great issues between nations at war have always been decided - except in the rarest of cases - either by what your army can do against your enemyís territory and national life, or else by the fear of what the fleet makes it possible for your army to do...".[10] Corbett's ideas were greeted with some scepticism by contemporary senior naval officers - he was even blamed by some for the failure to achieve decisive battle at Jutland - but his ideas of limited warfare and joint operations are much more in kilter with present ideas of expeditionary warfare. In conclusion, John Gooch is probably right in his view of the contribution of Mahan and Corbett to naval thinking, that "...Mahan's theories have worn less well than Corbett's ... but together the two men stand as the founding fathers - as well as rivals - of modern maritime strategic thought...".[11]

On the plane of pure theory of strategy, in Peter Paret's **Makers of Modern Strategy: from Machiavelli to the Nuclear Age** Mahan is the only naval strategist to be awarded individual treatment.[12] In **Masters of War: classical strategic thought** where George Handel compares Sun Tsu, Clausewitz, Jomini and others including Machiavelli, Mahan is only mentioned three times and Corbett never.[13] More recently Handel has ranked Sun Tsu, Thucydides, Machiavelli, Clausewitz, Jomini and Mahan as amongst the greats and Corbett as first among the also-rans. This interesting observation deserves a separate discussion since many of these authors are only known to us as aphorisms and Delphic sound bites.

Briefly, Sun Tsu was not translated until early this century and had no influence on the others; Thucydides never wrote about strategy directly so his ideas are only available by inference and implication; Machiavelli was a medieval statesman whose principle interest was in statecraft; Jomini (who certainly influenced Mahan in his early years) wrote in French and is today unfashionable, and Clausewitz never finished his **On War**, which was only translated from German into English in 1874, i.e. after the first "modern" wars of the 19th century. On Clausewitz's premature death his wife managed only to partly finish his work - a fact which some hold to be the reason why academics prefer him, since they can argue over what they think he would have said. So, even if Corbett is only first of the second division of military and naval philosophers, then he is still first amongst the useful strategists.

In the genus of maritime and naval strategy, there are many good books some of which have been popular in their time and whose authors have contributed specific ideas to the body of theory. However, since strategy and hence doctrine is affected by circumstances it is not surprising that few authors have been able to divorce themselves from their contemporary context, whether it is the dominant technology in use or the politics of the day. This is a besetting sin of, and should be a warning to, all retired admirals and captains, a sin committed by authors down the years such as Custance, Grenfell,[14] Richmond,[15] Scholfield,[16] Gretton,[17] Roskill,[18] and even Mahan. For example, few authors writing in the 1980s at towards the end of the Cold War could envisage a world without two or more superpowers in confrontation. Hence the advice of one eminent scholar that it is not worth reading anything written before 1989.

The two books on Mahan and Corbett which have been already mentioned come from the Classics of Sea Power series, edited by John Hattendorf and Wayne Hughes for the Naval Institute Press at Annapolis. This series also makes available to us much foreign thinking on the evolution of naval strategy and operations, including the Russian S.O.Makarov,[19] the French Raoul Castex,[20] and the German Wolfgang Wegener.[21] Other British authors in the same series include Philip Colomb,[22] and Charles Calwell,[23] as well, of course, as several American authors. For another, non Anglo-Saxon view of the world there is **Maritime Strategy and Continental Wars** by Rear Admiral Raja Menon, Indian Navy.[24]

In the Cold War strategy did tend to ossify, perhaps not unexpectedly since even in the late 1980s confrontation between superpowers seemed to be a permanent state of affairs. During this period and especially towards its end the US Navy developed a maritime strategy, which can be interpreted, in a crude way, as Mahanian. Good reading on this subject is Norman Friedman's **The US Maritime Strategy**,[25] and the subject is brought up to date and developed by Stewart Fraser in **US Maritime Strategy: issues and implications,** a short paper from the Centre for Defence and International Security Studies at the University of Lancaster.[26]

For the Royal Navy the Cold War was a lean time, its low point the 1981 Defence Review and the resignation of the then Navy Minister, Keith Speed. It did not help that in the circumstances of the time the then Secretary of State for Defence was probably right to commit British forces to the Continent and to disinvest in the Navy. Coincidentally it is possible to chart the rise of British naval, strategic thought. Sir James Cable had already published, in 1971, his first edition of **Gunboat Diplomacy** about the limited application of naval force (and is remarkable not least for its anticipation of the newly introduced British concept of *defence diplomacy*), but he was largely ignored by a service preparing for general war against the Soviet Union.[27] **Gunboat Diplomacy** is already a classic work that has been reprinted and updated in Britain and America several times, the latest in 1994. Then in the black night of the 1980s there were two or three landmark publications. Geoffrey Till, now professor and dean of academic studies at the Joint Services Command and Staff College, edited a volume, **The Future of British Sea Power**, proceedings of a conference in 1983, which opened with an important statement about the Government's policy towards the Navy by the new Secretary of State, Michael Heseltine.[28] In the same year Sir James Cable published **Britain's Naval Future**, which looks increasingly prescient in its arguments for a stronger maritime strategy.[29] Then in 1986 Rear Admiral Richard Hill brought out **Maritime Strategy for Medium Powers**, which recognised Britain's reduced role but also began to introduce new arguments and concepts such as *reach*.[30]

In this revival of interest in maritime history and strategy, other modern writers not mentioned elsewhere in this essay are Jan Breemer, Michael Duffy, Barry Gough, Andrew Lambert, Nicholas Lambert, Williamson Murray, Norman Polmar, Michael Pugh,

Nicholas Rodger, David Rosenberg, and Jon Sumida (this list of names is only meant to be indicative). There have also been several good anthologies about sea power, one being **Seapower and Strategy**,[31] edited by Colin Gray and Roger Barnet, and **Maritime Strategy and the Balance of Power:**[32] though both were published in 1989 and thus overtaken by the end of the Cold War, they provide good, coherent surveys of the subject. One more anthology is the 1995 **Navies and Global Defense: theories and strategy**, published in Canada and less well known than it deserves.[33] Another valuable contribution to debate is Geoffrey Till's 1994 **Seapower Theory and Practice**, in particular his own perceptive essay **Maritime Strategy and the Twenty First Century**.[34] In this essay, which has stood the test of time well, Geoffrey Till argues that the changed global security environment means back-to-basics for strategists - and thus for doctrine writers - and he predicts more use and utility of navies in the next century. However, perhaps the most significant post-Cold War work is Colin Gray's **The Leverage of Sea Power**, published in 1992 and reckoned to be essential reading for anyone thinking about the role of maritime power.[35] Gray's central thesis is that sea power grants the ability to control the geostrategic terms of war and that the state or coalition of states which most effectively harnesses sea power wins wars.

In the last few years strategic and doctrinal thinking in the world's navies has evolved rapidly. From India Admiral Raja Menon has already been mentioned, and Australia too has proved a particularly fertile ground for new ideas about maritime strategy and security, two leading authors being James Goldrick and Sam Bateman. Naturally however the evolution has been most marked and most fertile in the world's largest navy and the influences on and the process of making strategy have been very well described in David Rosenberg's essay on making modern naval strategy.[36] Most notably, "... **From the Sea - Preparing the Naval Service for the 21st Century**", a joint United States Navy/US Marine Corps paper was published in 1992 and its successor paper in 1994 "**Forward from the Sea**". The former paper describes how, in the changed strategic environment, the attention of the US Navy and Marine Corps would shift towards littoral warfare and manoeuvre from the sea: the latter assesses the two Services' contribution to the totality of American armed power. These two American papers give a high level concept compatible with the post Cold War era from which strategy and then doctrine can be derived: they have also had a considerable influence on British naval thinking. In 1996 the Commander in Chief Fleet, Admiral Abbott, argued that territorial defence was no longer necessary to Britain and Europe, who with allies in and out of NATO must now be ready to project visible and useable power in order to deter, dissuade, protect mutual interests and, if necessary, credibly coerce.[37] In **Dimensions of Sea Power: strategic choice in the modern world** it was argued that the qualities and capabilities of a maritime strategy are particularly suitable for use in the unpredictable and confused situations which might threaten Britain's interests, whether these are vital, secondary or altruistic.[38] Brigadier Rob Fry has perceived broad and enduring rhythms of strategy, and suggested that Britain's declared foreign policy must be active and occasionally militant if it is to be relevant and credible, that there is a growing consensus among professional military and defence-academics that future operations are likely to be expeditionary, and that a "maritime national strategy" is the appropriate response to the changed geopolitical environment.[39] This strategy, which has emerged afresh from the British government's Strategic Defence Review (SDR), is no other than the British way in warfare, for which Captain Sir Basil Liddell-Hart is best known (though in fact he synthesised the views of others including Herbert Richmond). For a historical overview of the British way in warfare see David French's book.[40] The immediate past First Sea Lord, Admiral Sir Jock Slater, has assessed that the changes which have taken place since 1989 caught the grand strategic mood of the time to which the Royal Navy has responded with its concept of the Maritime Contribution to Joint Operations.[41]

The SDR marks the end in Britain of a period of post Cold War thinking. It marks a significant and historic shift in British Defence policy, away from a continental commitment back to a more maritime, expeditionary role for British armed forces. Certainly the Royal Navy and Royal Marines, which during the Cold War sometimes had difficulty in putting their case, have emerged well from the SDR. In particular, several influential articles by senior officers in the RUSI journal have marked the changes and have armed the Navy with a new and more powerful rationale for its doctrine. What is now needed is a unifying theory to digest the changes which have taken place since the end of the Cold War and to encapsulate the present state of theory about maritime strategy. One candidate for this is clearly Cable's latest book, **The Political Influence of Naval Force in History,** in which he examines the use of naval force for political purposes and concludes that naval - he means maritime - force is attractive to politicians because it is easier to limit and control, inflicts no collateral damage, can poise and sustain a threat without perpetrating any warlike act, can deploy without commitment, or wait, gain time for diplomacy and withdraw without loss of face.[42] In short, the adoption by politicians of a maritime strategy allows them flexibility and choice.

One book deserves a separate category of its own, and that is Andrew Gordon's **The Rules of the Game: Jutland and British naval command**.[43] Gordon's book has probably been sold and read more widely amongst officers of the Royal Navy than any other book in recent times. It is a fascinating and controversial book which can be read and enjoyed at different levels. While dealing with the events and the personalities leading up to the Battle of Jutland in 1916, it is, as the subtitle warns us, about the development of the minds of and the mindset of senior officers and their approach to the problems of command, whether their actions should be ruled by doctrine or dogma. In **Rules of the Game** Gordon characterises commanders as rat-catchers or regulators, though in actuality any commander may have a mixture of both styles. It is an important book because it is the most recent and probably the best analysis of a fundamental problem which lies at the heart of all doctrine and strategy: how to encourage initiative and flexibility while maintaining effective command and control. In other words, how to institutionalise sound doctrine without turning it into rigid dogma. There are no black and white answers.

The subject continues to develop. Other books to look out for in 1999 are **The Changing Face of Maritime Power**, the proceedings of a conference held at the former Royal Naval College Greenwich to mark the translation to the Joint Services Command and Staff College, and **New Dimensions: the Royal Navy, maritime manoeuvre, and the Strategic Defence Review**, a collection of essays by distinguished military and civilian authors who assess the impact of the SDR one year on from the announcement of its findings.

This has been no more than a catspaw of wind across the surface of a huge subject. One of the purposes of this essay is to indicate that the subject is constantly under development and that there is yet more which can be read about and written upon sea power and maritime strategy. A score of authors and their books, essays and articles have been mentioned in the text and more in the footnotes, and many of the books listed have their own bibliographies. Yet the very book which the reader would recommend has probably been missed, however, just as students and practitioners, senior officials and politicians need to make up their own minds about what is an appropriate strategy, what doctrine should be associated with this, and how it should be applied in changing circumstances, so they should make up their own minds about what is the best to read on the subject. While the expert is presumably already well-read, it is suggested that the novice might wish to start with reading the essays in RUSI, then read Gray, Gordon, Hattendorf on Mahan, and Grove on Corbett, Fraser, Till, and Cable's latest book. A suggested short reading list therefore is:

THE RUSI ARTICLES

Admiral Sir Peter Abbott: *The Maritime Component of British and Allied Military Strategy*

Brigadier Rob Fry: *End of the Continental Century*

Admiral Sir Jock Slater: *The Maritime Contribution to Joint Operations*

BOOKS

Colin S. Gray: *The Leverage of Sea Power*

Andrew Gordon: *The Rules of the Game*

Alfred T. Mahan: *Mahan on Naval Strategy: selections from the writings of Rear Admiral Alfred Thayer Mahan* (Classics of Sea Power series)

Julian S. Corbett: *Some Principles of Maritime Strategy* (Classics of Sea Power series)

Geoffrey Till: *Seapower Theory & Practice*

James Cable: *The Political Influence of Naval Force in History*

OTHER PUBLICATIONS

Stewart Fraser: *US Maritime Strategy: issues and implications* (Centre for Defence and International Security Studies)

NOTES

1. Sir John Knox Laughton, ed., *The Barham Papers* (London: Navy Records Society, 1911; Lord Barham's instructions to Lord Nelson, letter dated 5 September 1805), XXXIX
2. Sir Eugene Millington-Drake, *The Drama of the Graf Spee and the Battle of the Plate* (London: Peter Davies, 1964), pp 165, 172, 222
3. Admiral of the Fleet Sir Philip Vian, *Action This Day: a war memoir* (London: Frederick Muller Ltd, 1960), p84
4. Vian, *Action This Day: a war memoir*, p57
5. Robert B. Vice Admiral Carney, *'Logistical Planning for War'*, Naval War College Review, October (1948)
6. John Gooch, *'Maritime Command: Mahan and Corbett'*, in *Seapower and Strategy*, ed. by Colin S. Gray and Roger W. Barnett (London: Tri-Service Press, 1989), pp. 27-46
7. Paul M. Kennedy, *'British and American Strategies, 1898-1920'*, in *Maritime Strategy and the Balance of Power: Britain and American in the Twentieth Century* (Oxford: Macmillan in association with St Antony's College, 1989), pp.165-88
8. John B. Hattendorf, *Mahan on Naval Strategy: selections from the writings of Rear Admiral Alfred Thayer Mahan*, Classics of Sea Power edn (Annapolis: Naval Institute Press, 1991)
9. Donald M. Schurman, *The Education of a Navy: the development of British naval strategic thought 1867-1914* (London: Cassell, 1965), p17, p19, p171, p174
10. Julian S. Corbett, *Some Principles of Maritime Strategy*, Classics of Sea Power edn, with an introduction and notes by Eric J Grove (Annapolis: Naval Institute Press, 1911), pp 15-16
11. Gooch, *Maritime Command: Mahan and Corbett*
12. Peter Paret, *Makers of Modern Strategy: from Machiavelli to the nuclear age* (Princeton: Princeton University Press, 1986)
13. Michael I. Handel, *Masters of War: classical strategic thought*, Second Revised Edition edn (Portland, OR: Cass, 1992)
14. R. Grenfell, *Sea Power by T124* (New York: Doubleday, Doran, 1941)
15. H. Richmond, *Sea Power in the Modern World* (London: G Bell & Sons, 1934)
16. B. B. Scholfield, *British Sea Power* (London: Batsford, 1967)
17. Peter Gretton, *Maritime Strategy: a study of British defence problems* (London: Cassell, 1965)

18 Stephen W. Roskill, *The Strategy of Sea Power: its development and application* (London: Collins, 1962)
19 S. O. Makarov, *Discussions of Questions in Naval Tactics*, Classics of Sea Power edn (Annapolis: Naval Institute Press, 1990; with an introduction by Robert B Bathhurst)
20 Raoul Castex, *Strategic Theories*, Classics of Sea Power edn (Annapolis: Naval Institute Press, 1994; selections translated by and with an introduction by Eugenia C Kiesling)
21 Wolfgang Wegener, *The Naval Strategy of the World War*, Classics of Sea Power edn (Annapolis: Naval Institute Press, 1989; with an introduction by Holger H Herwig)
22 Vice Admiral Philip H. Colomb, *Naval Warfare*, Classics of Sea Power edn (Annapolis: Naval Institute Press, 1891; introduced by Barry M Gough)
23 Charles E. Calwell, *Military Operations and Maritime Preponderance*, Classics of Sea Power edn (Annapolis: Naval Institute Press, 1905; edited and introduced by Colin Gray)
24 Rear Admiral Raja Menon, *Maritime Strategy and Continental Wars* (London: Frank Cass, 1998)
25 Norman Freidman, *The US Maritime Strategy* (London: Jane's, 1988)
26 Stewart Fraser, *US Maritime Strategy: issues and implications*, Bailrigg Paper, 25 (Lancaster: Centre for Defence and International Security Studies, 1997)
27 James Cable, *Gunboat diplomacy 1919-1991, political applications of limited naval force* (Basingstoke: Macmillan, 1994)
28 Geoffrey Till, ed., *The Future of British Sea Power* (Annapolis: Naval Institute Press, 1984)
29 James Cable, *Britain's Naval Future* (Annapolis: Naval Institute Press, 1983)
30 Rear Admiral J. R. Hill, *Maritime Strategy for Medium Powers* (London: Croom Helm, 1986)
31 Colin S. Gray, and Roger W. Barnett, eds, *Seapower and Strategy* (Annapolis, Md: United States Naval Institute, 1989)
32 John B. Hattendorf, and Robert S. Jordan, eds, *Maritime Strategy and the Balance of Power: Britain and America in the twentieth century* (Oxford: St Antony's/Macmillan, 1989; foreword by Robert O'Niell)
33 Keith Neilson, and Elizabeth J. Errington, eds, *Navies and Global Defense: theories and strategy* (Westport, Conn: Praeger, 1995)
34 Geoffrey Till, *Seapower Theory & Practice* (Ilford: Frank Cass, 1994)

35 Colin S. Gray, *The Leverage of Sea Power* (New York: The Free Press, 1992)
36 David A. Rosenberg, 'American Naval Strategy in the Era of the Third World War: an inquiry into the structure and process of general war at Sea, 1945-90', *Naval Power in the Twentieth Century*, ed. by Nicholas A. M. Rodger (London: Macmillan, 1996), pp. 242-54. A longer version of this essay also appeared in James Goldrick, and John B. Hattendorf, eds, *Mahan is Not Enough: the proceedings of a conference on the works of Sir Julian Corbett and Admiral Sir Herbert Richmond* (Newport RI: Naval War College Press, 1993)
37 Admiral Sir Peter Abbott, 'The Maritime Component of British and Allied Military Strategy', *Royal United Services Institute*, December (1996), pp 6-11
38 Eric Grove, and Peter Hore, eds, *Dimensions of Sea Power: strategic choice in the modern world* (Hull: Hull University Press, 1998), pp 3-25
39 Brigadier Rob Fry, 'End of the Continental Century', *Royal United Services Institute*, (1998),
40 David French, *The British Way in Warfare 1688-2000* (London: Unwin Hyman, 1990)
41 Admiral Sir Jock Slater, 'The Maritime Contribution to Joint Operations ', *Royal United Services Institute Journal*, (1998),
42 James Cable, *The Political Influence of Naval Force in History* (London: Macmillan Press Ltd, 1998)
43 Andrew Gordon, *The Rules of the Game: Jutland and British naval command* (London: John Murray, 1996)

EDITORIAL CONSULTATIVE BOARD

The Editorial Consultative Board for this Edition of BR1806: British Maritime Doctrine consisted of the following:

        Director Naval Staff (Chairman)
        Commander S W Haines Royal Navy (Editor and Principal Author)
        Director Navy Plans and Programme
        Director Naval Operations
        Director of Naval Logistics Policy (Operations and Plans)
        Director of Operational Requirements (Sea)
        Director Maritime Warfare Centre
        Assistant Chief of Staff (Warfare) to CinC Fleet
        Assistant Chief of Staff (J7) to CJO (PJHQ)
        Assistant Commandant (Navy) JSCSC
        Director of Academic Studies JSCSC
        Commodore BRNC Dartmouth
        Head of Naval Historical Branch
        Head of Defence Studies (Royal Navy)
        RN Liaison Officer, US Navy Doctrine Command
        Director of Land Warfare
        Director of Defence Studies RAF
        Dr Andrew Gordon
        Mr Nicholas Rodger
        Professor Colin Gray

The Board also acknowledge the significant contribution, through their development and editorship of the First Edition, made by Commander C M S Codner Royal Navy, Dr Eric Grove, Captain J C Kidd Royal Navy and Lieutenant Commander T J Peacock Royal Navy.

ABBREVIATIONS

ACNS	Assistant Chief of Naval Staff
ACSC	Advanced Command and Staff Course
ACT	Area Capability Training
AEW	Airborne Early Warning
AI	Air Interdiction
ALSS	Advanced Logistics Support Site
AAW	Anti-Air Warfare
ASW	Anti-Submarine Warfare
ASuW	Anti-Surface Warfare
ATG	Amphibious Task Group
BDD	British Defence Doctrine
BRNC	Britannia Royal Naval College
C2W	Command and Control Warfare
C4I	Command, Control, Communications, Computers and Information
CAG	Carrier Air Group
CAS	Close Air Support
CDL	Chief of Defence Logistics
CDS	Chief of the Defence Staff
CESM	Combat Electronic Support Measures
CIMIC	Civil-Military Co-operation
CJO	Chief of Joint Operations
COA	Courses of Action
CTCRM	Commando Training Centre Royal Marines
CTT	Command Team Training
CVS	Aircraft Carrier
DD	Destroyer
EA	Environmental Assessment
EEZ	Exclusive Economic Zone
EFZ	Extended Fisheries Zone
EXTACS	Experimental Tactics (NATO)
EW	Electronic Warfare
FAC	Fast Attack Craft
FA2	Sea Harrier
FCBA	Future Carrier Based Aircraft
FF	Frigate
FLS	Forward Logistics Site
FMRO	Forward Maintenance and Repair Organization
FRS	Forward Repair Ship

GR7	Ground Attack Harrier
HMS	Her Majesty's Ship
HNS	Host Nation Support
IHP	Initial Handling Point
ISC	Initial Staff Course
ISTAR	Intelligence, Surveillance, Target Acquisition and Reconnaissance
JDCC	Joint Doctrine and Concepts Centre
JF2000	Joint Force 2000 (Joint RN and RAF Fighter Aircraft Force)
JMC	Joint Maritime Course
JTFACC	Joint Task Force Air Component Commander
JTFHQ	Joint Task Force Headquarters
JOA	Joint Operating Area
JSCSC	Joint Service Command and Staff College
JTFC	Joint Task Force Commander
LCAC	Landing Craft Air Cushion
LPD	Landing Platform Dock
LPH	Landing Platform Helicopter
LSL	Landing Ship Logistics
MACA	Military Aid to Civil Authorities
MACC	Military Assistance to the Civil Community
MACM	Military Assistance to Civil Ministries
MACP	Military Aid to the Civil power
MCC	Maritime Component Commander
MCM	Mine Countermeasures
MCT	Maritime Counter Terrorism
MM	Mine Countermeasures Vessels
MMM	Multinational Maritime Manuals
MMO	Multinational Maritime Operations Manual
MNC	Major NATO Commander
MNLC	Multinational Logistics Commander
MOU	Memorandum of Understanding
MJLC	Multinational Joint Logistics Centre
MSC	Major Subordinate Commander (NATO)
NATO	North Atlantic Treaty Organization
NCS	Naval Control of Shipping
NEO	Non-Combatant Evacuation Operation
NGO	Non-Governmental Organization
OJT	On-Job Training

OPCOM	Operational Command
OPCON	Operational Control
OPS	Operational Performance Statement
OR	Operational Requirements
OST	Operational Sea Training
OSCE	Organization for Security and Co-operation in Europe
PGM	Precision Guided Munitions
PJHQ	Permanent Joint Headquarters
PJT	Pre-Joining Training
PSC	Principal Subordinate Commander (NATO)
PSO	Peace Support Operations
RAS	Replenishment at Sea
REA	Rapid Environmental Assessment
RM	Royal Marines
RMA	Revolution in Military Affairs
RMP	Recognised Maritime Picture
RN	Royal Navy
RNCS	Regional Naval Control of Shipping
ROE	Rules of Engagement
SDR	Strategic Defence Review
SF	Special Forces
SLOCS	Sea Lines of Communication
SOC	Scheme of Complement
SSBN	Ballistic Missile Carrying Submarine
STOVL	Short Take-off/Vertical Landing
STUFT	Ships Taken Up From Trade
TLAM	Tomahawk Land Attack Missile
TPS	Training Performance Statement
UK	United Kingdom
UKOPSDOC	United Kingdom Doctrine for Joint and Multinational Operations
UN	United Nations
UNCLOS	United Nations Convention on the Law of the Sea
UNCLOS III	Third UN Conference on the Law of the Sea
UNFICYP	United Nations' Force in Cyprus
UNPROFOR	United Nations' Protection Force
US	United States
WEU	Western European Union
WIGS	West Indies Guard Ship
WMD	Weapons of Mass Destruction

GLOSSARY

The Glossary that follows represents the best definitions of those terms included at the time that the book went to press. When the definition is taken from another publication, the source is placed in brackets at the end of the entry. Otherwise, definitions can be quoted as coming from **BR1806**.

Source Documents

AAP 6(V)	NATO Glossary of Terms and Definitions
ADP Vol 1	Army Doctrine Publications Volume 1:Operations
AJP 01(A)	Allied Joint Operations Doctrine
AP 3000	Royal Air Force Air Power Doctrine
BDD	British Defence Doctrine
BR 3012	Guide to Maritime Law
FM100-5	Field Manual 100-5: Operations (United States Army)
JP 1-02	The DOD Dictionary of Military and Associated Terms
JWP 0-10	UK Doctrine for Joint and Multinational Operations ***(UKOPSDOC)***
JWP 0-01.1	UK Joint Glossary of Joint and Multinational Terms and Definitions (replaces ***JSP110***)
JWP 3-50	Peace Support Operations
NDP 1	Naval Doctrine Publication 1: Naval Warfare (US Navy)
OED	Concise Oxford English Dictionary
SDE	Statement of Defence Estimates (Annual)
SDR	Strategic Defence Review
STANAG 1166	Standard Ship Designator System

A

Access (Military)
The freedom of action to manoeuvre to achieve control of a designated environment or to bring target sets within range of organic firepower or other military capabilities.

Administration
The management and execution of all military matters not included in tactics, [operations] and strategy; primarily in the fields of logistics and personnel management. (*AAP6*)

Administrative Authority
A commander vested with those aspects of command that are concerned with administration. (*JWP 0-01.1*) See also *full command*.

Advanced Logistic Support Site (ALSS)
The primary transhipment point for materiel and personnel destined to and from afloat units. In a NATO operation the ALSS commander reports to the *Multinational Logistic Commander* (MNLC). Daily co-ordination must be conducted with *Forward Logistics Sites (FLS)*. (*JWP 0-01.1*)

Advance Force Operations
Advance operations to prepare an amphibious objective area for the main assault by conducting such operations as *reconnaissance*, seizure of supporting positions, precursor mine countermeasures operations, preliminary bombardment (by *naval gunfire support*), underwater demolitions and air support. Suggest use the AAP 6 Advance Force definition below:

Advance Force
A temporary organisation within the amphibious task force which precedes the main body to the objective area. Its function is to participate in preparing the objective for the main assault by conducting such operations as reconnaissance, seizure of supporting positions, minesweeping, preliminary bombardment, underwater demolitions, and air support.

Advance Operation
Operation in advance of a main force. Advance operations include precursor operations and *advance force operations*. (*JWP 0-01.1*)

Aim (Military)
A single unambiguous military purpose that must be established before a plan can be developed at any level of command for a military operation. (*JWP 0-01.1*)

Airborne Early Warning (AEW).
Air surveillance and control provided by airborne early warning aircraft equipped with search and height finding radar and communications equipment for controlling weapon systems (*AAP6*)

Airhead:
A designated area in a hostile or threatened territory which, when seized and held, ensures the continuous air landing of troops and materiel and provides the manoeuvre space necessary for projected operations. Normally it is the area seized in the assault phase of an airborne operation.

A designated location in an area of operations used as a base for supply and evacuation by air. See also beach-head; bridgehead. (*AAP6*)

Air Interdiction (AI)
An air operation conducted to destroy, neutralize or delay the enemy's military potential before it can be brought to bear effectively against friendly forces at such a distance from friendly forces that detailed integration of each air mission with the fire and movement of friendly forces is not required. (*AAP6*)

Air Superiority
That degree of dominance in the air battle of one force over another which permits the conduct of operations by the former and its related land, sea and air forces at a given time and place without prohibitive interference by the opposing force. (*AAP6*)

Air Supremacy
That degree of air superiority wherein the opposing air force is incapable of effective interference. (*AAP6*)

Amphibious Assault
The principal type of amphibious operation which involves establishing a force on a hostile shore. (*AAP6*)

Amphibious Demonstration
A type of amphibious operation conducted for the purpose of *deceiving* the enemy by show of force, with the expectation of deluding the enemy into a course of action unfavourable to him. (*AAP6*)

Amphibious Feint
A ruse with the purpose of *distracting* the action of an enemy force by posing an amphibious threat to be countered. (*JWP 0-01.1*)

Amphibious Group
A command within the amphibious force, consisting of the commander and his staff, designed to exercise operational command of assigned units in executing all phases of a division-size amphibious operation. (*AAP6*)

Amphibious Objective Area (AOA)
A geographical area, delineated in the initiating directive, for purposes of *command and control* within which is located the objective(s) to be secured by the amphibious task force. This area must be of sufficient size to ensure accomplishment of the amphibious task force's mission and must provide sufficient area for conducting necessary sea, air and land operations. (*AAP6*)

Amphibious Operation
An operation launched from the sea by naval and landing forces against a hostile or potentially hostile shore. (*AAP6*)

Amphibious Raid
A type of amphibious operation involving the swift incursion into or temporary occupation of an objective followed by a planned withdrawal. (*AAP6*).

Amphibious Ready Group (ARG)
A high readiness amphibious force, based around a commando group with supporting joint assets, operating forward in the area of likely employment.

Amphibious Withdrawal
A type of amphibious operation involving the extraction of forces by sea in naval ships or craft from a hostile or potentially hostile shore. (*AAP6*)

Anti-Surface Air Operation
An air operation conducted in an air/sea environment against enemy surface forces. (*AAP6*)

Archipelagic State
An independent state consisting entirely of an archipelago of islands.

Archipelagic Sea-Lanes Passage
Under the terms of the *1982 UNCLOS* Archipelagic States may designate sea lanes and air routes suitable for continuous and expeditious passage of foreign ships and aircraft, in their normal mode of operation (this implying submarines may transit dived), through or over its archipelagic waters and the adjacent territorial sea outward. (***BR 3012***)

Archipelagic Waters
Waters over which an *Archipelagic State* claims increased sovereignty under the ***1982 UNCLOS (BR3012)***

Area Forces
Maritime forces declared to NATO at similar levels of readiness to the force categories of Reaction and *Main Defence Forces*, but not allocated to *Multinational NATO Maritime Forces*.

Area of Influence
A geographical area wherein a commander is directly capable of influencing operations, by *manoeuvre* or fire support systems normally under his command and control. (***AAP6***)

Area of Interest
That area of concern to the commander, including *area of influence*, areas adjacent thereto, and extending into enemy territory to the objectives of current or planned operations. This area also includes areas occupied by enemy forces who could jeopardize the accomplishment of the mission. (***AAP6***)

Armed Suasion
The use of military forces in support of diplomacy to influence the decisions of a government or quasi-governmental authority (such as the leadership of a faction). Suasion can be latent (as in *presence* and general *deterrence*) or active. Active suasion can be supportive (as in *coalition building*) or *coercive* in which case it can seek to *deter* or *compel*.

Armour
Tanks and armoured reconnaissance vehicles.

Assault
See *Amphibious assault*.

Attrition
The reduction of the effectiveness of a force caused by loss of personnel and materiel. (***AAP6***)

Attrition Warfare
A style of warfare characterized by the application of substantial combat power that reduces an enemy's ability to fight through loss of personnel and equipment. Essentially it aims at the physical destruction of the enemy. (***JWP 0-01.1***) (Contrasted with *manoeuvre warfare* in a debate that began during the First World War and has continued into the latter part of the 20th Century.)

Augmentation Force (AF)
Any force designated by a nation to strengthen its national forces. (*AAP6*)

B

Balanced Fleet
A naval force that can be generated and sustained with a full range of capabilities for such independent (unilateral) strategic and operational action as is envisaged in defence policy and national military strategy. (*JWP 0-01.1*)

Balanced Force
A military force that has all the necessary capabilities to carry out a particular *mission* without unnecessary redundancy. (*JWP 0-01.1*)

Balance of Advantage
The qualitative advantage of a force over an opposing force taking into account quantity, quality and categories of capability. (*JWP 0-01.1*) See *exchange ratio*.

Battle Damage Assessment
The timely and accurate estimate of damage resulting from the application of military force, either lethal or non-lethal, against a pre-determined objective assessment. (*JP 1-02*)

Battleforce
A force comprising several *battlegroups*. A battleforce is typically a three star command and equates in NATO Reaction Force parlance to a NATO *Expanded Task Force*.

Battlegroup
A standing naval task group consisting of a carrier, surface combatants, and submarines, operating in mutual support with the task of destroying hostile submarine, surface, and air forces within the group's assigned area of responsibility and striking at targets along hostile shore lines or projecting fire power inland. (*JP 1-02*) (Note that *JWP 0-01.1* has a UK Army definition)

Battlespace
All aspects of air, surface, subsurface, land, space and the electromagnetic spectrum that encompass the area of operations. (*JWP 01-1.1*)

Battlespace, Influence over the
See *influence over the battlespace*.

Battlespace Dominance
The degree of control over the dimensions of the *battlespace* that enhances friendly freedom of action and denies the enemy freedom of action. It permits *power projection* and force sustainment to accomplish the full range of potential missions. (*JWP 01-1.1* and *US NDP1*)

Beachhead
A designated area on a hostile, or potentially hostile, shore which, when seized and held, provides for the continuous landing of troops and materiel, and provides *manoeuvring* space required for subsequent projected operations ashore. (*AAP6*)

Benign Application
The use of armed forces solely for the capabilities not directly associated with combat that they can provide. The expression is used more broadly to mean a *combat* operation carried out to prevent access to, or departure from the coast or waters of a hostile state.

Blockade
A legal definition is "An operation intended to disrupt the enemy's economy by preventing ships of all nations from entering or leaving specified coastal areas under the occupation and control of the enemy. Blockade is an act of war and the right to establish it is granted to belligerents under the traditional laws of war. This law requires, inter alia, that the blockade must be effective, that it is to be declared by the belligerent so that all interested parties know of its existence and that it is confined to ports or coasts occupied by the enemy".

'Blue on Blue' Engagement
(colloquial) Incident involving casualties caused by friendly fire.

Branch (in operational planning)
A contingency plan or option built into a plan for changing the disposition, orientation, or direction of movement of forces, and also for accepting or declining battle (*US FM100-5*). A form of "what if?".

C

Campaign
A sequence of planned, resourced and executed military *operations* designed to achieve a strategic *objective* within a given time and area, usually involving the *synchronization* of maritime, land and air forces (*AJP1 (A)*). Campaigns may be *sequential* or *cumulative*. The orchestration of campaigns is the business of the *operational commander*.

Carrier Air Group (CAG)
Two or more aircraft squadrons formed under one commander for administrative and tactical control of operations from a carrier.(*AAP6*)

Carrier Group
Task group or *battlegroup* whose core is a carrier and whose function is principally to deliver carrier capabilities.

Catastrophic Damage
The sudden loss of a substantial collection of resources and capabilities, such as the sinking of a major warship.

Centre of Gravity
Characteristics, capabilities or localities from which a nation, an alliance, a military force or other grouping derives its freedom of action, physical strength or will to fight. (*AAP6*)

Civil War
War conducted largely within the boundaries of a state in which a significant part of the population is associated with opposing sides. One or both sides may have external help.

Close Air Support (CAS)
Air action against hostile targets which are in close proximity to friendly forces and which require detailed integration of each air mission with the fire and movement of those forces. (*AAP6*)

Close Blockade
A *blockade* that denies an enemy access to or from his ports. See *distant blockade*.

Close Escort
Escort of shipping where the escorting force is in company with escorted shipping and can provide a measure of direct defence.

Close Operations
Operations conducted at short range, in close contact and in an immediate timescale. (*JWP 01-1.1*)

Coalition Building
Military action in support of diplomacy to further the building of an ad hoc coalition by providing reassurance, evidence of support and, perhaps, the opportunity for military meetings in theatre.

Coercion
The use of force, or the threat of force to persuade an opponent to adopt a certain pattern of behaviour, against his wishes. (*JWP 01-1.1*)

Collateral Damage
Damage to personnel and property adjacent to, but not forming part of, an authorised target. (*JWP 01-1.1*)

Combat
Military combat is a contest in which the parties attempt to achieve mutually incompatible aims through the organized use of *violence* by armed forces.

Combat Air Patrol (CAP)
An aircraft patrol provided over an objective area, over the force protected, over the critical area of a combat zone, or over an air defence area, for the purpose of intercepting and destroying hostile aircraft before they reach their target. (*AAP6*) Patrols by fighter aircraft over an objective area, a force to be protected, over the critical area of a combat zone or over an air defence area for the purpose of intercepting and destroying hostile aircraft before they reach their targets. (*AP 3000*)

Combat Power
The total means of destructive and/or disruptive force which a military unit/formation can apply against the opponent at a given time. (*AAP6*)

Combat Service Support (CSS)
The support provided to combat forces, primarily in the fields of administration and logistics. (*AAP6*)

Combat Support Air Operations
Air operations designed to enhance or support the effectiveness of air, surface and sub-surface combat forces. (*AP3000*)

Combined
Between two or more forces or agencies of two or more allies (*AAP6*). The expressions "combined forces" and "combined operations" imply that the command and control of allied forces is integrated. (The term 'multinational' is preferred within the UK and Allied joint communities) See *co-ordination; concertation; integration;* and *multinational*.

Combined Joint Task Force (CJTF)
A multinational multi-service task force. The CJTF Headquarters Concept provides for deployable multinational multi-service headquarters of variable size formed to command and control CJTFs of NATO and possibly non-NATO nations. A CJTF HQ could also be deployed for WEU led operations.

Command
The authority vested in an individual of the armed forces for the direction, co-ordination and control of military forces (*AAP6*). See *full command*.

Command and Control (C2)
Expression used to mean:

The processes through which a *commander exercises command (whether full or operational* or *tactical command*) or *operational* or *tactical control* to organize, direct and co-ordinate the activities of the forces allocated to him.

The structures and systems through which these processes are exercised. A command, control, (communications) and information system (C3I) is an integrated system comprising *doctrine*, procedures, organizational structure, personnel, equipment, facilities, and communications, which provides authorities at all levels with timely and adequate data to plan, direct and control their activities. (*AJP1(A)*).

Command and Control Warfare (C2W)
The integrated use of all military capabilities including operations security (OPSEC), deception, psychological operations (PSYOPs), electronic warfare (EW) and physical destruction, supported by all-source intelligence and Communications and Information Systems (CIS) to deny information to, influence, degrade, or destroy an adversary's C2 capabilities while protecting friendly capabilities against similar actions. (NATO) (*JWP 01-1.1*)

Commander Allied Joint Force (COMAJF)
In NATO the commander appointed by a MNC or MSC to mount and sustain an Allied operation and to exercise OPCON of all the forces assigned to the operation.

Commander's Appreciation of the Situation
The classical British expression for what has come to be known in combined and joint parlance as the *Commander's Estimate of the Situation*.

Commander's Estimate of the Situation
A formal analysis of the situation, mission, enemy and own courses of action conducted in preparation for forming a *commander's intentions* and *concept of operations*.

Commander's Intent
A concise expression of the purpose of a *campaign* or *operation*,

the desired results and how operations will progress towards achieving the desired end-state. At the tactical level, the Commander's Intent should be focused on the effect that he wishes to achieve on the enemy. (*JWP 01-1.1*)

Commando
A Royal *Marines* formation of battalion size with combat support and *combat service support*.

Command of the Sea
The ability to use the sea in its entirety for one's own purposes at any time and to deny its use to an adversary. (*JWP 01-1.1*)

Command Post Exercise (CPX)
An exercise in which the forces are simulated, involving the commander, his staff and communications within and between headquarters. (*AAP6*)

Compel/Compellance
The *coercive* use of armed forces to persuade a government by the threat or isolated use of combat to desist from a course of action. (*JWP 01-1.1*)

Component Commander
The commander of the maritime, ground, air, or other component of a *Joint Task Force* (UK national) or *Combined Joint Task Force* (NATO/WEU) and reporting to the *Joint Task Force Commander* or *Combined Joint Task Force Commander* respectively.

Concept of Operations
A clear and concise statement of the line of action chosen by a commander in order to accomplish his mission. (AAP6)

Concerted Multinational Operations (basic co-operation)
Operations in which forces of more than one friendly or allied nation are operating in the same theatre but without formal arrangements to co-ordinate operations or an integrated command structure. They co-operate to the extent that mutual interference may be minimized, information may be exchanged and some logistic support and mutual training offered.

Conditions for Success
The situation and state of affairs that must pertain if a military campaign or operation can be considered successful. The conditions may be *military conditions* which are normally expressed as control of the environment, or may be non-military such as the decision of a hostile government to desist from action. (*JWP 01-1.1*) See *end state*.

Conflict
A situation in which violence becomes a possibility in the external relations between nations or violence is threatened or used within a state's borders between competing groups for political reasons beyond levels that might be controlled by levels of civilian policing that are normal for that state.

Conflict Prevention
Activities normally conducted under Chapter VI of the UN Charter, ranging from diplomatic initiatives to preventative deployments of forces intended to prevent disputes from escalating into armed conflicts or from spreading. Conflict prevention can include fact finding missions, consultation, warnings, inspections and monitoring. (*JWP 01-1.1*)

Consolidation
The replenishment of organic *logistic* shipping by freighting vessels.

Constabulary Application
The use of military forces to uphold a national or international law, mandate or regime in a manner in which minimum violence is only used in enforcement as a last resort and after evidence of a breach or intent to defy has been established beyond reasonable doubt. The level and type of violence that is permitted will frequently be specified in the law, mandate or regime that is being enforced. Also called policing.

Containment:
Military containment: The geographical restriction of the freedom of action of enemy forces.

Crisis containment: Measures to limit the geographical spread of a crisis.

Containment as grand strategy: Measures taken to limit the geographic spread of an ideology or the influence of a power.

Containment by Distraction
Containment achieved by posing so great a threat to an enemy in one area (particularly in home waters or close to critical interests) that enemy forces are retained in defence allowing friendly forces elsewhere to be unmolested.

Contiguous Zone
A belt of high seas immediately adjacent to the territorial sea and extending to a distance not more than 12 miles from the baseline of the territorial sea. (*BR 3012*)

Continental Shelf
Comprises an area of the sea bed and the sub-soil adjacent to the coast but beyond the territorial sea in which the coastal state has sovereign rights for the purpose of exploration and exploitation of the natural resources. (*BR 3012*)

Contingency Forces
Forces required to undertake *Military Tasks* to fulfil UK *Defence Roles* other than: those forces permanently stationed at home and abroad; and, those additional forces that would be *regenerated* and/or *reconstituted* in the event of general war. (*JWP 01-1.1*)

Control:
That authority exercised by a commander over part of the activities of subordinate organizations, or other organizations not normally under his command, which encompasses the responsibility for implementing orders or directives. All or part of this authority may be transferred or delegated. (*AAP6*)

The process through which the commander organizes, directs and co-ordinates the activities of the forces allocated to him.

Military control (of the environment) is the condition in which one protagonist has freedom of action to use one or more *warfare environments* (land, sea, air, space or electro-magnetic spectrum) for his purposes and to deny its use to an opponent. See *sea control; control of the air*.

Authority which may be less than full command exercised by a commander and part of the activities of subordinate or other organisations. (*ATP1C Gloss 5*)

Control of the Air
The three degrees of control of the air are: *favourable air situation*; *air superiority*; and *air supremacy*. (*AP 3000*)

Convoying
The aggregation of shipping to be protected into groups to reduce losses through enemy action, to make best use of protective forces and to increase losses of enemy attacking forces.

Co-operation, Multinational Operations Under Basic
See *concerted multinational operations*.

Co-ordinated Multinational Operations
Operations in which participating friendly or allied nations share objectives to the extent that formal arrangements can be made to

apportion tasks or areas of responsibility and to provide mutual assistance. However there is no integrated command structure.

Counter-Air Operations
Operations to achieve and maintain the required degree of *control of the air*.

Counter-Insurgency Operations
Military operations carried out to complement those political, economic, psychological and civic actions necessary to defeat an armed *insurgency* and thereby sustain an existing government's authority. (*ADPVol 1*)

Counter-Terrorism
Measures taken to prevent, deter, and respond to terrorism. (*US FM 100-5*)

Crisis
A situation, which may or may not be foreseen, which threatens national security or interests or international peace and stability, and which requires decision and action. (*JWP 01-1.1*)

Crisis Management
The co-ordinated actions taken to defuse crises, prevent their escalation into an armed conflict and contain hostilities if they should result. (*AAP6*)

Crisis Prevention
Diplomatic, economic and, on occasion, military measures to modify the causes of a potential crisis and prevent its onset. (*JWP 01-1.1*)

Culminating Point
An operation reaches its culminating point when the current operation can just be maintained but not developed to any greater advantage. (*JWP 01-1.1*)

Cumulative Campaign
A campaign the outcome of which is the result of the cumulative effect of a number of independent actions.
See *sequential campaign*.

D

Deception
Those measures designed to mislead *the enemy* by manipulation, distortion, or falsification of evidence to induce *him* to react in a manner prejudicial to his interests. (*AAP6*)

Decisive Points
Those actions, the successful completion of which are preconditions to the elimination of the enemy's centre of gravity. Decisive points are the key to unlocking the enemy's centre of gravity. (*AAP6*)

Deep Operations
Operations conducted against forces or resources not engaged in close operations. They expand the battle area in time and space, help to shape the close battle, make it difficult for the enemy to concentrate combat power without loss, and diminish the coherence and tempo of his operations. (*JWP 01-1.1*)

De-Escalation
A decrease in the level of extent of *violence* during *hostilities*. See *escalation*.

Defence Diplomacy
To provide forces to meet the varied activities undertaken by the MOD to dispel hostility, build and maintain trust and assist in the development of democratically accountable armed forces, thereby making a significant contribution to conflict prevention and resolution. (***SDR White Paper***)

Defence in Depth
The siting of mutually supporting defence positions designed to absorb and progressively weaken attack, prevent initial observations of the whole position by the enemy, and to allow the commander to manoeuvre his reserve. (*AAP6*)

Defensive Operation
Operation in which forces await for the approach of the enemy before attacking.

Demarche
Formal request or statement of policy or opinion issued through diplomatic channels by a government alliance, coalition or group of nations.

Demobilization Operations
In the context of *peace support operations*, the controlled withdrawal, demobilization and rehabilitation of belligerents. They might include *cantonment* of belligerents' vessels.

Demonstration
An attack or show of force on a front where a decision is not sought, made with the aim of deceiving the enemy. (*AAP6*)

Deterrence
The convincing of a potential aggressor that the consequences of coercion or armed conflict would outweigh the potential gains. This requires the maintenance of a credible military capability and strategy with the clear political will to act. (***AAP6***)

Directive:
A military communication in which policy is established or a specific action is ordered.

A plan issued with a view to putting it into effect when so directed, or in the event that a stated contingency arises.

Broadly speaking, any communication which initiates or governs action, conduct, or procedure. (***JWP 0-1.1***)

Dislocation
To dislocate is to deny another party the ability to bring his strengths to bear, or to persuade him that his strength is irrelevant. (***JWP 01-1.1***)

Disruption
Use of force to shatter the cohesion of a military formation and prevent it from functioning effectively in combat. (***JWP 01-1.1***)

Distant Blockade
A *blockade* that denies the enemy passage through a sea area through which all ships must pass in order to reach the enemy's territory.

Distant Escort
Escort of shipping where the protective forces are not sufficiently close to provide a measure of direct defence but effect protection by *deterrence* through the threat of reprisals.

Distraction:

Situation in which an enemy is unable to concentrate forces in a time and place of his choosing because of the threat of attack elsewhere. (***JWP 01-1.1***)
Measures taken to offer alternative targets to a weapons control or missile homing system so that a false target is selected. (***ATP1C***)

Doctrine
Fundamental principles by which the military forces guide their actions in support of objectives. It is authoritative but requires judgement in application. (***AAP6***)

E

Echelonment
The organization of formations at each level of command from lower level formations. (*JWP 01-1.1*) Echelonment of maritime forces is very flexible and makes use of *functional* or *task organization*.

Economy of Force Operation
A *distractive* or *defensive* maritime operation using modest resources so as to concentrate force for the main effort. Sometimes called a *holding operation* when associated with an offensive manoeuvre. (*JWP 01-1.1*)

Elan
Offensive spirit. Ardour.

Electronic Warfare
Military action to exploit the electromagnetic spectrum for the purposes of combat. (*ATP1C*) Military action to exploit the electromagnetic spectrum encompassing: the search for, interception and identification of electromagnetic emissions, the employment of electromagnetic energy, including directed energy, to reduce or prevent hostile use of the electromagnetic spectrum, and actions to ensure its effective use by friendly forces. (*AAP6*)

Embargo
A prohibition on the entry or egress of shipping into a port. Nowadays frequently used for prohibitions of certain categories of cargo such as munitions. (*JWP 01-1.1*)

Embroilment
Military embroilment is the involvement of forces in *conflict* at a level of *violence* that is greater than that for which they are equipped or prepared or that envisaged in their strategic *directive*.

End-State
That state of affairs which needs to be achieved at the end of a campaign either to terminate or resolve the conflict on favourable terms. The end state should be established prior to execution. (*JWP 01-1.1*)

Endurance
See *sustainability*   The time an aircraft can continue flying, or a ground vehicle or ship can continue operating, under specified conditions e.g. without refuelling. (*AAP6*)

Envelopment/Envelop
An offensive *manoeuvre* in which the main attacking force passes

around or over the enemy's principal defensive position to secure objectives in the rear. (*AAP6*)

Escalation/de-escalation
A qualitative transformation in the character of a conflict where the scope and intensity increases or decreases, transcending limits implicitly accepted by both sides. (***JWP 01-1.1***)   See *vertical escalation, horizontal escalation, qualitative escalation* and *prolongation*.

Escort:
A method of protection of shipping short of the establishment of full *sea control* in which protection is achieve primarily by the *deterrent* presence of protective forces.

Colloquial generic expression for a destroyer or frigate.

Exchange Ratio
The numerical ratio of friendly to enemy forces taking into account quantity, quality and categories of capability. See *balance of advantage*.

Exclusive Economic Zone (EEZ)
The zone of sea around a state over which it has exclusive rights under international law to exploit economic resources. (***JWP 01-1.1***)

Expeditionary Forces
Forces projected from the home base capable of sustained operations at distance from that home base. (***JWP 01-1.1***)

Expeditionary Operations
Military operations which can be initiated at short notice, consisting of forward deployed, or rapidly deployable, self-sustaining forces tailored to achieve a clearly stated objective in a foreign country. (See *maritime expeditionary forces; power projection*)

Extended Fisheries Zone (EFZ)
A zone declared for fisheries management purposes beyond the limit of the Territorial Sea but within what would be the permissible limits of the *exclusive economic zone* if the state were to declare one. The UK does not as yet have an *EEZ* but has had an *EFZ* since the 1 January 1977.

F

Fast Dash Role
The use of a United Kingdom carrier in an amphibious role to carry elements of a landing force, and assault helicopters as the principal component of the carrier air group.

Favourable Air Situation
An air situation in which the extent of air effort applied by the enemy air forces is insufficient to prejudice the success of friendly land, sea or air operations. (*JWP 01-1.1*)

Feint   (see *amphibious feint*)

Fighting Instructions
Classified publication containing Royal Navy operational and tactical doctrine.

Fire Support
The application of fire, co-ordinated with the manoeuvre of forces, to destroy, neutralize or suppress the enemy. (*AAP6*)

Flag Staff
The staff supporting a flag officer, who may be embarked at sea or based at a shore headquarters.

Fleet in Being
The use of options provided by the continued existence of one's own fleet to constrain the enemy's options in the use *of* his.

Fog of War
Uncertainty and confusion generated in wartime by a combination of limited, incomplete, inaccurate and contradictory information, deliberate deception and the mayhem and stress caused by combat. From Clausewitz' *On War*.

Force Generation
The process of providing suitably trained and equipped forces, and their means of deployment, recovery and sustainment to meet all current and potential future tasks, within required readiness and preparation times. (*JWP 01-1.1*)

Force Packaging
The process by which elements of those forces delivered by Force Generation are combined into a coherent, mission orientated, joint force in order to conduct a specific operation or campaign. (*MCJO Sub-Concept Paper*)

Force Projection
See *power projection* and *maritime force projection*.

Force Protection
Process which aims to conserve the fighting potential of the deployed force by countering the wider threat to all its elements

from adversary, natural and human hazards, and fratricide. (*JWP 01-1.1*)

Forward Line of Own Troops (FLOT)
A line which indicates the most forward positions of friendly forces in any kind of military operation at a specific time (*AAP6*). Primarily used in land operations.

Forward Logistics Site (FLS)
Normally the final land transhipment point for *materiel* and personnel which provides a bridge between an *Advanced Logistic Support Site* (*ALSS*) and the sea. (*JWP 01-1.1*) It will be linked to the ALSS by intra-theatre airlift. In a NATO operation the FLS commander reports directly to the *Multinational Logistic Commander* (*MNLC*). Daily co-ordination with the ALSS commander must be conducted.

Forward Presence
Strategic choice to maintain forces deployed at distance from the home base or stationed overseas to demonstrate national resolve, strengthen alliances, dissuade potential adversaries, and enhance the ability to respond quickly to contingencies. (*JWP 01-1.1*)

Fratricide
The accidental destruction of own, allied or friendly forces. A result of what is colloquially known as a *'blue on blue' engagement*. (*JWP 01-1.1*)

Freedom of Navigation (FON) Operations
Operations of *naval diplomacy* designed to challenge an attempt to restrict free use of the seas by the passage of combat forces. FON operations may be *symbolic* or *coercive*. (*JWP 01-1.1*)

Friction
Features of war that resist all action, make the simple difficult, and the difficult seemingly impossible. Friction may be mental (such as indecision) or physical (such as enemy fire). It may be extremely imposed by enemy action, geography or the weather, or self induced through a poor plan or clash of personalities (*ADP Vol 1*). The expression was used by Clausewitz in *On War*.

Full Command
The military authority and responsibility of a superior officer to issue orders to subordinates. It covers every aspect of military operations and *administration* and exists only within national Services (*AAP6*). In the UK full command is exercised by the single Service commanders (eg CINCFLEET) who report to the

United Kingdom Government through the Chief of the Defence Staff. See *administrative authority*.

Functional Organization
Command organization for maritime forces reflecting the functions, missions or tasks of the component elements. See *type organization*.

G

General War
A conflict between major powers in which their large and vital national interests, perhaps even survival, are at stake. (*JWP 01-1.1*)

Goal
An expression of broad meaning embracing *aim, mission, objective*, and purpose.

Grand Strategic Level
The level of command and planning for armed conflict (*level of war*) at which all national resources diplomatic, economic, military, political, informational and technological) are applied to achieve national security policy objectives.

Guerre de Course
A campaign consisting of attacks on enemy shipping.

Gunboat Diplomacy
Colloquial expression for *naval diplomacy*.

H

Handling Point 1 (HP1)
United Kingdom Logistics Start Point (such as a Naval Base, Royal Logistics Corps base, RAF Transport Command Air Station or UK commercial port).

Harmonization (of ROE)
The process whereby the *rules of engagement* of more than one national taking part in a *multi-national* operation are compared and altered where possible to achieve similar levels of permission and prohibition through the various national systems.

High Seas
All parts of the sea which are not included in the *territorial seas* or *internal waters* of States. All states have the freedom to navigate or conduct other activities, subject to certain restrictions, on the high seas. Where states have declared other zones beyond the terri-

torial sea (*contiguous zone, exclusive economic zone, continental shelf*) the traditional high seas freedoms are affected by the rights that coastal states can exercise in such zones.

Holding Area
Area of sea occupied by surface forces with a stationary speed of advance.

Holding Operation
See *economy of force operation*.

Horizontal Escalation
Escalation by extension of combat into new geographic areas or environments. (***JWP 01-1.1***)

Host Nation Support (HNS)
Civil and military assistance rendered in peace, crisis and war by a host nation to allied forces and NATO organizations which are located on or in transit through the host nation's territory. (***AAP6***).

Hostilities
Period between the onset of regular *combat* between parties and any cease fire or truce.

I

Immediate Reaction Forces (IRF)
NATO forces held routinely at the highest readiness. The *Standing Naval Forces* are maritime IRF.

Infiltration
A technique and process in which a force moves as individuals or small groups over, through or around enemy positions without detection.(***AAP6***)

Influence over the Battlespace
One of the *operational functions*. It describes the moulding of the situation in and around the operating area in order to prevent enemy action from *disrupting* the operation. Influence is achieved by a combination of *command and control warfare*, control of the electromagnetic *spectrum*, *interdiction* of enemy forces, and a responsive and agile force capable of acting faster than the enemy.

Innocent Passage
Defined as navigation through the *territorial sea* of a State for the purpose of either traversing that sea without entering *internal waters,* or of proceeding in either direction between the high seas

and internal waters. Vessels have the right to take innocent passage through *territorial seas* without interference by the coastal States concerned.

Insurgency
An organised movement aimed at the overthrow of a constituted government through use of subversion and armed conflict. (*AAP6*)

Integrated Military Structure (IMS)
See *NATO Integrated Military Structure (NIMS)*.

Integrated Multinational Operation
Operation in which forces of two or more nations operate under a *unified* command structure. Only integrated operations are truly combined. (*JWP 01-1.1*)

Interdiction
Actions to divert, disrupt, or destroy the enemy before he can affect friendly forces. (*JWP 01-1.1*)

Internal Conflict
Situation in which *violence* is threatened or used within a state's borders between competing groups for political reasons beyond levels that might be controlled by levels of civilian policing that are normal for that state. (*JWP 01-1.1*)

Internal Waters
All waters actually within the territory of a State such as harbours, rivers and lakes; together with all other waters to landward of the baseline from which the State's *territorial sea* is measured. They are an integral part of the territory of the State and in them the laws of the land are supreme.

International Strait
Considered to be a route which is used for international navigation which either connects one part of the *high seas* with another, or passes between one part of the high seas and the *territorial sea* of a State. Where there is no similarly convenient alternative route, the United Kingdom recognizes certain rights including unimpeded passage through international straits even where these pass through States' territorial seas.

Interoperability
The ability of systems, units or forces to provide services to and accept services from other systems, units or forces and to use these services so exchanged to enable them to operate effectively together. (*AAP6*)

Intervention
A *campaign* or *operation* with limited objectives, involving the entry of another state where opposition is expected. (*JWP 01-1.1*)

J

Joint
Connotes *activities*, operations, organizations etc in which elements of more than one Service of the same nation participate. (*AAP6*)

Joint Commander (Jt Comd)
The Joint Commander, appointed by CDS, exercises the highest level of operational command (OPCOM) of forces assigned with specific responsibility for deployment, sustainment and recovery. (*JWP 0-01.1*)

Joint Force Air Component Commander (JFACC)
The JFACC is responsible for planning, co-ordination and tasking of air missions to meet the *Commander Allied Joint Forces' (COMAJF')* objectives. (*AJP1(A)*). In national terms he would be responsible to the JTFC.

Joint Task Force Commander (JTFC)
The operational commander of a nominated joint force. (*JWP 0-01.1*)

Joint Task Force Headquarters (JTFHQ)
A purely national deployable joint headquarters of variable size commanded at the operational level by a Joint Task Force Commander. (*JWP 0-01.1*)

Joint Headquarters (JHQ)
A tri-Service staff organized on functional lines responsible for the planning and exercise of operational command of forces assigned to joint, potentially joint and multinational operations. (*JWP 0-01.1*)

Joint Operations Area (JOA)
An area of land, sea and airspace, defined by a strategic or a regional commander, co-ordinated with nations and approved by the North Atlantic Council or Military Committee, as appropriate, and in accordance with the agreed NATO's Operational Planning Architecture, in which a designated subordinate joint commander plans and conducts military operations to accomplish a specific

mission at the operational level of war. A Joint Operations Area and its defining parameters, such as time, scope and geographic area, is contingency/mission-specific and may overlap Areas Of Responsibility. NATO (*JWP 0-01.1*)

Joint Services Command and Staff College
The UK armed forces staff college was established in 1997 at Bracknell and is due to move to a purpose built building at Shrivenham in 2000. It is a combination of the former Joint Service Defence College at Greenwich, the RN Staff College at Greenwich, the Army Staff College at Camberley and the RAF Staff College at Bracknell. All UK armed forces staff training is now conducted on a joint basis at the JSCSC, including the Higher Command and Staff Course for those likely to fill higher joint command and staff posts.

Joint Theatre Plans
Contingency plans for specific crisis operations in various parts of the world (*JWP 0-01.1*).

L

Land Attack Missile
Submarine, surface ship, or naval air launched missile capable of engaging land targets.

Layered Defence
The disposition of protective assets possessing a mixture of anti-submarine, anti-surface and anti-air capabilities in layers of screens and patrol areas about units of high value or crucial waters.

Levels of Warfare (war)
The recognized levels of warfare from which the levels for the planning and command of operations are derived. They are *grand strategic, military strategic, operational* and *tactical*. (*JWP 0-01.1*)

Leverage (military)
Disproportionate strategic or operational advantage gained by the use of a form of military power to exploit its geographical circumstances.

Lift
The capability to move resources between two points. (*JWP 01-1.1*)

Limited War
War waged towards limited *war aims*, and/or in a limited geographical area and/or employing limits on means and methods of fighting. It is a phrase that came into currency after the Second World War to distinguish limited wars from the type of general war that was experienced between 1939-45. It also came to imply a restriction on means, in particular the non-use of nuclear weapons.

Linear Operation
Operation planned to proceed along a physical *line of operation*. (***JWP 01-1.1***)

Lines of Communications (LOC)
All the land, water and air routes that connect an operating military force with one or more bases of operations and along which supplies and reinforcements move (AAP6). See *line of support*, and *sea lines of communications (SLOC)*.

Line of Operation:
(US Army) A directional orientation that connects the force with its base of operations and its objective. (***FM 100-5***)

(UK) The link between decisive points in time and space on the path to the centre of gravity. (***JWP 01-1.1***)

Line of Support
A route (sea, land and air) that connects an operating military force with a logistics base and along which supplies move.

Littoral Region
Coastal sea areas and that portion of the land which is susceptible to influence or support from the sea. (***JWP 0-01.1***)

Lodgement Area
Following the invasion of a hostile coast and the establishment of a bridgehead ashore, the operations of invading forces are directed to the seizure of a lodgement area. This is an area which comprises adequate port, airfield and communications facilities and sufficient space for the assembly and maintenance of the total forces destined to take part in the campaign. (***JWP 0-01.1***)

Logistics
The science of planning and carrying out the movement and maintenance of forces. In its most comprehensive sense, those aspects of military operations which deal with:

- design and development, acquisition, storage, transport,

- distribution, maintenance, evacuation and disposition of materiel;
- transport of personnel;
- acquisition, construction, maintenance, operation and disposition of facilities;
- acquisition or furnishing of services.
- medical and health service support (AAP6)

M

Main Defence Forces (MDF)

Active and mobilisation capable NATO components which are assigned to MNCs/MSCs as appropriate in order to dissuade coercion, deter attack and defend against aggression.(***JWP 01-1.1***)

Main Effort

A concentration of forces or means, in a particular area, where a commander seeks to bring about a decision. (***JWP 01-1.1***) See *economy of force* and *holding operations*.

Major NATO Commander (MNC)

The highest level of NATO military command beneath the Military Committee. The two MNCs are the Supreme Allied Commander, Europe (SACEUR), and the Supreme Allied Commander, Atlantic (SACLANT).

Major Subordinate Commander (MSC)

Level of NATO military command directly subordinate to a *Major NATO Commander*. The Commander-in-Chief Eastern Atlantic Area (CINCEASTLANT) whose headquarters is at Northwood, Middlesex, is a MSC.

Mal-deployment

Force posture that is strategically or operationally disadvantageous in the pertaining circumstances. (***JWP 01-1.1***)

Manoeuvre:

A movement to place ships or aircraft in a position of advantage over the enemy

A tactical exercise carried out at sea, in the air, on the ground or on a map in imitation of war.

The operation of a ship, aircraft or vehicle to cause it to perform a desired movement.

The employment of force on the battlefield through movement in combination with fire, or fire potential, to achieve a position of advantage in respect to the enemy in order to accomplish the mission. (*AAP6*)

Manoeuvre Warfare
Manoeuvre Warfare is a war-fighting philosophy that seeks to defeat the enemy by shattering his moral and physical cohesion - his ability to fight as an effective, co-ordinated whole - rather than by destroying him physically through incremental attrition. (*JWP 01-1.1*) Capital initial letters are used in this publication to distinguish *Manoeuvre Warfare* from *manoeuvre* above.

Manoeuvrist
A term describing an approach that employs the principles of Manoeuvre Warfare.

Maritime Campaign
A connected series of operations conducted essentially by maritime forces including surface, subsurface, air forces and amphibious troops, for the purpose of gaining, extending, or maintaining control of the sea for power projection.

Maritime Component Commander
The Maritime Component Commander is an officer subordinate to the Joint Force Commander responsible for maritime operational advice to him and the tactical employment of assigned *maritime forces*. See *component commander*.

Maritime Domain
The series of jurisdictional zones that surrounds the coast of a state. It includes territorial seas and the *Exclusive Economic Zone*.

Maritime Exclusion Zone
Declaration by a state of sea areas, including parts of the high seas in which conditions are imposed on the passage of ship and aircraft.(*BR3012*)

Maritime Expeditionary Forces
A self-sustaining forward deployed joint maritime force which demonstrates UK interest with its physical presence and latent power. Operating from international waters, the joint maritime force is free of political and economic encumbrances, and independent of overseas bases or host nation support, which may not be accessible due to domestic or international concerns. (See also *expeditionary operations*)

Maritime Forces
Forces whose primary purpose is to conduct military operations at

and from the sea. The expression includes warships and submarines, *auxiliaries, Ships Taken Up From Trade, organic* aircraft, fixed seabed installations, fixed shore installations (such as batteries) for the defence of seaways, shore based maritime aircraft and other shore based aircraft permanently assigned to maritime tasks.

Maritime Force Projection
The ability to project, sustain and apply effective military force from the sea, at global range, in order to influence (effect) events on land. (***MCJO Sub Concept Paper***)

Maritime Power Projection (MPP)
See *power projection*.

Maritime Superiority
The capability of a state to establish *sea control* at will in any area of importance to that state.

Materiel
The stores and equipment (as opposed to personnel) available or required for an undertaking. (***JWP 01-1.1***)

Mexeflote
Large, powered pontoon capable of offloading heavy stores from amphibious shipping.

Military Aid to Civil Authorities (MACA)
This is a legal doctrine forming a part of the UK's constitutional and administrative law that regulates the domestic use of armed forces and maintains democratic and civil authority control of them when they are employed within the UK's domestic jurisdiction (including the *maritime domain*) The collective term covers three categories of activity: MACC, MACM and MACP. Each of these categories is defined below:

Military Aid to Civil Ministries (MACM)
The use of armed forces personnel to ensure the continued provision of essential services during industrial disputes. Personnel employed on such duties are invariably unarmed; if protection is required it is either provided by the civil power itself (the police) or, in exceptional circumstances (eg during the Ulster Workers Council strike in Northern Ireland in 1974) by other armed forces personnel who are deployed in an MACP role. MACM is not a common means of employing the armed forces in the *maritime domain*, the only real instance being the provision of essential transport to outlying islands in the Western Isles during seamen's strikes in the 1950s and 1960s. In recent years, the annual ***Statement on***

the Defence Estimates has often referred to the RN's fishery protection effort as a form of assistance to civil ministries. However, this use of the phrase in these policy documents is a descriptive one, referring to the RN's support to the fisheries ministries for law enforcement purposes, in which the use of force cannot be ruled out. It should not be confused with the legal meaning of MACM, which is very precise and exclusively to do with essential services provision during industrial action. The distinction is a vital one because personnel employed on MACM are emphatically not to be armed, whereas those employed on law enforcement activities (MACP) may, in certain circumstances, have to resort to armed force.

Military aid to the Civil Power (MACP)

The use of armed forces personnel to aid the civil power in the maintenance of law and order and the enforcement of law within the domestic jurisdiction. It is most often associated with the type of support provided by all three Services to the RUC in Northern Ireland since 1969. However, it extends also to such maritime activities as drug interdiction operations (in support of Customs and Excise) and fishery protection, the UK's longest running and permanent example of MACP, in which the RN provides support to the UK's fisheries ministries to enforce fisheries law in the EFZ (since 1977) and in the inshore fisheries zone (since 1964).

Military Application

Applications of armed force in which *combat* is used or threatened, or in which combat potential is a prerequisite for success.

Military Assistance:

Training, advice. and other forms of assistance rendered by a government through its military services to another government in the process of developing and/or improving the operational performance of its armed forces.

In the context of peace *support operations*, all forms of mandated military assistance rendered to a foreign civil authority including the supervision of a transfer of power, reforming security forces, and developing or supporting civil infrastructure facilities.

Military Assistance to the Civil Community (MACC)

The use of unarmed Servicemen to provide assistance to the community. This includes help in natural disasters and emergencies (search and rescue operations, for example). However, it can also be of a more routine nature and, in the *maritime domain*, includes the provision of hydrographic surveying and the provision of explosive ordnance disposal assistance to the fishing community, who still from time to time haul up First and Second World War mines in their nets.

Military Condition
A description of the degree of *military control* in a theatre possessed by protagonists in the five *warfare environments* of land, sea, air, space and the electronic spectrum. A primary planning task of an *operational commander* during *hostilities* is to define the military conditions that will achieve his given strategic *objectives*.

Military Containment See *containment*

Military Exclusion Zone (MEZ)
Geographical (usually maritime) area including parts of the high seas within which a government states its intention to enforce the exclusion of all military units of a designated nation or nations or other grouping, using force if necessary. See *maritime exclusion zone* and *total exclusion zone (TEZ)*

Military Strategic Level (of conflict)
The level of command and planning for armed conflict (*level of war*) at which military resources are applied to achieve policy objectives. (***JWP 01-1.1***)

Military Strategy
That component of national or multinational strategy, presenting the manner in which military power should be developed and applied to achieve national objectives or those of a group of nations. (***AAP6***)

Military Use of Force
See *military (or combat governed) application of force*.

Mission:
A clear, concise statement of the task of the command and its purpose.

One or more aircraft ordered to accomplish one particular task. (***AAP6***)

Mission Command
A style of command that seeks to convey understanding to subordinates about the intentions of the higher commander and their place within his plan, enabling them to carry out missions with the maximum freedom of action and appropriate resources. (***JWP 01-1.1***)

Mission Orders
A style of orders to subordinate commanders that specify what is to be achieved without constraining the subordinate as to how it is to be achieved.

Mobility
A quality or capability of military forces which permits them to move from place to place while retaining the ability to fulfil their primary mission. (*AAP6*)

Multi-National Logistic Commander (MNLC)
Assigned by the lead *Major NATO Commander (MNC)* for a NATO operation. The MNLC and staff plan, co-ordinate and control, based on NATO Military Authorities' and national prearranged agreement, all maritime *logistic* shore support for *Multinational NATO Maritime Forces (MNMF)*. Additionally he will assume responsibility for all shuttle ships not under the control of the MNMF commander. The MNLC will report to the NATO Commander having *operational control (OPCON)* of the MNMF.

Multi-National Maritime Forces (MMF)
Multinational NATO *Reaction Forces* consisting of *Standing Naval Forces, NATO Task Groups, NATO Task Forces* and NATO Expanded Task Forces.

N

NATO Expanded Task Force (NETF)
A force consisting of the elements of NATO *Task Forces* with multiple carriers, amphibious ships/landing forces and an enhanced complement of multi-mission capable escorts and submarines. It is a fully battle-capable force with a significant *maritime power projection* capability.

NATO Integrated Military Structure (NIMS)
The Integrated Military Structure of NATO comprises the NATO Military Command Structure (Including the Defence Planning Committee, Military Committee, *Major NATO Commanders* (MNCs) and subordinate commands), the associated command boundaries, the Integrated Military Staffs at NATO Headquarters and those of subordinate commands), the Defence Planning System, the NATO Force Structure and NATO Infrastructure Programme.

NATO Task Force (NTF)
A force consisting of the elements of a NATO *Task Group (NTG)* with amphibious ships/landing forces and a carrier, or both, to provide *control of the air* and limited *maritime power projection*.

NATO Task Group (NTG)
A *task group* of one or more cruisers, and destroyers and frigates with submarines, maritime patrol aircraft and mine countermeasures forces as required.

Naval Control of Shipping (NCS)
Control exercised by naval authorities of movement, routeing, reporting, convoy organization and tactical diversion of allied merchant shipping. It does not include the employment or active protection of such shipping (***AAP6***).

Naval Diplomacy
The use of naval force in support of diplomacy to support, persuade, *deter* or *compel*.

Naval Fire Support (NFS)
In naval operations, fire support to land operations provided from warships. (***AAP6***).

Naval Forces
Seaborne military forces including warships, submarines, amphibious forces, *organic* aircraft and *auxiliaries*.

Naval Service(s)
The *Naval Service* is the Royal Navy, Royal Marines, Queen Alexandra's Royal Naval Nursing Service, their respective Reserves, the *Royal Fleet Auxiliary*, the Royal Maritime Auxiliary Services and members of the Civil Service under the direct management of the Navy Board. The United Kingdom *Naval Services* are the Naval Service and the Merchant Navy.

Naval Staff
The staff serving in the Ministry of Defence and supporting the activities of the Navy Board. The core of the Naval Staff is in the Naval Staff Directorate, but other naval officers serving in naval directorates within the Central Staff are also a part of the broader naval staff.

Navy Board
The executive committee of the Admiralty Board. The Navy Board is chaired by the First Sea Lord in contrast to the full Admiralty Board which is chaired by the Secretary of State for Defence.

No Fly Zone
Zone of airspace established by international mandate (or conceivably unilaterally as a military or total exclusion zone) in which the flying of specified types of aircraft is prohibited. (***JWP 01-1.1***)

Non-Combatant Evacuation Operations (NEO)
An operation conducted to relocate (to a place of safety) non-combatants threatened in a foreign country.

O

Objective
The physical object of the action taken, e.g. a definite tactical feature, the seizure and/or holding of which is essential to the commander's plan. (*AAP6*) See *aim* and *mission*.

Offensive Operations
Operations in which forces seek out the enemy in order to attack him. (*JWP 0-01.1*)

Operation
A military action or the carrying out of a strategic, tactical, service, training, or administrative military mission; the process of carrying on combat, including movement, supply, attack, defence and manoeuvres needed to gain the objectives of any battle or campaign. (*AAP6*)

Operational Art
The skilful employment of military forces to attain strategic *goals* through the design, organization, integration and conduct of campaigns and major operations (*ADP Vol 1*). It is the essence of admiralship and general-ship.

Operational Command (OPCOM)
The authority granted to a commander to assign *missions* or tasks to subordinate commanders, to deploy units, to reassign forces and to retain or delegate *operational* and/or *tactical control* as may be deemed necessary. It does not of itself include responsibility for *administration or logistics*. (*AAP6*). This is usually exercised by a national Single Service or *joint* commander of Flag or equivalent rank (e.g. CINCFLEET) and is the highest degree of command authority that nations will delegate to a *Major NATO Commander (MNC)*.

Operational Commander
A commander exercising command at the *operational level*.

Operational Control (OPCON)
The authority delegated to a commander to direct forces assigned so that the commander may accomplish specific *missions* or tasks which are usually limited by function, time or location; to deploy units concerned, and to retain or assign tactical control of those

units. It does not include authority to assign separate employment of components of the units concerned. Neither does it of itself include *administrative* or *logistic* control. (*AAP6*)

Operational Function

To maximize success an operational commander and his staff should group and focus planning effort to address certain key aspects of a campaign or major operation and subsequently monitor and review their execution closely. These aspects, the operational functions, are *command and control (C2)*, intelligence and *surveillance*, protection, *combat power, logistics*, and *influence over the battlespace*.

Operational Level of war

The level of war at which *campaigns* and major operations are planned, conducted, and sustained to accomplish strategic objectives within theatres or areas of operation. (*AAP6*)

Operational Manoeuvre From The Sea (OMFTS)

A USMC concept which places emphasis on the rapid projection of combat power ashore at the right time and in the right place to accomplish an operational objective. OMFTS includes the sub-concepts of Over The Horizon (OTH) operations and Ship-To-Objective-Manoeuvre (STOM).

Operational Pause

A periodic pause in operations while initiative is retained in other ways. (*JWP 01-1.1*) Operational pauses may be required because a force has temporarily reached the end of its *sustainability*; because forces are exhausted; because of terrain or weather; because the character of the *campaign* has changed; (for political reasons); or for a combination of these factors. (*ADP Vol 1*)

Operational Requirement

An established need justifying the timely allocation of resources to achieve a capability to accomplish approved military objectives, missions, or tasks. Also called *military requirement*. (*AAP6*)

Operational Sea Training (OST)

Training of individual naval units and groups of *maritime forces* in their operational roles and tasks under the supervision of a sea training authority and with the assistance of specialist training staff and facilities. See *work up*.

Operations Security (OPSEC)

The process which gives a military operation or exercise appropriate security, using passive or active means, to deny the enemy knowledge of dispositions, capabilities and intentions of friendly forces. (*AAP6*)

Operation Other Than War (OOTW)

Those military operations which are conducted in situations of conflict other than war. Such operations, in which military activities are likely to be firmly subordinated to the political throughout, will be designed to prevent conflict, restore peace by resolving or terminating conflict before escalation to war, or assist with the rebuilding of peace after conflict or war. (*JWP 01-1.1*)

Organic

In a naval context used to mean capabilities and resources that are borne within a *naval force* or formation. Often used of aircraft, *logistics*, weapons and sensors.

P

Partnership for Peace (PfP)

This initiative provides for non-NATO European nations who are members of the Organization for Security and Co-operation in Europe to become individual partners of the Alliance. Each Partner agrees a specific programme with NATO Headquarters to meet its own needs and requirements. NATO will consult with a Partner who perceives a direct threat to its territorial integrity, political independence or security. Partners may participate in political and military bodies in NATO with respect to Partnership activities. They may take part in joint planning, joint military exercises and in creating an ability to operate with NATO forces in such fields as *peacekeeping*, search and rescue, humanitarian operations, and others as may be agreed.

Peace Building

Peace building covers actions which support political, economic, social and military measures and structures aiming to strengthen and solidify political settlements in order to redress the causes of conflict. This includes mechanisms to identify and support structures which tend to consolidate peace, advance a sense of confidence and well-being and support economic reconstruction. (*JWP 01-1.1*)

Peace Enforcement

Action including the use of military force on a multilateral basis to maintain or restore international peace previously agreed to be belligerents who may now be in *combat*; and to compel compliance with agreement to which parties have conferred or implied consent. Peace enforcement may entail the enforcement of *sanctions* and/or direct military *intervention* to impose peace by the threat, or the actual use of force.

Peace Imposition

Use of force to *compel* compliance with internationally expected patterns of behaviour, sanctions or resolutions, without any previously conferred or implied consent.

Peacekeeping

Measures by third parties to achieve and maintain peace taken with impartiality and with the full consent of parties involved.

Peacemaking

The diplomatic activities conducted after the commencement of a conflict aimed at establishing a cease-fire or a rapid peaceful settlement. They can include the provision of good offices, mediation, conciliation and such actions as diplomatic pressure, isolation or sanctions. (*JWP 01-1.1*)

Peace Support Operations (PSO)

Multi-functional operations involving military forces and diplomatic and humanitarian agencies. They are designed to achieve humanitarian goals or long term political settlement and are conducted impartially in support of an appropriate mandate. These include *peacekeeping, peace enforcement, conflict prevention, peacemaking, peacebuilding* and humanitarian operations.

Permanent Joint Headquarters

This is the HQ of the Chief of Joint Operations (CJO) located at Northwood in North London. All UK joint operations commanded through the HQ, with the in theatre commander reporting to the Joint Commander at PJHQ. For most operations the designated Joint Commander will be the 3 Star CJO himself. However, the option is retained of appointing one of the 4 Star single Service CinCs as the Joint Commander if the scale and nature of the operations being commanded warrant a more senior officer in the chain of command.

Phase

A phase is a discrete and identifiable activity along a Military Line of Operation in time and/or space that allows for the reorganisation and redirection of forces as part of the superior commander's plan. (*JWP 01-1.1*)

Piracy

As defined in *1982 UNCLOS*, piracy is an act that can only be committed on the high seas and for which universal jurisdiction applies (that is to say, any state can apprehend a pirate vessel, regardless of its flag state). As defined, piracy consists of the following:

(a) Any illegal acts of violence, detention or any act of depredation, committed for private ends by the crew or passengers of a private ship or private aircraft, and directed:

> on the high seas against another ship or aircraft, or against persons or property on board such ship or aircraft;

> against any ship, aircraft, persons or property in a place out side the jurisdiction of any State.

(b) Any act of voluntary participation in the operation of a ship or of an aircraft with knowledge of facts making it a pirate ship or aircraft.

(c) Any act of inciting or of intentionally facilitating an act described in a. and b. above.

Such acts of piracy committed by a warship, government ship or government aircraft whose crew has mutinied and taken control of the ship or aircraft, are treated in the same way as acts committed by a private ship.

Poise
An attribute of a *maritime force* which permits it to remain in international waters for long periods while retaining the ability to become engaged in events ashore or withdrawn without risk of *embroilment*.

Policing See *constabulary applications*.

Power Projection
In maritime terms, power projection is the ability to project force from a maritime force into the territory of another state. It is any deployment of force ashore or the provision of fire to influence events ashore. Power projection operations are one of the two main categories of military operations (the other being sea control) in which maritime forces can be utilised.

Pre-Emption
To pre-empt the enemy is to seize an opportunity, often fleeting, before he does, in order to deny him an advantageous course of action. (*JWP 01-1.1*)

Precursor Operation
An *advance operation* to eliminate enemy sea denial forces such as conventional submarines, fast attack craft and mines from the path of the main force, a *holding area* or *amphibious objective area* (*AOA*).

Presence
The exercise of *naval diplomacy* in a general way involving deployments, port visits, exercising and routine operating in areas of interest to declare interest, reassure friends and allies and to *deter*.

Preventive Deployment
Deployment of forces to avert a conflict. (*JWP 01-1.1*)

Principal Subordinate Commander (PSC)
A NATO commander operationally responsible to a major subordinate commander for a given mission and geographical area. (*AAP6*)

Principles of War
The Principles of War are guides to action and fundamental tenets forming the basis for appreciating a situation and planning, but their relevance, applicability and relative importance change with circumstances. (*JWP 01-1.1*)

Proactive
Action that seeks to pre-empt and control rather than respond to events by seizing and maintaining the initiative. The antithesis of "reactive".

Prolongation
The deliberate extension of the length of a *conflict* as a means of outlasting or wearing down an enemy, or to provide an opportunity for new allies or reinforcements to be brought to bear. It can be considered as a form of *escalation*. (*JWP 01-1.1*)

Psychological Operations (PSYOPS)
Planned psychological activities in peace and war directed at enemy, friendly and neutral audiences in order to influence attitudes and behaviour affecting the achievement of military and political objectives. They include strategic psychological activities psychological consolidation activities and battlefield psychological activities. (*AAP6*)

Q

Qualitative escalation
Escalation between categories of warfare, for instance from conventional warfare to chemical and then to nuclear warfare.

Quarantine
Expression used loosely to mean a restriction on the egress of certain types of cargo. Also used to mean embargo enforcement.

R

Raid see *Amphibious raid.*

Rapid Environmental Assessment
The rapid collection of relevant information about the characteristics of the sub-seabed, seabed, waters, atmosphere and land of a potential battlespace and its immediate assimilation into products and databases for use by warfare commanders and in weapons and command support systems.

Rapid Reaction Forces (RRF)
NATO *Reaction Forces* at longer *readiness* than *Immediate Reaction Forces (IRF)* and available to respond to a *crisis* which exceeds the capacity for IRF to *deter* or counter. (***JWP 01-1.1***)

Reach
The ability to operate for extended periods at considerable distance from shore support. (***JWP 01-1.1***)

Reaction Forces (RF)
Highly mobile and capable multinational land, air and maritime forces allocated to major NATO commands and available at short notice, in order to provide an early military response to a crisis and demonstrate NATO's cohesion and resolve and, if required, facilitate the timely build-up of forces in the crisis area. They are composed of smaller *Immediate Reaction Forces*, and more capable *Rapid Reaction Forces*, both with maritime, ground and air components. (***NATO***)

Reactive
The state that exists when a force is responsive to enemy activity. The antithesis of proactive.

Readiness
The time within which a unit or formation can be made ready to perform unit-type tasks. This time is amplified or measured by

indicators of its current personnel, materiel and training state. The time does not include transit time. (*JWP 01-1.1*) Ships and their *organic* air units will have the required *combat* load and other *logistic materiel* embarked or appropriately positioned. A Royal Marine formation will have the required weapons and equipment, as well as basic loads of supply, collocated or appropriately positioned.

Rear Operations
Operations which establish and maintain our own forces in order to generate the freedom of action to allow for the conduct of close and deep operations.
(*JWP 0-01.1*)

Recognized Maritime Picture (RMP)
The fullest achievable agreed level of identification and tracking of all surface and sub-surface contacts in the area of interest. The RMP is normally associated with the Recognized Air Picture (RAP) of the same area.

Reconnaissance
A mission undertaken to obtain, by visual observation or other detection methods about the activities and resources of an enemy or potential enemy, or to secure data about meteorological, hydrographical or geographic characteristics of a particular area.(*AAP6*) See *surveillance*.

Reconstitution
The expansion of force structures and infrastructure beyond existing levels, including the raising of new units and formations and the expansion of industrial capacity to support the procurement of equipment and stocks. (*JWP 01-1.1*) See *regeneration*.

Regional Naval Control of Shipping
Voluntary participation in *Naval Control of Shipping* by ship owners and operators within a clearly defined geographical region or regions.

Regeneration
The timely activation, in full or in part, of existing force structures and infrastructure, including the restoration of manning, equipment and stocks to designated levels. (*AAP6*) See *reconstitution*.

RO-RO Ferries
Roll on-Roll Off ferries into and from which vehicles can be driven from and to a wharf or jetty.

Roulement
The rotation of personnel or units in the front line with those in

reserve in order to maintain the fighting effectiveness of the forces engaged in an operation. (*JWP 01-1.1*)

Royal Fleet Auxiliary (RFA)

The Royal Fleet Auxiliary (RFA) is a civilian manned flotilla owned and operated by the Ministry of Defence to provide *logistic* support for the armed services but primarily the Royal Navy.

Rules of Engagement (ROE)

Direction and guidance provided to commanders by ministers which control the application of force by UK Forces. Issued as a set of parameters to inform commanders of the limits of constraint imposed or of the freedom permitted when carrying out these assigned tasks. (*JSP 398 (new)*)

S

Sanction (United Nations)

A penalty imposed on a state with the intention of influencing that state to comply with a Security Council Resolution or otherwise to abide by international law.

Screening

System of defence of a force or area using protective units deploying sensors and weapon systems in sectors or patrol areas around the force. See *layered defence*.

Sea Communications

See *sea lines of communications (SLOC)*.

Sea Control

The condition that exists when one has freedom of action to use an area of sea for one's own purposes for a period of time and, if necessary, deny its use to an opponent. Sea control includes the airspace above the surface and the water volume and seabed below. (*JWP 01-1.1*)

Sea Denial

The condition short of full *sea control* that exists when an opponent is prevented from using an area of sea for his purposes. (*JWP 01-1.1*)

Sealift

The movement of resources between points by carriage in shipping.

Sea Lines of Communications (SLOC)

The sea routes that connect an operating military force with one or more bases of operations and along which supplies and reinforcements move. The expression is sometimes used more broadly in a strategic sense to include commercial shipping routes.

Sequel
Subsequent operation based on the possible outcomes of the current operations. The execution of a sequel normally means beginning another *phase* of a *campaign*. A form of "what if?. (*US FM 100-5*)

Sequencing
The arrangement of activities within a *campaign* in the order most likely to achieve the elimination of the enemy's *centre of gravity.* (*JWP 01-1.1*)

Sequential Campaign
A campaign which consists of a series of discrete *phases*, steps or actions each of which is shaped to some extent by the outcome of those preceding. (**JWP 01-1.1**)

Shakedown (colloquial)
Period of basic sea or harbour training for naval units after a period without training or operation experience, or for a naval force on first assembling to build interoperability. Shakedown may be part of or precede *operational sea training* or it may be informal.

Ship-To-Objective-Manoeuvre (STOM)
Force projection from maritime sea based platforms of joint assets by surface or air assault direct to objectives.

Ships Taken Up From Trade (STUFT)
Merchant ships chartered or requisitioned for maritime operations.

Simultaneity
Element of campaign and operational design that seeks to disrupt the decision-making process of the enemy commander by confronting him with a number of problems simultaneously. (*JWP 01-1.1*)

Spectrum of Conflict
The full range of levels of *violence* from stable peace up to and including *general war*. (JWP 01-1.1) Often displayed graphically relating military tasks and types of operation to levels of violence, and sometimes also to probability of occurrence.

Standing Naval Forces (SNF)
NATO's maritime multinational *Immediate Reaction Forces*. They are the Standing Naval Force Atlantic (STANAVFORLANT),

Standing Naval Force Mediterranean (STANAVFORMED) and Standing Naval Force Channel (STANAVFORCHAN, which is shortly to be redesignated, Standing Naval Mine Countermeasures Force or STANAVMINFOR). The first two are principally frigate and destroyer formations. The third is a mine countermeasures force.

Statement on the Defence Estimates (SDE)
Annual statement presented to Parliament by the Secretary of State for Defence which may include the public presentation of Defence Policy. Also known as the Defence White Paper.

Straits Transit Passage
This is a right of passage through international straits used for navigation between different areas of high seas. It exists when a strait is narrower than 24 nautical miles wide and when the coastal states on both sides of the strait have territorial waters extending out to the maximum permitted limit of 12 nautical miles. The resultant lack of a high seas corridor through the straits would have restricted rights of passage to those allowed for in territorial sea (innocent passage). However, awareness of this difficulty led to the idea of straits transit passage being enshrined in ***1982 UNCLOS***. In effect, it provides the right of unimpeded passage through a strait, a right that cannot be suspended.

Strategic Air Offensive
The use of airpower to strike directly and with precision at the enemy's strategic *centres of gravity* including leadership, military forces, infrastructure and research and production facilities. (***AP3000***)

Strategic Defence Review (SDR)
The comprehensive defence policy review conducted by the Government following the General Election of 1997.

Strategic Level
See *grand strategic* and *military strategic levels*.

Strategic Nuclear Deterrence
Deterrence of aggression effected by the existence of long range nuclear weapons capable of holding at risk objects of value in the homeland of any possible aggressor. (***JWP 01-1.1***)

STUFT
See *ships taken up from trade*.

Suasion See *armed suasion*.

Sub-Strategic Nuclear Deterrent Capability
The capability to deliver more limited nuclear attacks than that

maintained for *strategic nuclear deterrence* to provide nuclear deterrence in circumstances in which the threat of strategic nuclear attack may not be credible. (*JWP 01-1.1*)

Surveillance

The systematic observation of the aerospace, surface and sub-surface areas, places, persons or things by visual, aural, electronic, photographic or other means. (*AAP6*)

Survivability

The ability of a ship to continue fighting when it has suffered damage.

Sustainability

The ability of a force to maintain the necessary level of combat power for the duration required to achieve its objectives (*AAP6*). See *endurance*.

Symbolic Use of Force

A form of *naval diplomacy* in which naval forces can be used purely to signal a message to a specific government while not in themselves posing any threat to an opponent or providing significant military assistance to a friend.

Synchronization

The focusing of resources and activities to produce maximum combat power at the decisive time.(*JWP 01-1.1.*) *Synchronization* differs from *simultaneity* as the purpose is to achieve decisive coincidence of the effects of activities rather than the activities themselves.

Systemic Disruption

Reduction by the selective use or threat of *combat* of the cohesion of an enemy forces total combat system to the extent that it is unable to deliver combat to achieve the military objectives required of it. See *disruption*.

T

Tactical Command (TACOM)

The authority delegated to a commander to assign tasks to forces under his command for the accomplishment of the *mission* assigned by higher authority. (*AAP6*)

Tactical Control (TACON)

The detailed, and usually, local direction and control of movements or manoeuvres necessary to accomplish *missions* or tasks assigned. (*AAP6*)

Tactical Level of war
The tactical level of war at which battles and engagements are planned and executed to accomplish military objectives assigned to tactical formations and units. (*AAP6*)

Task Element (TE)
The fourth and lowest level of *echelonment* in a *task organization*.

Task Force (TF)
A temporary grouping of units, under one commander, formed for the purpose of carrying out a specific operation or *mission* (*AAP6*) In a *functional* or *task organization* a TF is the highest level of *echelonment*. See *battleforce*.

Task Group (TG)
A grouping of units under one commander subordinate to a *task force* commander, formed for the purpose of carrying out a specific function or functions. The second highest level of *echelonment* in a *task organization*. See *battlegroup*.

Task Organization
Functional command *organization* in which the component units and formations are organized according to task into *task forces, task groups, task units* and *task elements*.

Task Unit (TU)
The third level of *echelonment* in a task *organization*.

Tempo
The rate or rhythm of military activity relative to the enemy, within tactical engagements and battles and between major operations. (*JWP 01-1.1*)

Territorial Sea
The territorial sea of a state consists of a belt of water adjacent to the coast of the state and extending up to a maximum distance of 12 nautical miles to the seaward of the baselines drawn in accordance with the accepted principles of international law. It forms part of the sovereign territory of the state and is under that state's control and jurisdiction. (*BR 3012*)

Theatre of operations
A geographical area defined by the military-strategic authority which includes and surrounds the area delegated to the operational commander within which he will conduct operations - known as the *joint operations area*. (*JWP 01-1.1*)

Total Exclusion Zone (TEZ)
Maritime geographical area including parts of the *high seas* within which a government states its intention to enforce the exclusion of all ships and aircraft, both military and civilian, of a designated nation or nations or other grouping, using force if necessary. See *maritime exclusion zone* and *military exclusion zone (MEZ)*.

Total War
General war waged towards unlimited objectives. (***JWP 01-1.1***)

Turning Movement
A variation of the envelopment in which the attacking force passes around or over the enemy's principal defensive positions to secure objectives deep in the enemy's rear to force the enemy to abandon his position or divert major forces to meet the threat. (***AAP6***)

Type Organization
Command organization of *naval forces* by type or class of unit normally used for *administrative* purposes. See *functional organization*.

U

Unified
Forces under the command or control of a single commander. A command that includes forces from different Services and/or nations. An imprecise expression variously meaning *joint, combined,* and *integrated*.

V

Versatility
The ability to change fighting posture quickly without recourse to outside resources.

Vertical escalation
An increase in intensity of *combat* during *hostilities*. It is sometimes understood to include *qualitative escalation*. (***JWP 01-1.1***)

Violence
Conduct involving the use of great physical force. In the military context violence may result in injury and damage to or destruction of resources.

W

War

The most extreme manifestation of armed conflict, characterised by intense, extensive and sustained combat, usually between states. (*JWP 01-1.1*). The expression is normally associated with combat at high levels of intensity but criteria of intensity would exclude some *civil* and guerrilla wars. Whether or not a state of war exists is very much in the perception of the parties involved. One party may believe that it is at war, for instance a group of *insurgents*, while the other party, in this case a government, may consider that it faces a problem of peace disorder. To Thomas Hobbes (Leviathan) the relationship between combat and war is that of a shower to bad weather. *Hostilities* is a more precise expression for any period between the onset of regular combat between parties and any cease-fire or truce. See *general war, limited war, civil war,* and *operations other than war (OOTW)*.

War Aim

The *grand strategic* or political aim of a government or faction on outbreak of war and during its conduct and termination phases. *War aims* are loosely used to mean grand strategic *objectives* generally that are being pursued during *hostilities*.

Warfare Environment

The five warfare environments are sea, land, air, space and the electromagnetic spectrum.

Withdrawal

See *amphibious withdrawal*.

Work-Up

Colloquial expression for *operational sea training*. It is also used for a period of informal sea training.

INDEX

Access 22,30
Accompanying 55, 129
Advance force operations 134
Advance sea control operations (Shaping operations) 134
Advanced Command and Staff Course (ACSC) 5
Advanced Logistic Support Site (ALSS) 84
Afloat logistic support 153
Afloat support 134-5
Aims 9, 110-12
Air Interdiction (AI) 138, 168
Air Power Doctrine 6
Air superiority 34-5
Air supremacy 34
Aircraft 152-3
Aircraft carriers (CVS) 148
Alanbrooke, Field Marshal Viscount 83
Amphibious forces 167
Amphibious operations 136-8
    assault 136-7
    demonstration 136
    raiding 136
    withdrawal 137
Amphibious shipping 149-50
    landing platform helicopter (LPH) 149, 150
    landing platforms dock (LPDs) 149, 150
    landing ships logistic (LSLs) 149, 150
Amphibious Task Group (ATG) 136
Anti-Air Warfare (AAW) 132-3
Anti-piracy operations 64
Anti-submarine warfare (ASW) 3-4, 133
Anti-surface force operations 138
Anti-Surface Warfare (ASuW) 133
Antwerp 105
Archipelagic sea lanes passage 18
Area operations 131
Area sea control operations 52, 130
Arms control 60
Asymmetric campaign 162
Attributes 30
Attrition warfare 21, 41, 47

Balance of advantage 47, 122-3
Ballistic missile carrying submarine (SSBN) 4
Baltic States 62
Barnet, Roger 180
Barrier operations 54, 131
Battle of Leyte Gulf 95
Battlespace 138
    dominance 35
    influence over 121
Benign operations 65-7, 74, 75, 141, 150
Biological warfare 124
Blockade 54, 130-1
Branches 115
Britain's Naval Future 179
British Defence Doctrine 6
British Military Doctrine 6
Britannia Royal Naval College (BRNC) 5
Bryant, Sir Arthur 83

Cable, Sir James 179, 181
Campaign 41, 74, 90, 111, 112
    planning 40, 109-39
Carrier air group (CAG) 148
Catastrophic damage 30
Centre of gravity 40, 112
Changing Face of Maritime Power 182
Chemical warfare 124
Chief of Defence Logistics (CDL) 78
Chief of Defence Staff (CDS) 90, 142
Chief of Joint Operations (CJO) 110
Churchill, Sir Winston 83
CINCFLEET 79
Civil authorities 123
Clausewitz, Karl Marie von 178
Close Air Support (CAS) 168
Close blockade 47
Close escort operations 129
Co-operation 11
Coalition building 56-7
Coalition operations 100-5
Coercion 26, 38, 58, 111
Collateral damage 29
Collective performance 153-6
Colomb, Vice Admiral Sir Philip 33

Combat
    operations against the land 59
    power 120
    stress/fatigue 146-7
    support air operations 59
    support operations 138
Combined Joint Task Force (CJTF) 101, 148
Command and Control organization 19, 43, 60, 89-107, 101-2, 118, 168-9
    example 107
    failure 105
    integrated 102
    lead nation 102
    national 106
    parallel 102
    see also Control; Sea control
Command and control warfare (CW2) 121
Command of the sea 33
Command Team Training (CTT) 154-5
Commanders 102-3
Commander's Estimate 117
3 Commando Brigade 149
Commando Training Centre, Royal Marines (CTCRM) 5
Communications 91-6
Compel 58
Concentration of force 10
Concept of operations 110
Concluding operations 104-5
Conditions for success 111-12, 127
Conflict 52
    control 29
    prevention 68
Conjunct Operations 28
Consolidation 78, 135
    shipping 25
Constabulary operations 63-5, 74, 75, 111, 141, 150, 152
Consumer logistics 78
Containment 35, 48-9, 54, 131
Contiguous zones 18
Continental shelf 18, 73
Control 34
    see also Command and Control organization; Sea control
Control of electromagnetic spectrum 168
Convoying 45-6, 55, 128-9
Corbett, Sir Julian 28, 33, 176-7
Counter air operations 138

Counter-air, anti-surface force 59
Counter-contraband 64
Counter-insurgency operation 64
Cover 37-8
Covering force 37-8
Crisis
    identification 126-7
    management 38, 124
    prevention 58
Cruise missiles 161
Culminating point 40, 82, 114, 115
Cumulative campaign 111, 114, 115
Current situation 160-3

De-escalation 96
Decision-making 91-3
Decisive points 40,112-13
Defence in depth 49
Defence diplomacy 56, 60-2, 179
Defensive action 45-6, 52
Delegation 92
Deployment 124, 128-9
Destroyers 150
Deterrence 26, 111
Dimensions of Sea Power 181
Diplomacy 55-62, 149
Disaster relief operations 65, 66
Discipline 146
Dislocation 121
Disruption 27, 121
Distant blockade 47
Distant operations 129
Distraction 27, 47
Doctrine 43, 78, 100, 155
    bibliographic essay 172-83
    context 2-11, 167-70
    hierarchy 6-7
    joint approach 3-4
    nature 5-6
    purpose 4-5
Domestic jurisdiction 72-3
Drug interdiction 64, 73

Economic sanctions 63
Economy
    of effort 10
    of force operations 121
    logistics 81
The Education of a Navy 176
Education and training 4-5, 124, 154-5
Effort 125

Elan 47
Embargo operations 15, 63
Embroilment 29
End-state 127
   conditions for success 111-12
Envelop 27
Environment 14-22
   economic 14-16
   legal 17-18
   military 18-19
   multi-dimensional battlespace 21-2
   physical 19-21
   political 16-17
   tactical exploitation 120-2
   warfare 118
Equipment 147-53, 161
   afloat logistic support 153
   aircraft carriers/organic air 148
   destroyers/frigates 150
   hydrographic vessels 151-2
   maritime patrol aircraft 152-3
   mine countermeasures vessels 151
   nuclear powered attack submarines 148-9
   nuclear powered ballistic missile submarines 148
   patrol vessels 152
   ships taken up from trade (STUFT) 153
   specialist amphibious forces 149-50
Escalation 96
Escort 55, 134
Evacuation 135
Exclusion zones 54
Exclusive economic zones (EEZs) 15, 18
Exploitation 122
Extended fisheries zone (EFZ) 72, 73

Falklands campaign 114
Fast attack craft (FAC) 133
Fatigue 146-7
Favourable air situation 34
Fighting Instructions 6, 174-5
Fire support 167
Fishing 15-16
   protection 152
Fleet 147
Fleet in being 35-7, 47
Flexibility 10-11, 122
   logistics 81
Force co-ordination 103

Force generation 127-8
Force packages 165-6
Force protection 52, 53, 131-2
Forward from the Sea 180
Forward line of own troops 39
Forward Logistics sites (FLS) 84, 153
Forward Maintenance and Repair Organization (FMRO) 153
Forward presence 58
Forward Repair Ship (FRS) 153
Fraser, Stewart 179
Fratricide 130
Freedom of navigation operations 54, 63
Friedman, Norman 179
Frigates and destroyers (FF/DD) 150
From the Sea - Preparing the Naval Service for the 21st Century 180
Future of British Sea Power 179
Future Carrier Based Aircraft (FCBA) 170

Gallipoli 121-2
Gordon, Andrew 182
Grand-strategic level 8, 78, 110, 122
Gray, Colin 27, 180
Grove, Eric 177
Guerre de course 35, 114
Gulf War 116-17, 161-2
Gunboat Diplomacy 179

Handel, George 177
Harriers 170
Hattendorf, John 176
High seas 29
   freedom 17
Hill, Rear Admiral Richard 179
HMS Naiad 175
Holding operations 121
Host Nation Support (HNS) 82-3, 161
Hostilities 27, 56, 111, 141
Humanitarian operations 65, 70-1
Hydrographic survey vessels (SVs) 151-2
Hydrographic surveying 66-7

Immigrants, interception of illegal 64
Influence over battlespace 121
The Influence of Sea Power upon History 176
Information 169
   exchange 103

operations 99-100
public 123-4
Initial Handling Point (IHP) 84
Initial Staff Course (ISC) 5
Initiative 48
Innocent passage 18
Insurgency 114
Integrated multinational forces 100
Intelligence 118-19, 126-7, 169
Interception of illegal immigrants 64
Interdiction of enemy's maritime forces 53
Interdiction operations 131, 168
Internal waters 18, 123
Intervention 38
Iterative planning 126

Joint campaign 39, 54, 112
Joint Commander 90
Joint doctrine 7, 169
Joint forces 22
Joint integration 22
Joint operations 3-4, 24, 25, 29, 35, 42-3, 85
Joint Operations Area (JOA) 60
Joint Services Command and Staff College (JSCSC) 5
Joint Sub-Regional Commands/Component Commands 101
Joint Task Force Air Component Commander (JFACC) 138
Joint Task Force Commander (JTFC) 80, 91, 109
Joint Task Force Headquarters (JTFHQ) 148
Joint Task Force Headquarters (JTFHQ) (Afloat) 139, 168
Joint Theatre Plans 135
JWP 3-50 Peace Support Operation 67-8

Land attack missiles 59, 138
Landing Craft Air Cushion (LCACs) 150
Landing force movement assets 150
Landing platform helicopter (LPH) 148, 149, 150
Landing platforms dock (LPDs) 149, 150
Landing ships logistic (LSLs) 149, 150
Language 103
Law, influence 8

Layered defence 48, 54
Leadership 143-4
Level of war 41
Leverage 26, 26-7, 31, 129
The Leverage of Seapower 27, 180
Liaison 123
Liaison officers 103
Life at sea 142-3
Lift capacity 26, 31
Lines of support 29, 39, 78, 135
Littoral operations 3-4, 14, 17, 19, 21-2, 27-8, 35, 112, 163-4
Logistic support 25, 120-1
Logistics 39-40, 78-85, 104
    maritime operational pipeline 84
    multi-national 80
    operational level 79-80
    principles 81-2
    roulement 82
    shore support 82-3
    strategic level 78
    sustained reach 83-4

Mahan on Naval Strategy 176
Mahan, Rear Admiral Alfred Thayer 33, 176, 177-8
Main effort 40, 121
Maintenance 96
Major NATO Commander (MNC) 100-1
Major Subordinate Commander (MSC) 101
Makers of Modern Strategy 177
Maldeployment 58
Manoeuvre from the sea 27, 39, 42, 53
    as combat function 44
Manoeuvre warfare 25, 39-41, 41-4, 113, 122, 164, 166
Maritime campaign 33
Maritime Component Commander(MCC) 109, 148
Maritime counter-terrorism (MCT) 73
Maritime domain 16, 65, 72, 152
Maritime forces 33, 147
Maritime manoeuvre 43-4, 160, 164-5, 170
Maritime Patrol Aircraft (MPA) 133, 152-3
Maritime Power projection 38-9
Maritime Strategy and the Balance of Power 180
Maritime Strategy and Continental Wars 178

Maritime Strategy for Medium Powers 179
Maritime Strategy and the Twenty First Century 180
Masters of War 177
Memoranda of Understanding (MOU) 83
Menon, Rear Admiral Raja 178
Micro-management 91-2
Military Aid to the Civil Power (MACPA) 73
Military Assistance to Civil Authorities (MACA) 51, 72-3
Military conditions 111
Military operations 52-62, 74, 75, 150
   levels 8
Military-strategic level 5, 6, 8, 20, 78, 121
   aim 110-12
Mine Countermeasures (MCM) 134
Mine countermeasures vessels (MMs) 151
Mission 110
Mission command 93-4
Mobility 22-3, 30
Molyneux, Thomas More 27-8
Morale 9, 145-6
Multi-dimensional battlespace 21-2
Multi-national logistics 80
Multinational Joint Logistics Centre (MJLC) 80
Multinational Logistic Commander (MNLC) 80
Multinational Maritime Manuals (MMMs) 103
Multinational Maritime Operations document 103
Multinational operations 100-5
   co-operation 101
   key factors 102-5
   principles 101

NATO 80, 100-1, 110
NATO doctrine 6-7
NATO Expanded Task Force 147
NATO Task Force 147
Naval 160
   diplomacy 38, 55-6, 111, 149
   force 29, 82
   platform 160
   support 134
Naval Control of Shipping 55
Naval C41 systems 97-9, 161
   characteristics 98-9
   functions 97-8
Naval Service 79
Navies and Global Defense 180
Navy Board 4
Nelson, Horatio 172-3, 174
New Dimensions 182
Non-combatant evacuation operations (NEOs) 39, 59, 135
Non-governmental organizations (NGOs) 123
Nuclear Powered Attack Submarines (SSNs) 148-9
Nuclear powered ballistic missile submarines (SSBNs) 148

Offensive action 10, 45-6, 52
On Job Training (OJT) 154
On War 178
Operational
   art 112-14
   commander 110
   organization 90-1
   pause 82, 115
   sea training 124
Operational capability 142-57
   collective performance 153-6
   equipment 147-53
   people 142-7
   sustainability 156
Operational Command (OPCOM) 90, 100
Operational Control (OPCON) 91, 100, 101
Operational functions 117-18
   command/control 118
   intelligence/surveillance 118-19
Operational level 4, 8, 20, 35, 39-40, 74, 110
   logistics 79-80
Operational logistics pipeline 84, 86-7
Operational Manoeuvre From the Sea 167
Operational Performance Statement (OPS) 154
Operational Requirements (OR) staff 5
Ordnance disposal 66-7
Organic 131
   air 148
   logistics 38, 39
   shipping 25

Organization 123
Outreach activities 60-1, 62

Pacific area 95-6
Paret, Peter 177
Patrol vessels 152
Peace building 69
Peace enforcement 68
Peace Support Operations (PSOs) 51, 62, 67-72
   maritime tasks 71-2
Peacekeeping 67-8
Peacemaking 68-9
People 142-7
   combat stress/fatigue 146-7
   discipline 146
   leadership 143-4
   life at sea 142-3
   morale 145-6
Performance 153-6
Permanent Joint Headquarters (PJHQ) 90, 110
Philippine Sea 95-6
Piracy 129
Planning 104, 109-39
   process 117-26
   stages 126-39
Platforms 148, 149, 150, 160, 169
Poise 26, 31
Political Influence of Naval Force in History 181-2
Power 28-9
   application 75
   attributes 22-7
   benign 65-7
   combat 120
   constabulary 63-5
   domestic 72-3
   impact 27-8
   maxims 29
   military 52-62
Power projection 52
   forces 60
   operations 135
Pre-emptive naval diplomacy 58
Pre-Joining Training (PJT) 154
Precautionary diplomacy 58
Preparation 124
Presence 49, 57-8, 111
Preventive deployment 58
Preventive diplomacy 58

Principal Subordinate Commander (PSC) 101
Principles of Maritime Operations 48-9
Principles of Maritime Strategy 177
Principles of War 9-11, 48-9, 145
Proactive choice 45-8
Production logistics 78
Protection 120, 168
Protection of joint forces 60
Public information 123-4

Quarantine enforcement 63

Rapid Environmental Assessment (REA) 151
Reach 25, 56, 179
Reactive choice 45-8
Readiness 24, 124
Recognized Maritime Picture (RMP) 118-19
Reconnaissance 134
Regeneration 78
Regional Commands 101
Regional Naval Control of Shipping (RNCS) 55,123
Replenishment at Sea (RAS) 83
Resilience 25-6, 31
Revolution in Military Affairs (RMA) 161
RN's Handbook on the Law of Maritime Operations (BR3012) 17-18
Ro-Ro ferries 153
Roulement 25, 82, 124
Royal Air Force (RAF) 169-70
Royal Fleet Auxiliary (RFA) 26, 83
RUKUS Talks 61, 62
Rules of Engagement (ROE) 8, 58, 96, 104
Rules of the Game 182

Safety issues 104
Scheme of Complement (SOC) 154
Screening 47-8
Sea basing 25, 78
Sea control 19, 33, 34, 35, 38, 47, 47-8, 52, 54
   operations 129-35
   see also Command and Control organization; Control
Sea denial 29, 35, 36, 52, 54
Sea lines of communication (SLOCs) 39, 54, 79, 134
Sealift 26, 123
Seapower and Strategy 180

Seapower Theory and Practice 180
Search and rescue 66
Second World War 115, 174-5
Security 9
Sequels 115
Sequential campaign 111, 115, 116-17
Shakedown 124
Shaping operations see Advance sea control operations
Shared doctrine and publications 103
Ships Taken Up From Trade (STUFT) 83-4, 153
Shore support 82-3
Short take-off and vertical landing (STOVL) 148
Simplicity (logistics) 82
Simultaneity 40, 126
Some Principles of Maritime Strategy 28
Space systems 100
Spanish Civil War 59-60
Specialist amphibious forces 149-50
    3 Commando Brigade 149
    landing force movement assets 150
    shipping 149-50
Specific doctrine 74
Straits transit passage 18
Strategic air defensive 59
Strategic Commands 101
Strategic Defence Review (SDR) 60-1, 181, 182
Strategic level 4, 39-40, 126
Strategic nuclear deterrent 56, 148
Strategy (history) 172-4
Stress 146
Sub-strategic component 56
Sub-strategic nuclear deterrence 148
Sub-surface land attack 138
Submarines 133
    types 148-9
Support
    by organic air 138
    combat 59, 138
    fire 167
    lines 29, 39, 78, 135
    logistic 25, 120-1
    naval 134
    shore 82-3
    to joint operations 59
Surface land attack 138
Surprise 9-10
Surveillance systems 118-19, 126

Sustainability 11, 125, 155, 169
Sustained reach 25, 31, 83-4
Sustainment of operations 138-9
Symbolic use of force 58
Symmetric campaign 162
Synchronization 135
Systemic disruption 41

Tactical exploitation 120-2
Tactical level 8, 20, 35, 39, 110
Tactical organization 90-1
Task
    forces 24
    groups 19, 24, 160, 165-6
    organization 123
Technology 161
Tempo 40, 125-6
Termination 123
Territorial waters 18, 73, 123
Till, Geoffrey 179, 180
Trade 14-16
Training see Education and training
Training Performance Statement (TPS) 154
The Turn of the Tide 1939-1943 83

UN Charter 63
UN Convention on the Law of the Sea (1982 UNCLOS) 17, 65
United Kingdom Doctrine for Joint and Multinational Operations (UKOPSDOC) 6, 59, 111, 117
Unity of effort 101, 125
US Maritime Strategy (Fraser) 179
US Maritime Strategy (Friedman) 179

Versatility 23, 23-5, 31
    adaptability in roles 24
    flexibility in response 24
    joint/multinational attributes 24-5

Warfare environment 118
Weapons of mass destruction (WMD) 26
Weather 20
"What if's" 126
Withdrawal 139
Work-up programmes 124, 126

Yugoslavia 69, 74